The Japanese

The Japanese

by Jack Seward

William Morrow & Company, Inc.
NEW YORK 1972

Seward, Jack.
    The Japanese.

    1. National characteristics, Japanese. I. Title.
DS821.S39 1972   915.2'03'4   75-182973
ISBN 0-688-00003-7

To Mother, with love

Contents

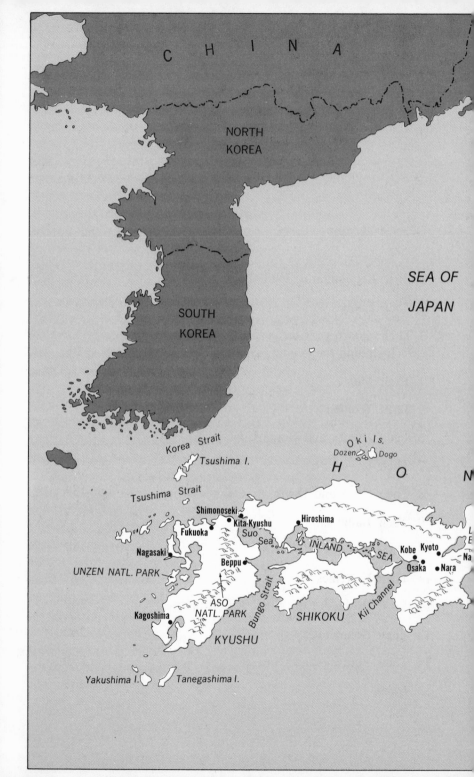

CHINA

NORTH
KOREA

SOUTH
KOREA

SEA OF

JAPAN

Korea Strait

Tsushima I.

O k i I s.
Dozen   Dogo

H

O

N

Tsushima Strait

Shimonoseki
Kita-Kyushu
Fukuoka
Suo
Sea

Hiroshima

INLAND

SEA

Kobe Kyoto
Osaka
Nara

L
E

Na

Nagasaki

UNZEN NATL. PARK

Beppu

ASO
NATL. PARK

Bungo Strait

SHIKOKU

Kii Channel

Kagoshima

KYUSHU

Yakushima I.

Tanegashima I.

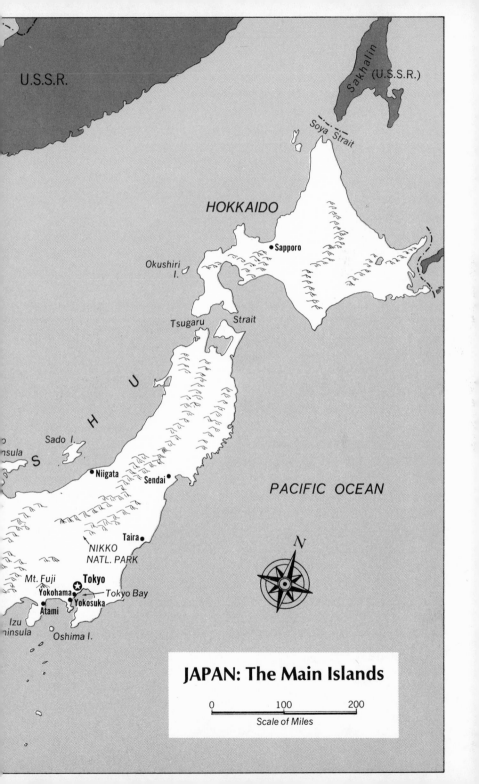

U.S.S.R.

Sakhalin (U.S.S.R.)

Soya Strait

HOKKAIDO

Okushiri I.

• Sapporo

Tsugaru   Strait

U

Sado I.

nsula

S

• Niigata   • Sendai

PACIFIC OCEAN

Taira•

N

NIKKO
NATL. PARK

Mt. Fuji   **Tokyo**
Yokohama•   — Tokyo Bay
Yokosuka
• Atami

Izu
ninsula   Oshima I.

JAPAN: The Main Islands

0   100   200

Scale of Miles

The Japanese

1

First Acquaintance
with the Japanese

A few years ago I returned to my home in the United States after twenty years of living in Japan. These years had been spent in six Japanese cities and small towns as a writer, businessman, Army officer, and intelligence agent, and during that time I think that I may have submerged myself in Japanese society as deeply as any Westerner before me.

From the day of my arrival in Yokohama, in early 1946, I tried to live in the Japanese style as completely as possible, at some times in one cramped room and at others in a small, flimsy house with a single hibachi for both heating and cooking. I rode the incredibly crowded subways, trains, and buses to work and ate mostly Japanese food. I listened only to programs in Japanese on the radio, associated mostly with Japanese, and read Japanese newspapers and magazines much more frequently than periodicals in English.

These things I did deliberately, although my preferences might have dictated otherwise, because I believed that this was the only way by which I could ever come to achieve a significant understanding of all that Japan is: by simply being a part of it and letting it sink in.

After twenty years of this kind of life I went back to the small town in north Texas that is my home, where the contrast between what had and had not happened there and what had happened in Japan during those years was extreme and startling. If anything, my home town had retrogressed (although I must say that I sometimes prefer such retrogression to what passes these days for progress). The population had declined. Most young people were moving away soon after graduation from high school. Businesses were decreasing in both number and scale. Television and the automobile had completely changed the style of social life. While land prices were increasing, the rate was painfully slow: land values had not even doubled in twenty years—in sharp contrast to Japan, where increases of several hundredfold were not at all uncommon.

In Japan (where I am now living again) the movement had been forward, at breathtaking speeds. When I first passed through the southern sections of Tokyo in 1946, I wondered in bemusement if this were not an agricultural district devoted entirely to the cultivation of just one crop, a crop called rubble—rubble that sprouted profusely in all directions, adorned here and there by a rusty safe that alone told the previous whereabouts of a now-pulverized shop or office. By 1966—and even more so now, in 1972—the pendulum had swung a long, long way in the opposite direction. The Japanese had wrought history's most amazing national economic recovery, and wrought it largely with their own skills and energy, though backed by more than a little American aid and direction.

My acquaintance with Japan, however, did not begin in early 1946 with the arrival of my transport in Yokohama harbor. Rather, it started six years before that in a far less likely location: a cattle ranch near Bartlesville, Oklahoma, where I was working during summer vacations from college. The ranch owner was an oilman whose staff included two Japanese valets. I've long since forgotten their family names, but Henry and Dan taught me—against their better judgment, I suspect—a magnificent array of at least twelve Japanese words, mangled perhaps beyond recognition by my Texas-Oklahoma drawl. Why I badgered them for this knowledge, I can't now remember. I would like to think that I was inspired by a premonition of things to come, but it was more likely just the curiosity of a country boy in initial contact with envoys from the mysterious Orient.

Anyway, college classes resumed and the war started, and then in early 1943, Howard Van Zandt—an American recently repatriated from Japan—began teaching spoken Japanese at the University of Oklahoma. As my schedule wasn't too crowded, I elected to take the course. In the meantime, I had signed up for the Enlisted Reserve Corps and was called to active duty in the Army just as my first semester of Japanese was ending.

Six months in the infantry gave me a lot of other things to think about besides the Japanese language, so it was with considerable—and most grateful—amazement that I learned one day that a sharp-eyed records clerk had spotted my one-semester course in that language on my college transcript and I was to be transferred to a Japanese language school sponsored by the Army on the University of Michigan campus. Here I entered the first of what became a series of three Army schools, which provided me with more than two years of intensified training, first in the written and spoken language of Japan, then in its history, economy, geography, literature, and social structure.

This schooling came to a close shortly after the war ended, and we graduates were commissioned and sent to Japan to staff military government and assorted intelligence units under Douglas MacArthur's command.

In Japan I was struck, as almost all visitors are, by the many differences from my own country—differences that will be one of the major themes of this book. Many of these distinctions and variances were immediately discernible, while others eased their way into my consciousness only after several months or even years. But there was one most important difference of which I did not become fully aware until twenty years later, when I returned to the United States and found life-styles (at least around my home in Texas) to be comparatively relaxed, friendly, and pleasure-oriented. It was only then that I began to realize fully the extent and the seriousness of the strains and stresses that living in Japan involves, both for long-term foreign residents and for the Japanese themselves.

I remember when this realization first began to take concrete form. One morning as I was driving to Dallas, I found myself *whistling*. I was whistling, I suppose, merely because I was relaxed and comparatively happy and reasonably free of the many minor irritations that beset one so often in Japan. What was surprising was that I could not even remember when I had whistled last.

It was then that I began to formulate my Taut Rubber Band Theory. As the days passed and I relaxed and whistled—and even hummed—more and more, I theorized that every day of my years in Japan had twisted an imaginary rubber band within my mind—turn by slow turn—until in time it became so tense that it trembled with annoyances, vexations, and social inflammations. Depending on the quality of the rubber and on the degree of tension and the length of exposure, such a band may break—occasioning unpleasantness, irrational acts, and even tragedy. But if it is removed from the arena of irritation it will gradually become untensed and finally return to a normal state, or one as near normal as is possible after such strain. This is what, I believed, was happening to me. I was relaxing and slowly returning to a near-normal condition, which was being evidenced by such unfamiliar symptoms as whistling and humming. I found that I seldom if ever got angry anymore. Weeks and months went by without the temperamental reactions to the exacerbations that had savagely twisted this mental rubber band almost daily back in Japan.

Partly, I know, these irritations stemmed from the fact that I was a Westerner trying to live as a Japanese in a society where even foreigners with twenty years of residence are treated (sometimes, admittedly, to their advantage) as if they

First Acquaintance with the Japanese 5

had just got off the boat that very morning; but mostly they arose from the same factors that militate against the peace of mind of the Japanese themselves.

In January, 1972, for example, Tokyo newspapers reported the results of an international survey sponsored by the Sanwa Bank, one of Japan's leading financial institutions. While granting that it is difficult to accurately measure such factors as human happiness, this survey is nonetheless notable and interesting in what it suggests, if not proves. Selecting thirty-three contributing causes and conditions, such as longevity, working hours, crime, living space, wage levels, education, increased costs of living, old-age pensions, and public facilities, the survey then grouped these into six categories: social satisfactions, working conditions, personal satisfactions, presence or absence of irritant factors, safety and a sense of security, and the feeling of worthwhile living.

Assigning a base figure of 100 to Japan, the surveyors gave the United States top listing in this welfare and happiness index with a rating of 253. Great Britain followed with 213, then West Germany with 190, and France with 187.

Japan's overall low rating (which suggests that the Japanese are less than half as happy as Americans) derived principally from such factors as pollution, traffic congestion, lack of parks and public libraries, shortage of paved roads, inadequate drainage and sewage systems, commuting problems, soaring prices, population congestion, and varied serious neuroses arising from the tense preoccupation with individual image and stance on the social scene.

With this background, it is hardly surprising to find another survey (based on a poll of 8,429 junior-high-school students taken by the Japan Emigration Service in the spring of 1971) projecting that 46 percent of such students throughout Japan "would rather live in a foreign country than spend their lives in tradition-bound, feudalistic Japanese society." (Imagine, if you can, the furor that would be aroused in the United States if we Americans were to be authoritatively informed that nearly one-half of our young people would rather live away from their own country.)

Strangely enough, when older Japanese are able to realize their long-cherished desires and go abroad for short visits, they often come home disappointed, but the explanation for this seeming contradiction can be found—partly, at least—in the above Theory of the Taut Rubber Band, because such travelers do not stay in foreign countries long enough to allow their mental rubber bands to untense. Even in my own country, it took me several months, whereas it should take much longer for a Japanese, coping with strange customs, unfamiliar places, and a language in which he or she may be far from perfect.

To understand why it is difficult for the Japanese to accustom themselves to the life-styles of the Western world, one should first try to see the Japanese as they see themselves. They believe that as a race they are emotional (as opposed to logical), diligent, polite, kind, conformist, loyal, patient, humane, just, and responsive to a sense of obligation toward others. A majority of them believe that they are superior to all other races, with the possible exception of the Germans.

They are intensely concerned with their image, both at home and abroad. In a recent list of the ten best-selling books in Japan, *six* were devoted to surveys, analyses, and commentaries on the nature of the Japanese themselves. And yet they are capable of large-scale self-deception. For example, they fancy themselves kind and are puzzled (nowadays as well as before World War Two) by the failure of other nationalities to view them in the same light. When they have the upper hand, they do not realize that their efforts at kindness smack too much of condescension, of the superior who is doing a favor for an inferior and wants that superior-inferior relationship clearly acknowledged, on bended knee and with cap in hand. Or else.

In dealing with the West, they see themselves as being

guided by high moral principles, to which we may or may not
be responsive. They like to say that we do not understand their
position, but in Japan "to understand" is often taken as meaning "to agree with." In their view, if we really understood
their position, we would have to agree with it, for they are
acting under the guidance of Japanese principles of behavior,
which are to them obviously right and true and proper. In
business and personal dealings in Japan, I have occasionally
been asked if I understood so-and-so's position, and when I
answered, "Yes, I understand it—but cannot agree with it,"
I was more often than not rewarded with looks of puzzlement. How could I possibly *not* agree if I understood, they
wanted to know.

Despite this self-deception, there are, of course, more than
a few Japanese who do not see things "in the Japanese way."
For the most part, these are men and women of considerable
intelligence who have been exposed to Western thinking, but
when they venture to criticize the "Japanese way" in print,
they often take care to do so under some guise, or to attribute
these criticisms to someone else, preferably a Westerner.

For example, during most of 1971 the best-selling book
in Japan was one called *Nihonjin to Yudayajin (The Japanese
and the Jews),* by "Isaiah Ben Dasan." While not at all harshly
critical, it does at times cast the Japanese in a not entirely
favorable light. The author's true identity still remains a mystery, but he is almost certainly a Japanese masquerading as
an American Jew. . . . And for years a weekly magazine
called *Shukan Shincho* has been running a column that re-
views and criticizes the Japanese character. The writer signs
himself "Yan Denman" (written in the *katakana* script, it is
obviously meant to be a foreign name) but is actually a Japanese member of the publication's staff.

Even when using a foreign name, one must exercise extreme
caution in being bluntly factual about the Japanese. Although
they are intently interested in what foreigners think of them,
they are even more anxious that they be admired—but from

a distance. If foreign observers get too close, the Japanese fear, what may appear from afar to be dimples will turn out to be pockmarks. This is why one can often find in Japanese publications commentaries about the Japanese by tourists and other short-time visitors, but seldom indeed does one ever see observations written by Old Japan Hands.

Recently I was urged by a Tokyo magazine to write for them in Japanese an article about the reactions of Americans to Japanese travelers as I observed those reactions during my recent time in Texas. I complied, submitting my article ten days later. A mixture of the favorable and unfavorable, it evidently caused something of a shock among the magazine staff. I had reported the facts as I had seen them, but the magazine editors evidently did not want facts, only praise. Eyeing me rather uneasily, they apologized but explained that an unexpected increase in space needed for advertising had made it impossible for them to carry my article "for some time."

While the Japanese people are not at all hard to understand (using *understand* in the non-Japanese sense, of course), it has become advantageous for them to assist in the perpetuation of the tired old half-myth about the Inscrutable Japanese and Their Islands of Mystery. True, in one sense the Japanese remain generally uncomprehended—but merely because so few Westerners really know their language well. And certainly their islands were a land of mystery only a century or so ago to all but a handful of Westerners. Now, however, millions of us have visited their archipelago since World War Two, and many of the veils of mystery and clouds of myth are being swept away. Still, it is convenient for the Japanese psyche to let the mystique run on, for then they can say to us in the West, "Look, you fellows just don't understand us. That's what the trouble is." When faced with persistent misunderstandings with the West, they can thus justify to themselves what they might otherwise be forced to consider stubbornness, insular egoism, or even failure to understand on their own part—an alternative too unbearable to support, of course.

Such misunderstandings are still all too frequent. Although Japan is our second-best customer (after Canada), and although we buy more from her than from any other country, little cultural or spiritual communion exists between the two countries, separated as they are by an abyss of incomprehension—which is deeper and more difficult to cross from our side than from theirs. For though it must be granted that it may be imperfect at times, their cumulative knowledge of us is fifty or even a hundred times greater than ours of them. (In illustration, consider this: Almost any Japanese can name at least five or ten of our states and five of our presidents besides the present one. How many Americans can name even one Japanese prefecture or prime minister?)

Considered in this light, the careful observer cannot regard the future of U.S.-Japan relations with the placid confidence that our economic and security ties would otherwise inspire. Obviously what is needed is an intensified effort at understanding.

And understanding is what the following chapters—in a modest way—are all about.

2

Their Land

Whether the traveler's jet approaches Tokyo from the direction of North America with the rising sun at his back or from Hong Kong and beyond with the setting sun to his left, he has a fair chance of viewing that Queen of Mountains, Fuji, depending upon the courtesy of the weather and the discourtesy of an increasingly polluted atmosphere.

If he fails to see her in her awesome twelve-thousand-foot majesty, he can get another chance by taking any of the trains out of Tokyo for Nagoya, Kyoto, Osaka, Kobe, and beyond, all of which will sweep down the coast past the foot of this extinct volcano which—with geisha and cherry blossoms—has too long and too simplistically characterized Japan to the Western world. And if he doesn't catch a glimpse of her even then, he would be well advised to content himself with a picture postcard showing the mountain. (One Japanese photographer has devoted his entire career to taking pictures of Mount Fuji from every possible angle and at all possible hours and seasons. This in itself is a revealing comment on the philosophy of Japanese art, in which the native artist does not try to innovate, to pioneer new art forms, but rather only to do better what others have already done before him—or what he himself has done before.)

No matter what part of Japan's geography the traveler is able to see from the window of his jet or train, three features will stand out: its greenness, its mountainous terrain, and its clear, fast rivers. Coming as I did from north Texas with its monotonous flatness and muddy, sluggish streams, these three prominent features of the Japanese landscape made an indelible impression on me and are responsible, I am sure, for a considerable portion of the hold that Japan has had on me for so long.

With more than three thousand islands, this archipelago—called *Nihon,* or "The Source of the Sun," by its people—extends along the eastern rim of the Asian continent from the northeast to the southwest for about 1,350 miles. At the closest points it is 124 miles from Korea and 186 from Russia. In area 140,000 square miles, it is not quite so large as California (an oft-used but nonetheless still useful comparison) with its 19,000,000 inhabitants, in contrast to Japan's 103,000,000.

The four main islands of Honshu, Hokkaido, Shikoku, and Kyushu (in order of size) comprise 98 percent of the total area of Japan. The capital is Tokyo, located in central Honshu at about the same latitude as Fresno, Nashville, Newport News, and Seville.

With an abundance of evergreens, most of Japan's foliage remains verdant throughout the year, watered by reliable and plentiful rainfall and by the electricity-producing rivers and streams that rush down from the hills. Two parallel chains of mountains, broken here and there, follow the curve of the islands and occupy so much space that only 16 percent of the country is cultivated, although more than half of the land that slopes no more than 15 percent is tilled.

Much of this tilled land (of which more than half is devoted to the raising of irrigated rice) centers around the large industrial areas of Tokyo-Yokohama, Nagoya, Kita-Kyushu, and Osaka-Kyoto-Kobe, which four contain about three-quarters of the country's total population, as well as around Sapporo (where the 1972 Olympic Winter Games were held), Niigata, and Sendai. In terms of arable land and population,

Japan leads the world with a density of nearly five thousand souls per square mile.

While its rivers are generally not navigable, no place in Japan is more than ninety miles from the open sea, whose waves beat against a coastline nearly 17,000 miles long. This coastline is more irregular along the Pacific coast of southwestern Honshu and western Kyushu, and provides many excellent harbors. Indeed, the lovely, island-dotted Inland Sea could accurately be called one mammoth harbor.

Hot springs (about which more later in the book) and volcanoes are prominent features of the green landscape, there being 160 of the latter. Twenty of these have erupted during the twentieth century, but not Mount Fuji, whose last eruption was in 1707, when she covered Tokyo with six inches of volcanic ash.

Japan's climate is somewhat comparable to that of the eastern coast of North America from Nova Scotia south to Georgia, modified by continental and marine influences. The summers are humid, hot, and comparatively short, and they start off with the major rainy season, brought by predominant winds that blow up from the Pacific to the south and east. Except for Hokkaido, the winters are mild and sunny, influenced by winds off the continental mass of Asia. One southbound ocean current—the Oyashio—cools northeastern Honshu, while the northerly-flowing Kuroshio warms the Pacific coast of the islands as far as Tokyo. At Japan's northern tip, Hokkaido has four months of the year in which mean temperatures drop to below freezing, while on the southern island of Kyushu the climate is mild enough to permit two rice crops annually.

Such climatic distinctions constitute Japan's principal regional differences, the others mostly involving agricultural, fishery, and industrial products, dialects, and traditional folk crafts.

Climate permitting, the airborne traveler should be able to see, in addition to Mount Fuji, a good deal of Japan's capital city as his jet crosses over Tokyo Bay in its approach pattern. The most arresting physical feature of Tokyo's low-lying urban sprawl (consonant with Japan's low political posture of recent years) is the orange-and-white Tokyo Tower, built in 1958 at a cost of $2,800,000 and visited by four million paying customers annually. At 1,092 feet, it is—after one in Moscow—the second-tallest tower in the world. Its local rivals in stature are the thirty-six-story Kasumigaseki Building, the forty-story World Trade Building, and the forty-seven-story Keio Plaza Hotel. Otherwise, the city is noted for its lack of high buildings, their statutory ceiling having been 102 feet, or about ten stories, until 1963.

High or low, this mass that sprawls out to the west and north of Tokyo Bay is the world's largest city, a monstrous, teeming megalopolis at the northeastern end of the 366-mile-long Tokaido (Eastern Road) Corridor. Its "city tree" is the gingko and its bird is the *yuri-kamome,* a species of sea gull. Within its boundaries can be found more than a hundred universities (plus ninety junior colleges) and nearly one-half of all the university students in Japan; the world's largest police force; five full-scale symphony orchestras; five hundred movie theaters; more than one thousand pachinko (pinball) parlors; three opera companies; 30,000 taxis (12,000 in New York); nearly one hundred newspapers; and three baseball parks, each drawing crowds of up to 45,000 nightly. This exuberant jumble of uncoordinated concrete construction is the center of the country's culture—and of its commerce, where most success-oriented Japanese strive to live and long to thrive. It is, above all else, a city of contrasts, of variety, vitality, and more than a little venery. Of renewal and almost reckless resurgence. Of nocturnal delights and daylight drive. Of rawboned excitement and drab ugliness and rare beauty and exotic quaintness. A city to be loved or hated but never ignored. . . .

When Westerners come to Tokyo to live, they usually experience a kind of cultural shock, a wrench of acclimatization varying in severity with the dissimilarity of their points of origin. They find themselves strained and unsettled by the turmoil, the tumult, and the never-ceasing clamor of cars and chaotic construction, of cabaret music, of Klaxons and swooshing jets and of the curious cacophony of sounds of the Tokyo night: the noodle peddler's flute, the clack-clack of clogs on the cement, the eternal barking and howling of the ubiquitous watchdogs, the sirens and fire engines and police patrols, the *blok-blok-blok* of the fire-watch as he signals "All's well!" by knocking his two sticks together, the rolling rumble of the wooden shutters being shoved shut. They are angered or amused—or both—at absurd attitudes and accidents and antiquities. Their credulity challenged, they are puzzled and perplexed by peculiarities light years outside their ken. They are frustrated by language barriers and buffeted by the brusque urgency and hustle of pushing, prosperous, pulsating crowds. But in time the initial shock diminishes, becomes tolerable, and then these newcomers reach an individualistic compromise, an accommodation of life-styles with this, the earth's biggest, noisiest, most dynamic and contrast-packed human habitation.

Because there are no residential zoning regulations as we know them, you will find in Tokyo that the mansions of the affluent and mighty stand jowl to cheek with the sleazy stalls of fishmongers and miniature temples of exquisite beauty. And in the business district an ex-geisha may manage a 150-year-old *sushi* shop right next door to a brightly lit, chrome-plated Kentucky Fried Chicken dispenser. You can take a picture of the ancient stone walls of the Imperial Palace and find soaring Tokyo Tower in the background. Undeniably disharmony has arisen from this attempt to blend the West with the East, but it is disharmony with a certain appeal, compounded of ever-changing patterns and sudden, unexpected green oases and charming retreats, of rickshaw and monorails, of the most subtly tasteful and the most blatantly meretricious.

It is a city where high-speed freeways let you glide low over rooftops, looking right into modern apartment bedroom windows and down on a tousled ancient network of narrow, jagged, ill-lit streets and flimsy native houses made of wood, bamboo, and paper, which in turn lie above the world's most advanced subway network. It is a city of elegant tea ceremonies and poetry-reading contests and geisha-graced banquets, of flower-arranging classes and compulsive viewing of cherry blossoms and polynational restaurants, of jarring rhythms and tattooed toughs and mad, lemminglike dashes for the sea in the summer. It is a delightful but bedeviling, intricately wrought mosaic that sprawls unique among the metropolitan centers of the world.

Within this one giant of a city are to be found the seven cosmopolitan areas of Shinjuku, Shibuya, Ikebukuro, Ueno, Asakusa, Gotanda, and Ginza, each of which is a respectable "city within a city." For example, one of the smaller ones—Ikebukuro—has 60 mah-jong parlors, 4 mammoth department stores, 120 hotels, 135 coffee shops, 436 bars, 27 cabarets, 19 theaters, 24 dancing schools, 191 restaurants of many types, 12 Turkish baths, 32 pachinko parlors, and 820 shops, 100 of which are underground. Shinjuku has even more of each, including the world's tallest hotel, a complex of subway stations through which two and a half million passengers pass each day, and plans for a tower that will stand 1,815 feet high (in contrast to the 1,092-foot Tokyo Tower).

The most overwhelming aspect of Tokyo is, of course, the prodigious number of people who live (if, indeed, *live* is the right word) within its borders—the largest congregation of human beings in one spot in the history of this earth. People in streams, clumps, masses, avalanches, floods, rivers, armies, hosts, and multitudes. Almost all of them have black hair and dark eyes, but there the similarity halts, for we see people ranging in shape, dress, and life-style from gigantic sumo wrestlers with topknots and in native dress to tiny, wizened old women stooped over almost double from long, arduous years in the rice paddies; from teen-age swingers in hot pants to beggars with rented children; from golfing geisha to deaf shoeshine women; from financial magnates in Mercedes-Benz limousines to blind masseuses and masseurs being led down neighborhood streets at night by flute-blowing escorts; from the colorful but raucous *chindon-ya* (street bands) to begrimed ragpickers; and from harried housewives out for their afternoon shopping to the ubiquitous office workers in their white shirts and conservatively colored suits.

Their numbers literally boggle the mind. The zeroes pile up in such rows that the eyes begin to lose touch with reality. In January of 1972 it was estimated that they numbered 11,600,000. They live in 3,664,000 households, and men outnumber women by about 200,000. Their annual per capita earnings for 1970 were ¥ 567,929 (approximately $1,893 at the early 1972 rate of exchange). Each of these men and women (and children) has a theoretical allotment of 0.4 square meters of living space, in contrast with 8.7 square meters in Paris, 9.2 in London, 11.9 in New York, and 45.2 in Washington, D.C. One block in the Sumida Ward of Tokyo holds the dubious honor of having the highest population density in the world, that of 24,320 persons per square mile, which is all the more remarkable when one considers that Sumida does not have many buildings over a few stories in height.

Dotted here and there across Tokyo's flat countenance are spots of greenery, the largest of these being the 250 acres that form the city's—and the nation's—spiritual heart: the low-lying, unobtrusive, mysterious Imperial Palace area, with its circumambient moat and massive fifteen-feet-thick stone walls that have stood and withstood for nearly four hundred years. Within these walls but largely concealed from view by the many gnarled old pine trees are the Imperial Household Ministry, a rice paddy, a biological research laboratory, bomb shelters, a chicken house, riding stables, tennis courts, garages housing one Cadillac, one Daimler, and several Rolls-Royces and Mercedes-Benzes, and the new Imperial Palace itself. In the days when it was called Edo Castle, the site was four or five times its present size, was protected by three moats, and was entered through one of thirty-six gates. When Edo Castle was constructed in 1457, the waters of Tokyo Bay lapped at the base of its eastern battlements.

Other smudges of green on the metropolitan face are public parks (which are small in size and few in number) and private gardens, walled off from outside view and a world in themselves.

These gardens are a reflection of the reverence in which the Japanese hold nature and of their desire not to conquer it, as in the West, but to commune with it and, when necessary, submit to its demands. Depending upon the historical period in which they were developed, these gardens may be designed in any of several styles, such as the Shinden, Shoin, hill, castle, tea, and stroll. They eschew the formality (and the utility) of Western gardens and are carefully planned to appear completely unplanned. They are the great outdoors in miniature, a distilled essence of nature where one can get away from the workaday world and confirm man's oneness with nature in quiet reflection.

While these "vignettes of nature" may be small, they are often constructed to appear larger when viewed from proper vantage points. The ends of paths and tiny streams, for example, are often concealed to give the impression that they extend much farther. Reflecting the Shinto belief that natural spirits exist in all things, much of the material used in their design is symbolic: the pine stands for longevity, the plum for beauty and esthetic perfection, the bamboo for pliable strength, and water for purification. In this way the garden may tell or at least suggest a story. And this story may vary somewhat with the viewer because only its barest elements are told, like those of a sailing ship vaguely sighted through the distant mist, leaving the viewer to fill in the details as suits his fancy. In this way, the famous Ryoanji Temple Garden in

Kyoto can be interpreted in at least two ways: its carefully raked sand and fifteen rocks in three groupings may be seen as islands in the sea or as mountain peaks emerging from the morning mist.

Japanese gardens are in themselves a mirror of the geography of Japan and the character of its people and their passion for understatement. Their spareness reflects the scarcity of arable land and mineral resources as well as the comparative poverty of the common people until recent years. Having done without for so long, the Japanese learned to make a little do in place of a lot. They learned to let one flower stand for a dozen, one tree for a forest, one pebble for a boulder. A hint was always better than a bold statement. A delicate color blended better with humility than bright reds and golds.

This principle was also followed in flower arranging, at which the Japanese excel. No need to place two dozen red roses in the tokonoma (alcove) in the living room when only one—enhanced by a green sprig of this and a brown twig of that—would do quite well by inviting the viewer's participation through use of his imagination. Also, the flower arrangements are often symbolic and as such are made up of three elements—*ten, chi,* and *jin,* or heaven, earth, and man—which inhibits profuse use of materials.

With land as costly as it is, not many Japanese these days can afford such gardens, so, in addition to such floral arrangements, they may also adorn their homes with bonsai and bonkei. The former are dwarfed trees (some only a foot high and five hundred years old) and the latter are miniature gardens in boxes, often incorporating bonsai. To men and women who have no gardens and who miss daily communion with nature, these carefully nurtured trees and box gardens offer some compensation.

There was much more greenery but far fewer gardens in Tokyo that day in 1456 when Dokan Ota started to build his castle there. Edo (Tokyo) was then nothing more than a mud flat with about one hundred houses and a clutch of largely indifferent peasants who amused themselves by watching whales cavort in the then-clear waters of the bay. Ota, however, was one of the early civic boosters. He looked at the vast, fertile Kanto Plain, the rivers watering it, the immense bay, the seven hills upon which future battlements and homes of the wealthy could be constructed, and the mild weather, and decided that with the right kind of promotion this wretched little hamlet might someday dominate the Kanto Plain. Or, his imagination really running riot, it might even advance so far as to become the central city of all of Japan, although he doubted, in soberer moments, that it would ever really be able to compete with the splendor of Kyoto off to the southwest.

Choosing as the site a place where an old fort had stood, Ota began to build his castle when he was but twenty-four years of age. Completed in April of the following year (1457 is generally accepted as Tokyo's birth date, making it at this writing 515 years old), the castle became the focal point of the prosperous community that Ota went on to develop during the twenty-nine years of life remaining to him. In 1486, Sadamasa Uesugi—Ota's liege lord—became suspicious of his vassal's ambitions and arranged his assassination. After Ota's death, commerce declined, the castle fell into disrepair, and the inhabitants returned to their earlier lackadaisical ways.

One hundred years passed. In May of 1590, Hideyoshi—the five-foot-tall peasant-general and de facto ruler of Japan—was standing on a hill near Odawara, at the southern edge of the Kanto Plain, and looking to the north. He was there to lay siege to the mighty Odawara castle of the Hojo family. At his side stood Ieyasu Tokugawa, his second-in-command.

"When we defeat the Hojos, I shall give you this region to administer as your own," Hideyoshi said to Tokugawa, who bowed in silent appreciation.

Hideyoshi thought for a moment, then asked: "From where will you govern these lands?"

"From here in Odawara, my lord," said Tokugawa, soon to

be the founder of the dynasty that was to rule Japan for 264 years with a degree of strict control seldom achieved anywhere else in the world.

But Hideyoshi was both cautious and crafty. He knew that, after himself, Tokugawa was the most formidable military commander in Japan as well as an individual of vaulting ambition. If anything, he wanted Tokugawa even farther away than Odawara from his own stronghold in Kansai.

"No, not here," Hideyoshi said. "Build your bastion in Edo instead."

"Edo, my lord?" Tokugawa asked to be sure he had heard right. He was not at all enthusiastic, for he knew the half-ruined castle standing there at the edge of the mud flats.

Concealing his satisfaction, Hideyoshi nodded, then turned away from the still-kneeling Tokugawa.

Determined to make the best of a poor situation, Tokugawa Ieyasu had the old Edo castle torn down and, summoning some ten thousand laborers from the eight fiefs newly under his control, launched the construction of a larger, mightier castle, bringing the massive stones for the thick walls by ship from distant Hyogo and surrounding it with three deep moats two hundred feet wide in some places. Not long after the castle was completed, Hideyoshi died; and after some internal scuffling to see who would succeed him as the "Barbarian-Subduing Generalissimo," Tokugawa became, in 1603, the Shogun himself.

One of the first things he did—after putting down on paper a set of "House Laws" by which his descendants were to govern themselves (and Japan) for the next 264 years—was surely a stroke of administrative genius that was to shape the character of Edo—and present-day Tokyo—more than any other single factor. He instituted the system of *sankin-kotai*.

It was brilliant in its simplicity but massively burdensome in what it demanded of others. Japan was then divided up among more than three hundred fiefs—feudal kingdoms of varying sizes ruled by daimyo, or territorial barons. The *fudai* daimyo were those closely allied to the Tokugawa house, while the *tozama* (or outer) daimyo were the more distant, sometimes hostile, and often powerful clan chieftains. Tokugawa had decided to order all of them to build residences in Edo and to spend part of each year there under the watchful eyes of his magistrates—and to leave their families behind as hostages during those months when they were back home attending to local affairs (and perhaps plotting his downfall, he thought darkly).

The foundation of what was to become the world's largest metropolis was therewith accomplished by a few strokes of the pen. More than three hundred daimyo and eighty thousand of their samurai poured into the burgeoning city, together with their families and many of the most capable administrators from each fief. Large-scale construction was launched. Battalions of builders, then artisans and merchants, gathered. Persons long immured in the hinterlands were exposed to new tastes, fashions, pleasures, and philosophies. They wanted more—and there was always someone there to cater to their desires. Keenly aware of the unrelenting hostility of many of the outer daimyo, Tokugawa demanded of them ever-increasing expenditure on ceremonies, staff, shrine construction, and civic repairs—to keep their resources in a state of near-depletion. He then decided that one Edo residence was not enough, that each daimyo should maintain two: one near at hand, so that the daimyo could be within easy fetching distance, and the other farther off, where most of his warriors would be stationed—outside the protective walls of the moat. Provincial revenues poured into Edo to cover these costs. Cash-and-credit finances replaced the rice-and-barter economy of the countryside. New ideas, strange sights stimulated the peoples who came into Edo in a steady stream. The city began to call itself *O-Edo,* or Great Edo, and took on the not-entirely-unjustified airs of a progressive, vigorous, and sophisticated city. In short, the city boomed.

And so it was throughout the 264 years of the so-called

Tokugawa Era. While rural Japan toiled in the fields and rice paddies and slept—and, in many ways, stagnated—Great Edo continued to reign as the economic, cultural, political, and military heart-and-brains of Japan. There were, of course, setbacks, delays, detours, and distractions, but in general the movement was steady and forward. Against the background of the marvelous political stability of the Tokugawas there was enacted a continuing drama in which disastrous fires, assassinations, vendettas, and earthquakes figured strongly.

But in 1853, Commodore Matthew Perry's "black ships" anchored off Uraga (south of Yokohama) and presaged the downfall of the Tokugawa regime, which was already harassed by domestic discontent. Pressured by gunboat diplomacy into ratifying the unpopular foreign treaties, the last Tokugawa Shogun was forced by dissident elements into abdicating his de facto throne so that the way might be paved for the "Imperial Restoration" of 1868, the beginning of the new Meiji Era. The Emperor Meiji moved from Saikyo ("western capital"), or Kyoto, to Edo, took over Edo Castle as his residence and palace, and renamed the city Tokyo ("eastern capital").

The new emperor lost no time in seeing to it that his administration lived up to its ambitious name, "The Era of Enlightened Government." Gathering about him some of the most intelligent and farsighted young men in his realm, he decided that Japan would have to meet the Western world on its own terms. In order to do so, she would have to learn a great deal from the West, so foreign teachers, specialists, engineers, and consultants were invited to Japan in droves. Displaying their talent for adaptability on an as yet untested scale, the Japanese decided that since they obviously could not beat the West, they would, if not join it, at least learn from it. They hoped, however, to avoid sinking to slavish imitation. They would regard the models held up for their consideration with a critical eye, accept or reject, and then, perhaps, alter those found acceptable to suit their own national character. They would follow the principle of *Wakon-yosai* and blend the Japanese spirit with Western knowledge, just as they had done centuries before when they melded the Japanese spirit with Chinese learning (*Wakon-kansai*).

In this effort, Japan was blessed with the talented leadership of a group of extraordinary men who were farsighted, devoted, and brilliant: Ito, Okubo, Kido, Okuma, Itagaki, Iwakura, Inoue, and Yamagata. A group of men comparable, in several senses, to those who managed the American Revolution, wrote our Constitution, and steered the young republic through its unsteady infancy. These Japanese leaders traveled to Europe and to the United States to see for themselves the sources of the power that had produced Perry's black ships and the naval squadrons that had bombarded Kagoshima and Shimonoseki. They arranged for a continuing influx into Japan of Western teachers, experts, and technicians: Englishmen, who supervised the construction of a modern navy and the development of a system of coinage; Americans, who reformed the educational machinery and taught Western agricultural methodology; Frenchmen and Germans, who both contributed to the codification of Japanese law and the organization of a new army. And again, Germans, who directed the establishment and administration of medical schools.

Postal and telegraph systems, modern mining, national and international finance, development of harbors, paper mills, scientific laboratories, construction of modern office buildings and government edifices, sanitation, railroads, prison reform (including the abolition of torture), cotton mills, water works, steam-powered factories—all these and more were substantially the creations and contributions of Westerners employed and directed by Japan's leaders, who managed at the same time to stifle efficiently and thoroughly the strong opposition of those samurai who wanted to retain their two swords, topknots, and sinecures as idle vassals of feudal lords, of those lords themselves who did not wish to relinquish the control of their fiefs to central authority, and of a varied lot assembled under the banner of *"Sonno! Joi! Sakko!* (Revere the Emperor! Expel the barbaric Westerners! Close the ports!)"

While this miracle of internal transformation was taking place, Japan was also displaying its newly acquired military prowess on the international scene. After unilaterally annexing Okinawa from China in 1872, she dispatched, in May of 1874, a force of three thousand samurai to Formosa to punish the natives there for killing several Okinawan sailors, and then forced the Chinese government to pay an indemnity and to admit the culpability of her Formosan subjects in the incident. In 1894–95, Japan fought her first major foreign war of the Meiji Era with China and won the island of Formosa, with its considerable natural resources, as spoils of her victory. But many Western observers regarded this as merely another internal squabble in Asia and did not consider Japan's victory as meaningful proof of her strength in a larger international arena. The proof they lacked was not long in coming. In 1904–05, Japan challenged Czarist Russia over spheres of influence on the continent of Asia and, by destroying the Imperial Russian fleet at the Battle of Tsushima Strait with a classic crossing of the T, won the southern half of Sakhalin together with the respect, if not the friendship, of the world.

In 1910, only two years before the death of the Emperor Meiji, Japan annexed Korea. When the First World War came along like an encore to the Meiji drama, she sided with the Allied Powers, assisted the French in the Mediterranean, and saw minor military action in the Indian and Pacific Oceans, thereby securing for herself—at a cost of only three hundred men killed in battle—a position as one of the Big Five Powers and as one of the Big Three in terms of naval strength. As a bonus, Japan also earned a degree of prosperity that pushed her growing industry much farther along its path of competition with the West and that sowed some of the seeds of the disastrous ambitions that were to follow.

Hakko ichiu is what they called the concept in Japanese: the eight corners of the world under one roof. For the somewhat less megalomaniacal, there was the *Dai-Toa Kyoeiken,* or Greater East Asia Co-Prosperity Sphere. The successes of the Meiji, Taisho, and early Showa Eras had served to persuade many Japanese militarists, politicians, and industrialists that Japan's unique status as the Land of the Gods imbued her people with a charismatic quality that enabled—indeed, compelled—them to lead the less fortunate and often incomprehensibly recalcitrant races of the Far East to a better way of life, whether they wanted to be led or not.

As with Japan's previous era, the curtain on this one rose auspiciously enough, if somewhat slowly and fitfully. The Greater Japan National Essence Society (*Dai-Nihon Kokushi-kai*) was formed in 1919 and the National Foundation Society (*Kokuhonsha*) in 1924. In 1929, staff members of Japan's Kwantung Army arranged the murder of Chang Tso-lin, a Manchurian war lord, in an unsuccessful attempt to force their government into war with China. In 1931, Premier Hamaguchi was assassinated, and a military takeover of the government by a group of army officers (the *Sakura-kai*) and certain civilian extremists was barely averted. On September 18, 1931, without prior consultation with the Cabinet in Tokyo, the Kwantung Army arranged the Mukden Incident on the South Manchurian Railway and used this as a pretext to overrun Manchuria. In 1932, Premier Inukai was assassinated, spelling the end to party government in Japan. Other assassinations and incidents, such as those of the *Panay* and the Marco Polo Bridge, followed as the Thirties wore on.

Although in 1941 Japan was still far from conquering all of China, she controlled, albeit at times not so securely, enough of China's coast, industry, population, and major cities to earn respect for her boast that she would eventually dominate it all. On December 7, 1941, she threw all of her might into a series of military attacks and campaigns that encompassed the near-destruction of the U.S. Pacific Fleet and much of its finest naval facility away from the American mainland, the subjugation of Singapore (which British leaders had long boasted was impregnable), the sinking of the British battleships *Repulse* and *Prince of Wales* by air power, the capture of Hong Kong, the subdual of Corregidor, and the eventual conquest of the Philippines, Indonesia, Southeast Asia, and many Pacific islands, large and small.

The Japanese had risen high. Too high, as it turned out. And they had ridden roughshod over the backs of too many people. Their descent was, fittingly, more precipitate than their climb. After the cessation of hostilities and the signing of the surrender document aboard the battleship *Missouri* in Tokyo Bay, the Japanese lifted their heads to see their cities devastated, their property and wealth stripped from them, millions dead, and more millions homeless and hopeless. Few peoples had ever been so thoroughly beaten.

The problems they then faced—and how the Japanese overcame them—are the subjects of another chapter herein. But having solved these, the Japanese of the Seventies faced still another set of problems—admittedly less formidable than defeat, poverty, and starvation, but exasperating nonetheless because many of the new set were derived from success, prosperity, industrialization, Westernization, and technical advance.

Pollution plagued the land. Tokyo's smog overcast was worse than that of Los Angeles; twice as many noxious pollutants fell on the city as on an equal area in New York City. Inflation rode close behind, never quite under the control of a government that seemed to be able to control so much else. A massive migration from farms to factories was taking place, with resulting abrasions and imbalances. When Japanese exporters had been at last about to lay to rest the old bugaboo of "cheap Japanese goods," they found themselves facing instead increasing resentment of their success in raising quality and keeping prices reasonably low. Having so long neglected the welfare of its citizens to build up its industrial base, the nation found their living standards extremely low in many sensitive areas. (Only 20 percent of Japanese homes, for instance, have modern sewage disposal.) Here, too, were a pronounced generation gap and erosion of the traditional family system, while people of all ages faced individual and collective decisions of how to blend the new with the old, how to adapt the good being introduced from the Western world to Japan's framework without spoiling too many of the old traditions. And they were puzzled by a suddenly changed Uncle Sam, who had turned cold and hard (it seemed) in commercial and financial dealings.

Serious though these problems were, however, there was little doubt that the Japanese would overcome them. If you consider the problems that faced them when they emerged from 250 years of national isolation in the middle of the past century, and those confronting them in September of 1945 after the surrender, those of the Seventies fall into a less alarming perspective.

3

Their Courtesy, Customs, and Curious Ways— Including the Communal Bath

After a few days or weeks in Japan, most foreign visitors leave content in the conviction that they have witnessed some of the world's politest people in action: smiling elevator girls who bow hundreds of times daily, watchful waitresses who await the guest's every command in hushed expectation, first-time acquaintances who—it would seem—are quite prepared, even eager, to sacrifice anything short of the family honor to insure the visitor's comfort and tranquillity of mind.

After returning home, these good people spread the word: "Talk about being polite! Well, you've never seen anything till you've been to Japan. Sakes alive, Sarah, those people are just so polite it hurts to watch them!"

But then there is the inevitable other side of the coin. Ask the opinion of a long-time foreign resident of Japan, someone who has really lived *among* the Japanese and not just in their country, and don't be surprised if he tells you that, in his carefully considered opinion, the Japanese may well be the rudest people on the globe.

Why this dichotomy? How can such extreme differences of opinion exist, both being defended and clung to tenaciously by sizable groups of sober, serious citizens?

Part of the answer lies in definitions: To Westerners, kindness and sincere concern for the welfare of others—including, importantly, persons with whom we have no particular relationship—are integral parts of politeness. A man gives his seat on a bus to an old lady whom he has never seen before because he genuinely wants her to be comfortable.

But few Japanese would feel that way about it. Giving one's seat on a bus to a complete stranger—male or female, young or old—was not a point specifically raised when they were taught "good manners," and, besides, such a person stands too far outside their own orbit.

The Japanese concept of etiquette is, first and above all, a matter of demarcation. Lines—many lines—have to be drawn. Persons on this side of the line are in; those on the other, are out. Utterly, irretrievably out. Westerners would say that courtesy—if it is to be genuine—must be extended to all; the Japanese would protest that in their crowded islands it is simply not possible to be really courteous to so many.

To them, courtesy is *not* in limitless supply. Only by withholding it from strangers can they offer it lavishly to acquaintances, that is, those on the right side of the lines mentioned above. If given to friend and stranger alike, then the worth of the gift is diluted. And wherein, they ask, lies the value of being a friend?

The rest of the answer lies in the degree of exposure and the angle of vision. Let's say that Tom Wentworth typifies the former point of view; he spent two weeks in Japan recently and swears that the Japanese are the politest, friendliest people anywhere. In Tokyo, he stayed in the Hotel Okura, where his needs and comfort were ministered to by a highly trained, cordial staff. Letters of introduction opened to him the homes of two cosmopolitan Japanese families who vied with each other in entertaining the visitor, in assisting him in his business mission and personal errands, and in smoothing the way in many of his other proposed undertakings. Even when he left the warmth of their protection and guidance, he still did not stray far from the paths trodden by most visitors—to certain restaurants, bars, night clubs, and scenic attractions. With one or two minor exceptions, he was never really on his own or among strangers at any time he was in Japan. He was either in the company of a benefactor or guide or in a situation in which his comfort and convenience had been carefully pre-arranged.

But then there is Harry Sloughwit, who was discharged from the U.S. Army twelve years ago in Japan to be with his Japanese girl friend and whose mechanical aptitude got him a bread-and-butter job with an American business-machine dealer in Tokyo. Although Harry has been promoted twice over the years, the fact that he is still paying a whopping alimony to his ex-wife keeps him far from the "rich foreigner" category. He has to ride the trains and buses to and from work and gets shoved around ferociously in the process. On the way to work, he may stop in a store to buy a package of cigarettes and have a stranger come charging from behind and quite unconcernedly elbow him aside to demand prior service. At the entrance to his office building, no one will dream of holding the door open to keep it from closing in the face of others (unless they are acquainted). At noon he fights his way through crowds, being slammed into several times without apology, to a small restaurant down the street. No sooner does he find a table to himself off in one corner, however, than someone comes along and plops himself down at the same table without so much as a by-your-leave. When he walks to Yuraku-cho Station to catch a train home in the evening, one or more Japanese men will likely shove into the ticket line ahead of him, just as if they were Rulers of the Universe. (The insufferable arrogance of the Japanese at such times has made more than a few long-time foreign residents pull up stakes.) Reaching his own neighborhood, Harry may find that the Japanese children on the streets treat him with a degree of contemptuous familiarity that, if directed at a Japa-nese male of his age and dress, would surely earn them nothing less than an instantaneous and barbarous drubbing. If he is foolish enough to take his Japanese wife out for a stroll in the park on Sunday, idle laborers will likely shout something obscene at her, and college students may snicker and point when they pass.

Harry, of course, does not think that the Japanese are a polite people. In fact, he might even become violent if you suggested such a possibility to him.

Many foreigners explain the distinction by saying that the Japanese are wonderfully polite when they have their shoes off. What is meant, of course, is that the Japanese usually have their shoes off when in the presence of persons within the inner circle, on the right side of those all-important lines: neighbors, classmates, co-workers, relatives.

We in the Western world have tended to base actions on certain abstract principles while paying only incidental mind to manners, while in Japan the opposite emphasis has prevailed. The Japanese have concerned themselves more with the form than with the substance. For centuries they trained themselves to perform a great many acts, large and small, in a precisely specified manner, the slightest divergence from which was not only frowned upon but could even be, in serious cases, classified as a crime. This led to what Inazo Nitobe, author of *Bushido: The Soul of Japan,* characterized as "coercive etiquette."

This coercive etiquette toward only those with whom a relationship has been established is behind the typical Japanese failure to help anyone who is injured or taken suddenly ill on the streets or is in any kind of danger. The desire in this instance is to avoid the establishment of a relationship and its concomitant responsibilities. While most Westerners believe that the more friends we have, the better off we are, the Japanese tend to shy away from additional acquaintances, feeling that each is more of a burden than a pleasure or source of gain. Each requires much attention, and one can do only so much. Furthermore, the social values involved are so delicate, so subject to varied interpretations and evaluations, that the associations governed by them require the concentration

of a tightrope walker. To maintain each of several social relationships in proper balance and in a state of good repair is
not, as the Japanese would say, an *asameshimae no shigoto*—
an easy, "before-breakfast" job. They require much delibera-
tion, concentration, time, worry, and expense. Although there
may be pleasant moments, these are incidental. The Japanese
regard the proper servicing of a social connection as a duty,
and their attitude toward duty is manifest in the Imperial Rescript to Soldiers and Sailors: "Be resolved that duty is heavier
than a mountain, while death is lighter than a feather."

Perhaps the most important single key to an understanding
of the national character and the customary attitudes of the
Japanese can be found in their set of social values identified individually by the names *on* (kindness, obligation), *giri* (duty,
justice), *ninjo* (humanity), *seii* (sincerity), *makoto* (sincerity), *kao* (face), *sekinin* (responsibility), *gimu* (duty),
and *nimmu* (mission, assigned task). These are the ligatures
that hold the framework of Japanese society together, each
making active demands on its members. And if only each had
its own clear-cut area of operation, the troublesome friction
within and among groups would be considerably alleviated.

Unfortunately, the vectors cross and tangle only too often,
providing the plots for much of Japan's literature. Does duty
to liege lord outweigh obligation to one's teacher? Must human feelings be cast aside in favor of responsibility to one's
parents? Must the young man obey his father and abandon
the girl he loves? Should the young mother tell her husband
that the baby she has just borne is not his if, by so doing, she
may cause him to resign from his teaching job in shame?
These and similar threads of indecision are what form the
warp and woof of many literary classics as well as less pre-
tentious stories—and, even more important, what represent
the evaluations and decisions which typify actual social con-
course in present-day Japan.

While each of the above social values can be translated into

English fairly adequately, these English translations often do not encompass all that the original Japanese is meant to convey. This is especially true of *sekinin, seii* or *makoto,* and *on.*

Sekinin is a word used to describe the depth of a man's awareness of his various obligations and the extent to which he repays them. *Seii,* or *makoto* (described in more detail in the chapter "Their Men" herein), means the zeal with which a Japanese undertakes to do whatever is expected of him according to the Japanese code. *On* are obligations which the Japanese believe they incur passively or automatically just by being Japanese—these include obligations to their parents, teachers, and the Emperor. They must try to repay, at least in part, these obligations, and such efforts can be categorized into specific duties: a man's obligation to maintain his professional reputation, loyalty to Japan and to the Emperor, duty to his employer (in feudal times, to his liege lord), strict observation of community customs and cooperative life, and filial piety.

The Japanese adopted the Confucian ethic of filial piety from China, and it has long been a mainstay in their social morality, although perhaps not so strong as in its country of origin. (A picture illustrating this ethic—seen in both China and Japan—shows a sixty-year-old man romping like a baby on the floor in front of his parents, who are both in their doddering eighties. By acting much younger than his age, this son is trying to delude his parents into happily believing that they are not yet so very old themselves.) Because of this sense of duty, parents in Japan may lead less lonely lives in their declining years than their counterparts in the United States. In Japan, parents normally remain in the *honke* (the principal family seat) even after turning over the reins of familial control to their eldest son. Or, if this is not possible, a place is found for them in the home of another of their children. They seldom go to rest homes or retirement colonies.

Ancestor worship in Japan is an extension of filial piety about which a good deal of comment, mostly unfavorable, has been made by Westerners, who often seem somehow offended by the notion of worshipping one's ancestors. Here again, however, we have another of those many problems whose roots are fundamentally linguistic. Both of the words (*ancestor* and *worship*) are, in fact, inadequate translations. The Japanese do not "worship" their ancestors. To worship means to perform acts of adoration and veneration, and few Japanese feel that strongly about their forebears. What they do feel is that they are indebted to them and that they respect their memories, but the words *veneration* and *adoration* express much more than what is meant in this instance. Furthermore, the word *ancestor,* which implies distant progenitors, is itself excessive. The Japanese concern with "ancestors" is mostly limited to those who can be remembered by the oldest living member of the family. Were he asked if he worshipped his forefathers of eight or ten generations ago, the average Japanese would laugh at the idea. In fact, the Japanese are much less concerned with such genealogical matters than are many Westerners. Occasionally one may meet a Japanese who will make reference to his forefathers having been samurai, but usually he will be very vague and unconcerned about the details. Nor do I know of any Japanese equivalents, for example, of our Pilgrim Society, Daughters of the American Revolution, General Society of the War of 1812, or any other organization primarily concerned with distant progenitors.

Throughout the history of our relations with Japan, Western observers have frequently questioned her conception of truth, have, in fact, suggested or even averred that lying was a leading custom of her people. In his diary Townsend Harris, the first American consul in Japan, wrote, "All these bare-faced lies were a fair specimen of Japanese diplomacy." Sir Rutherford Alcock, the first British consul general in Japan, wrote of "the incorrigible tendency of the Japanese to withhold from foreigners or disguise the truth on all matters great and small." Even discounting a certain amount of exaggeration, these two men —and many who followed them during Japan's subsequent century of Western contacts—must have had some cause for such a jaundiced view of Japanese veracity. And yet, for example, during my almost thirty years of close association with the Japanese people, I have found them to be neither noticeably more nor less truthful than we are. It may be that the difference can be explained by the fact that I have always dealt with the Japanese in their own language and within the framework of their own social values. Admittedly, they may tend to avoid the truth if it is so unpleasant that it could damage the harmony of a relationship, but such a tendency is not entirely unknown in the Western world, either. The Japanese may often prefer to say what will please the hearer. The truth, to them, is not an absolute, abstract value but rather something that should be revealed, or at times concealed, according to the circumstances involved.

We might say that such an off-and-on attitude toward truth destroys its value almost as effectively as does an outright preference for falsehood. Be that as it may, the Japanese have ways of revealing the truth among themselves and among those Westerners who are privy to their psychology. If some of us think them mendacious, it may be because we are trying to make the Japanese play the game according to our rules instead of their own.

The Japanese have also been accused of being both two-faced and inscrutable (although the two adjectives are somewhat contradictory), but the latter allegation is hardly supportable nowadays—especially not if one knows how to read the signs. And if the Japanese do occasionally conceal their emotions, it may be only to protect the other party from exposure to them. This now largely undeserved reputation for inscrutability must have been formed when Westerners first came to Japan in large numbers about the time of the Meiji Restoration and the close of Japan's feudal era. Until then, it was customary for superiors to demand unquestioning obedience from those beneath them. When commands were given, inferiors were not allowed to show pleasure or distaste, surprise or curiosity, anticipation or disappointment. If they did, severe punishments were meted out, which could have understandably given rise to a decided preference for noncommittal inscrutability.

To say that the Japanese are two-faced is also inaccurate. What would be nearer the mark would be to say that they have *many* faces. Nor would such a description be regarded by them as derogatory. To the Japanese, it is only natural that the face one shows to a policeman be different from the face that he shows to a local shopkeeper, which in turn should differ from the one he shows to his son's teacher at school. And so on and on. Most of them are very adept at changing faces quickly, from the most humble to the most arrogant, from the most benign to the most petulant.

In this respect, I have in mind a not-so-unusual Japanese friend whose Tokyo office I visited quite often at one stage of my life in Japan. He was what we Americans would call colloquially a wheeler-dealer, although on a rather limited scale. At the time he was operating out of one large room that served him as office space, private bar, and occasional bedroom. He would often have three or four or even more business visitors in this room at the same time, but he would seldom introduce one to another. It was his custom to spread them as far apart as the space permitted and then to make his rounds from one to the next, conversing with each in confidential tones. It was invariably an enjoyable study in character to watch how completely he could change his expression, bearing, and general attitude between one visitor and another, depending, of course, on the variations in each visitor's position and situation vis-à-vis himself. With the first, he might be the embodiment of servility: bowing, scraping, and touching his forelock. To the next—only three steps beyond—he might be cold, haughty, gruff, and rancorous. With the third, he might be the incarnation of high good humor, laughing, joking, and nudging him in the ribs while reminiscing conspiratorially over their adventures on the Ginza two nights before. His features were superbly nimble. He never smiled when he should have frowned or grimaced when he should have guffawed. It was always a remarkable performance, especially since it was carried out in full view of all of his other visitors.

Their smile baffles many of us Westerners because the Japanese not only smile when amused or pleased, just as we do, but also as a distinct signal to others that they should go no farther with the present inquiry, line of conversation, or actions; that they should suspend or postpone judgment on the matter under discussion. And the smile is often used by the Japanese as a device to protect the privacy of the individual. Suppose that when you invite Mr. Tominaga and his wife to dinner, he replies that he will come but that he will not be able to bring his wife. If you ask him why and he smiles but does not answer, then you should not pursue the matter. It means that he does not want to tell you exactly why he will not bring her. He smiles instead of saying, "I'm sorry, but that is a private matter."

Likewise, the laugh can be used as a means to conceal or gloss over embarrassment or sadness or even incipient anger. It is another of those gossamer veils of reserve that partly— but only partly, for the meaning is nevertheless visible—cover certain emotional reactions.

One Japanese characteristic that seems to have irritated Westerners perhaps more than any other is their alleged imitativeness. (When we Americans copy things, we say we are following the fashion; if the Japanese do it, they are *imitating*.) For many years, we heard the old joke about the Japanese who, during the war, raised a sunken British battleship and copied it exactly—right down to the hole in its hull that caused it to sink. (The Japanese already had battleships like the *Yamato* that far outclassed any other naval vessel then afloat—or sunk.)

While no one would seriously try to deny that the Japanese have copied a great deal from the Western world, there are several points involved here that should be judiciously considered before a blanket condemnation is made: First, there is very little that the Japanese have borrowed from any foreign culture without having altered it—extensively in some cases, only slightly in others—to fit into their own milieu. Second, it was the West that forced Japan to open its doors to the world. (Then, as now, people should have had the right to be left alone.) Having been pushed against its will into the nineteenth-century arena of international intrigue, imperialism, and industrialization, Japan was brought face to face with a sink-or-swim situation—and the only way she could swim was to persuade the West to show her how. To have done otherwise would have been insane. Third, in its struggle to recover after the war, Japanese industry could seldom afford, until recent years, to budget funds for research and development, so inevitably the West stayed far ahead of Japan in the creation of new products. Nowadays, however, the Japanese are earmarking more money for research and development and are not only devising a respectable number of new technological processes of their own but are also beginning to export these to the West, which trend should exhibit a marked increase in the future. And, fourth, this Japanese willingness to learn from us is proving very profitable: Japan paid the Western nations—principally the United States—$433,000,000 (mostly net profit) in 1970 for technological assistance, and this sum increases yearly.

Akin to Japanese imitativeness is their curiosity, one commendable facet of which is their interest in international affairs and their willingness to open their minds and consider that which is new or different. Unfortunately for Westerners living in Japan, this curiosity becomes white-hot when focused on us. Anything that we do or show interest in suddenly becomes a very exciting object or action to the Japanese. As an experiment, I have occasionally stopped in front of a Japanese show window that no one had even glanced at until I came along. Almost immediately, at least three or four—

and often more—Japanese would then stop and stand shoulder to shoulder with me trying to see what it was that had attracted the attention of the American.

Often the very intentness of this curiosity is fatiguing. At first, such attention may be rather ego-gratifying to the foreigner in Japan, but soon this palls, and he then goes through a stage of wondering if he forgot to wipe the shaving cream off his neck that morning or if his ears might have turned green overnight. After that, he may become hypersensitive to being stared at and begin to deliberately seek out little-used streets and nearly empty stores.

The Japanese custom of the bath has deservedly been called the Grand Passion of the people, who embrace it because they are addicted to cleanliness and because it is as relaxing as two or three Martinis at the end of the day. If you are invited to dinner in a Japanese home and your host urges you to bathe shortly after arrival, you need not take umbrage at what you might construe as a totally unnecessary comment on the state of your hygiene. He will be only following the dictates of his code and suggesting that you indulge in what to him is a most pleasant and relaxing predinner custom.

In the winter a long, hot bath keeps the Japanese warm (in their chilly houses) long after the event, and in the summer, the air of the evening feels somehow less hot and oppressive after a long soak in 105°–110° water.

American and Japanese attitudes toward the bath and its uses diverge largely at three points. One is the shower, that embodiment of the American dream of antiseptic efficiency. Granted, the Japanese say, it gets you clean, but ridding one's body of dirt, sweat, and germs is only part, albeit an essential part, of the cult of the bath. It does not relax the bather, they say, nor does it accomplish any of several other desiderata.

We, in turn, question that anyone who bathes in the same water with others can really get clean, even granting that each bather scrubs himself outside on the title floor before entering the tub. This habit of having a number of persons bathe in the same water had its origin in the urgent necessity to conserve fuel, which is still a valid reason, together with the fact that, given typical Japanese water-heating equipment, it would take entirely too long to heat (and to refill) a tub for each member of the family.

In addition to the shower, the Japanese also raise dubious eyebrows at our juxtaposition of the bathtub or shower and the toilet bowl. We consider that both are integral parts of the internal and external cleansing of the body and that it is only right (or at least not shocking) that they should stand side by side. The Japanese, on the other hand, see less essential connection between the two and feel, in fact, that the sight of a toilet bowl so close at hand can crush the aesthetic pleasure to be had from a leisurely, contemplative soaking. They would prefer that their baths be adjacent to flowers, moonlight, wind-bells, and nightingale song.

My first encounter with a Japanese bath occurred shortly after my arrival in Japan, when I still didn't know how really hot such a bath can be. (Japan's hottest public baths are to be found in the resort town of Kusatsu, north of Karuizawa, where the water temperature hovers around 120 degrees Fahrenheit and where professional bath-masters are employed to lecture first-time bathers on the safest way to enter the caldrons and lead them in by the numbers, like Army drill sergeants. During the first inundation, which is limited to only three or four minutes, the bath-masters hover over their submerged platoons shouting encouragement, cautioning all to remain still to lessen the searing effect on the skin, and counting off the seconds remaining until the blessed reprieve of complete emergence. In Basil Hall Chamberlain's day, according to his *Things Japanese,* the bath-masters used trumpets to urge their phalanxes in and out of the waters, but this practice is now passé, so perhaps progress is a word with some meaning, after all.)

Blissfully ignorant of such temperatures, two of my class-mates and I made a weekend trip to the hot springs resort of Tsuetate in the mountains of central Kyushu. In those difficult days, there were almost no Japanese guests in any of the inns, so we were largely on our own when we strolled into the spacious communal bathroom of our inn for the first time. One of my classmates, Huntley, lowered himself blithely into the inviting expanse of bath water and then climbed right back out again, only with much greater alacrity.

Aghast at his broken whimpering and the bright red hue of his lower parts, Bill and I were backing away from the pool-sized bath when the door opened and two maids of the inn entered, both naked.

As I recall that scene today, I find it difficult to recognize myself, the intervening twenty-six years and hundreds of other sexually desegrated baths having completely revised my fundamental thinking about such matters. I was then a twenty-one-year-old Army lieutenant who had never before bathed in the buff with any woman whose name I did not at least know, but getting into the same bath toward which these two unconcerned and unclothed maids were obviously headed seemed somehow better than standing there face to face with them, with much to conceal (at least in terms of total epidermal area) but nothing to conceal it with.

After a few minutes of searing torture in the water, Huntley saved the day by shouting *"Jishin da! Jishin da!* (Earthquake! Earthquake!)," whereupon the two maids reacted as most Japanese would and fled with the same precipitate haste that we instantly emulated in getting out of that tub of thermal torment.

Perhaps the widest area of disagreement about Japanese and American bathing practices is, indeed, whether or not men and women, otherwise strangers to each other, should bathe together. Given their naturalistic acceptance of nudity (again, in its proper place), the Japanese custom of *konyoku,* or mixed bathing, should not be at all surprising. It has often been said that in Japan a naked person is seen but not really looked at. There are places and times in Japanese life in which it is necessary—or at least much the easier course—to appear wholly or partly unclothed before strangers (in unsegregated toilets and baths, aboard Pullmans, and in the pursuit of certain occupations). When this is the situation, the Japanese have learned to accommodate others by not taking careful notice. They are taught that to ogle nudity is the epitome of barbarism. Obviously, they see what they see, but they reflexively glance elsewhere as a courtesy and in acknowledgment of the fact which they must all accept: that far too many Japanese are living in far too little space.

The Japanese are conditioned to expect this courtesy from other Japanese, but many of them have also come to expect intolerance, misunderstanding, shock, amusement, or possibly delight from us. To them, therefore, standing naked in front of another Japanese and standing naked in front of an American may be entirely different.

From the very beginning of our relationship with them, we have tended to give the Japanese a hard time about their penchant for nudity, although it was really none of our blue-nosed business. Ensign McCauly, an American sailor who served under Perry on his first voyage to Japan, wrote in his diary, "I went into a bath house where girls of seventeen, old women, young women, old men were squatting on the stone floor, without rag enough to cover a thumbnail. . . . they invited us to join in and take a wash—but I was so disgusted with the whole breed, with their lewdness of manner and gesture, that I turned away with a hearty curse upon them." Fortunately, one would have to go a long way to find a reaction like that among the men of today's navy.

In the Yokohama of 1862, mixed bathing in public baths was banned "by force of public opinion as expressed by the foreigners then resident there." Evidently not much heed was paid to the opinion of the vast majority, e.g., the Japanese, who just happened to own the country and who had not wanted the foreigners to come there to begin with.

Right thinking and good taste must have prevailed, however, for mixed bathing—at least in the resorts and in city hotels—was certainly in style when I arrived in Japan just after World War Two. Mixed bathing had been prohibited in the public bathhouses since long before the war, and efforts have been made periodically to extend this ordinance to *all* bathing facilities . . . but without notable success, I am happy to report.

Even as accustomed to such coeducational facilities as I thought myself to be, I had an experience several years ago in Hokkaido (Japan's "last frontier") that was admittedly an eye-opener—although by no means an unpleasant one. I had decided to spend several days in the Daisetsuzan National Park on that northern island and arrived one afternoon at a large inn where I had a reservation. As I was unpacking in my second-floor room, I heard from the ground floor below the sound of a great many young, exuberant voices. In a few minutes a maid came to lead me to the bath, as is the custom upon arrival, and as we approached that area on the ground floor, I realized that the tumult I had heard came from the bath, which the inn brochure had depicted as being of Olympic-pool size.

I undressed in the men's dressing room and then opened the bathroom door into a charming scene.

About one hundred and fifty boys and girls were bathing together and apparently enjoying themselves immensely. They were all, I learned later, first-year students from a middle school in Sapporo, which meant that most of them were thirteen years old, give or take a year. They had come to the national park on a school-sponsored excursion together with a dozen or so male and female teachers. Nor were these teacher-chaperones shirking their duties. All of them were right there in the bath with their charges—and just as bare.

Japan has 13,300 hot springs, of which 1,400 have mineral properties that are of medicinal value. A spring is generally considered to be one localized underground source of hot water (the temperatures range from 80 to 226 degrees Fahrenheit), although several wells may tap the same source and two or three inns or a dozen or so homes may use the supply from a single well. Around the more plentiful sources of supply, hot springs resorts, called *onsen-machi,* have grown up, especially where the scenery is noteworthy. The best known of these *onsen-machi* include Beppu, Noboribetsu, Atami, Ikao, Miyanoshita, Kusatsu, Arima, Dogo, and Unzen.

Within each *onsen* inn, which can be identified by a mark that looks like an upside-down jellyfish and by the steam rising from a vent on its roof, the emphasis has always been on relaxation and submersion in the curative waters, with perhaps secondary attention paid to romance and partying. Nowadays, however, the restless and increasingly affluent younger people are demanding more than these simple, old-fashioned pleasures. In response to this pressure from youth, the operators are adding bowling alleys, go-go parlors, pachinko games, Ping-Pong tables, and other such exhilarating cultural facilities.

The average *onsen* inn will have one large communal bath, where all are welcome, and two or three *kazoku-buro* (family baths), in which three or four persons can bathe at the same time. The latter can be locked from inside, and some inns have taken to calling them, in their seductive literature, *romansu-buro* (romance baths), but I doubt that many Japanese couples would have any real reason to insist on such privacy. Again, we have here the principle of everything in its proper place, which, in the case of sex, is in their rooms upstairs.

Many inns offer rooms with private baths, e.g., with their own *kazoku-buro* attached. These are arranged so that one and sometimes two sides of the bathroom can be glassed-in. By building the inn on a slope, the various elevations are utilized so that the bathers are offered panoramic views of mountains or sea or both.

The list of the mineral properties of these *onsen* and of the ailments they are reputed to cure is too long to quote, but many minerals and most complaints (including—wistfully—pregnancy) are included.

After my first year in Japan, I returned to the United States and spent a month in southern California near one of our American hot springs. Although I had visited many *onsen* in Japan during that first year, I had never been to one in my own country, and I was shocked by the difference. In the one in California, the atmosphere was suffused with the sad pungency of illness and age, of antiseptic decay. There, stoop-shouldered oldsters talked endlessly about their ailments and their doctors. I never entered the town without thinking of the laughter and ease, of the steamy cheerfulness of Japan's *onsen,* where man and nature appeared to coexist on terms more amiable than elsewhere.

The foreign visitor to Japan would do well to find his own special *onsen*—or Bali H'ai or Shangri-la, if you prefer. I have mine: three of them, in fact, one of which is so remote that the last leg of the journey is a forty-five-minute walk uphill. In this one, I find seclusion. In the second, I find magnificent scenery. In the third, I find extraordinary seafood and an old gentleman who raises bear cubs and spins me tales of his boyhood around the turn of the century.

The list from which you may choose is truly startling in its variety. For example, in the town of Arita in Wakayama Prefecture, an enterprising hotel offers a so-called Apollo Bath, which consists of ten tubs in a glassed-in cable car which moves horizontally along the coastline, some fifty yards up in the air. Passenger-bathers undress outside the cable car, then get aboard and ensconce themselves in cozy tubs in preparation for a leisurely round trip above breath-halting scenery. The Meitetsu Inuyama Hotel on Honshu has a bath that envelops its bathers in musical vibrations from loudspeakers installed underwater. The Kowakien Hotel in Miyanoshita boasts the largest single bath in Asia. The Dai Ichi Takimoto Hotel in Noboribetsu, however, is the largest *onsen* establish-

ment under one roof in the world: it has twenty-three separate baths, one of which is fifty yards long. In the middle of a
broad, shallow river that flows through Shuzenji in the Izu
Peninsula, there rises a spring that pours forth its hot water
to blend with the chilly stream as both flow on. The munici-
pality of Shuzenji has constructed a wooden walkway from
the bank out to this *onsen,* which was discovered by a Buddhist priest in the ninth century. The dressing rooms, however,
are on the river bank, so that those who would take advantage
of this free municipal bathing must walk twenty yards in plain
view of fishermen, loafers, tourists, and bright-eyed foreigners
like myself—as naked as God or Buddha made them. Again,
no Japanese appears to think anything of it.

Even more memorable, however, is an *onsen* inn on the
Chita Peninsula, north of Nagoya, where man, not nature,
made the physical arrangements. This inn has a mammoth
communal bath, sixty yards long, in a room whose ceiling is
three stories high. When the men and women emerge from
their separate dressing rooms, they must walk across an ele-
vated path that is rather like a stage-passage through the
audience, only higher. Because the male and female walkways
are no more than fifteen yards apart, the men already in the
bath are given a good upward view of all women—of necessity, naked—approaching and leaving their side of the bath,
and vice versa. This particular bath is a recent construction,
and it appears to be somewhat out of tune with the traditional
Japanese attitude toward nakedness outlined earlier. One wonders if the efforts of the police to puritanize Japan, beginning
in 1964, the year of the Tokyo Olympics, may not already
have aroused the Peeping Tom instinct in the breast of some
Japanese men, with larger disasters to follow. (Peeping Toms
have been so rare in Japan that it takes most English-Japa-
nese dictionaries several sentences to define this unheard-of
creature.)

My own most unforgettable *onsen* night was passed in the

small resort town of Atagawa (meaning Warm River) on the eastern coast of the Izu Peninsula in 1954. Several American friends and I had gone hunting in the mountains that day and had returned to the inn at nightfall to dine on boar sukiyaki. For some now-forgotten reason, I decided to bathe before my friends, so I asked my room maid to take me to the *roten-buro*, or outdoor bath. Having been clambering up and down wet, slippery mountain paths most of the day, I was close to exhaustion and so took to the bath with me a bottle of Kirin beer, a fine local brew, hoping that it would help me relax and recuperate.

It being the dinner hour, I was alone in the bath, once my maid had left. It was a night in November, which is perhaps the best month of the year in Japan, when the cool hand of autumn is felt but is softened by clear skies and a palpable sun. Above and to my right rose the now-dark shapes of the mountains, dominated by Mount Amagi, that form the spine of the Izu Peninsula. To my left and below lay the Pacific, upon whose surface dancing lights had begun to appear. These were the lanterns that are hung from the prows of fishing boats to attract the squid. The number of boats shortly doubled, then tripled, until soon there were more than a hundred of them bobbing about on the dark surface of the sea.

The bath itself was designed to resemble a natural pool that one might stumble on in the deep mountains, studded with large rocks and half-hidden by foliage. After four or five minutes in its hot water, the bather could stand up and then, but only then, find the chill night air a welcome relief. Alone there in the relaxing water, with the sound of revelry from the inn faint enough to enhance, not diminish, the sense of pleasure to come, I slowly felt myself becoming more and more an integral part of nature instead of a mere intruder. The mountain and the sea, the moon and the stars, the cool autumnal evening and the hot spring pool amid the natural foliage—I felt that I was one with them, and I remained there for nearly an hour, unconscious of time and enthralled by an insight into what nature and the *onsen* may mean to the Japanese.

Sento (written "money" and "hot water") is Japanese for public bath, of which there are 2,578 in Tokyo and comparably more throughout the rest of the country. Usually these are large low buildings with towering chimneys. On the average of a thousand bathers will visit one daily, since 70 percent of all homes in Tokyo, for example, do not have their own baths. The *sento* open at three in the afternoon, which is when most mothers bring their babies to take advantage of the cleanest water, and close at eleven-thirty at night.

At the entrance, the bather removes his shoes and pays the fee of fifteen cents or so (for adults) to the cashier on duty at a lecternlike counter overlooking both the male and female sides of the bath. Inside he takes a basket, undresses, and places his clothes in the basket, which he then leaves on a shelf. From this dressing room he steps down a few inches onto the tiled floor of the bath proper, a spacious room with a 10- by 12-foot pool on the far side and with water faucets placed low all along its walls. The pool will hold up to twenty bathers at one time, and there may be even more squatting on small wooden stools and scrubbing themselves (obligatory before entering the bath) near the faucets, from which they can draw hot and cold water to ladle over themselves from wooden pails with handles. One essential item of equipment is the *tenugui,* a small towel that the Japanese use as wash cloth, drying towel, and, at times, fig leaf. (A wet cloth, incidentally, dries better than a dry one.)

Most public baths—and *onsen* as well—employ *sansuke,* men who scrub the backs of bathers of both sexes. There are no professional female *sansuke,* although a maid in an *onsen* inn may perform this service for the guest as one of her duties. The girls who work in Turkish baths might, however, be technically classed as *sansuke,* although they admittedly wash much more than just the back.

During the peak hours of use, men and women intent on advertising consumer products, political philosophies, or retail stores may appear in these public baths to strike up apparently casual conversations with fellow bathers and then proceed, in voices that carry afar, to wax eloquent—as disinterested private citizens, of course—about the wonders of socialism or a certain toothpaste or the friendly local abortionist. Among their captive audiences, these touts hope that there will be some who will tell their families at home later, "Say, I heard a fellow down at the bathhouse tonight say that Brand X is just one hell of a lot better than this stuff we've been using."

Among the minority of families who have their own baths, the housewife must begin her preparations for the evening ablutions about four in the afternoon. First, she drains the water from the night before (which she may have used for various cleaning purposes during the day), washes out the wooden tub, and refills it, which takes fifteen or twenty minutes. Then she puts the cover on the bath and lights the fire. It will take twenty or thirty minutes to heat most baths, but some take longer. (When we lived in Kamakura, it took forty minutes, my wife reminds me, to heat our bath, and this chore had to be done outside the house in all seasons.)

While most baths are made of wood (cypress is best), there is another kind that resembles a large iron laundry pot and is called a *Goemon-buro.* The origin of the name is worth, I believe, at least this brief paragraph: Japan's Robin Hood was a robber named Goemon Ishikawa, who, when at last captured, was sentenced to be boiled to death in oil in such a pot, together with his very small son. (I suppose the authorities wanted to stamp out his breed forever.) With his son in his arms, Goemon was forced to stand in the pot, under which a fire was kindled. As the heat became increasingly unbearable, Goemon lifted his little boy over his head to keep him as far from the heat as possible, but when he felt himself begin to weaken, he suddenly and resolutely plunged his son deep into the bubbling oil, to kill him as quickly as possible and thus shorten his suffering. Then, with his dead son in his arms, he stood up to shout defiance at his jeering enemies encircling him until he succumbed to the pain and sank beneath the surface. Subsequently, cast-iron baths of that particular potlike shape have been called *Goemon-buro,* or Goemon baths, in Japan, except in the Choshu district, where they may also be called *Choshu-buro.*

In the rural districts, where there are fewer public baths, many farmhouses have their own, but they rotate the bath night in their immediate neighborhood. My wife's parents, who are farmers, live in an isolated community with only three neighbors, and so they heat up the bath in their home every fourth night for all four families to bathe there. I have been there often when their turn came around, and it was always something of a festive occasion. Although the families did not bathe together (the bath was too small for that), they usually had tea together in their bathrobes before or after immersion, while the smaller children gamboled about in considerably less clothing, at least in the warmer months.

When I was a boy in Texas, we believed that the Japanese (and the Chinese) did almost everything in precisely the opposite way from that of Americans. It was perhaps in reaction to this early conviction that the Japanese were utterly different from us that I devoted much of my first several years of acquaintance with things Japanese to attempts to disembarrass myself of the remnants of this childhood fancy. After all, I argued, we are all human beings and essentially the same, except·for a few minor discrepancies in cultural overlay.

As might be expected, however, the passage of years brought an understanding that lies somewhere between these

two extremes: While they don't do *every*thing differently, they
do . . .

. . . believe that the initial step in etiquette is the removal
of their shoes, while we believe that it is the removal of our
hats. . . . The Japanese prefer to dine in privacy but bathe in
public, while we tend to the opposite arrangement. . . . We
believe that love should lead to marriage, whereas they believe that marriage should lead to love. Or, put more cynically,
we look for love inside marriage, and they look for it outside. . . . We narrow our eyes in anger; they narrow theirs
in pleasure. . . . They put their babies to sleep face up; we
usually put ours to sleep face down.

Normally the Japanese write from top to bottom and from
right to left. . . . Their books begin where ours end. . . .
Footnotes in Japanese books come at the top of the page
(head-notes?). . . . We consider ourselves liberated by education, while the Japanese find themselves confined by it.

We beckon others to come to us with our palms up, the
Japanese with their palms down. . . . We point to our chests
to indicate ourselves; the Japanese point to their noses. . . .
Japanese carpenters cut wood by pulling saws and planes toward them; we cut by pushing these tools away from us. . . .
The Japanese consider it impolite to fill a guest's cup or glass
too near the brim; we consider it impolite not to. . . . The
Japanese think it rude to open presents in front of the givers,
while we think it rude to fail to do so.

In mourning, we wear black, and the Japanese white. . . .
We say northeast and southwest while they say (the equivalents of) eastnorth and westsouth. . . . We carry babies in
our arms, whereas they strap theirs to their backs. . . . We
regard black cats at bad luck; the Japanese say *"Kuroneko
wa mayoke ni ii* (Black cats keep devils away)". . . . At
o-zashiki parties in Japanese-style resturants, hosts leave before
their guests.

In counting on their fingers, the Japanese open their hands

first, then bend the fingers to their palms one by one, while we close our hands first and then extend our fingers. . . . At least until recently in the United States, Americans saw more nudity in art than in real life, whereas the Japanese have always regarded nudity in real life as more permissible than nudity in art. . . . The Japanese strive for efficiency in space, and we strive for efficiency in time. . . . The Japanese drive on the left-hand side of the street, so their cars are steered from the right-hand side.

The Japanese draw arrows against the right side of the bow, we against the left. . . . We row boats backwards, they forwards. . . . They beach their boats stern-first, while we pull ours up by the prow. . . . They mount horses on the right, we on the left. . . . Their light switches, doors, faucets, and door handles are usually operated in opposite directions from ours.

The Japanese can be carried away by the beauty of the moon but seldom heed that of the sunset. . . . They often measure distance in terms of time, where we would measure it in miles. . . . To the Japanese, wives are not to be used for display purposes. . . . In seasons of slow business, we sometimes lower our prices to build up trade, whereas the Japanese tend to raise theirs, to cover the deficit.

In Japan, the twin who is born second is considered the older. . . . Japanese men strike matches away from themselves, American men toward themselves. . . . Japanese horses are backed, not led, into stalls. . . . The garden and better rooms of a house in Japan are in the rear. . . . When the Japanese keep accounts, they list the amounts first, then the corresponding items. . . . Whereas we whistle at girls, they whistle only at dogs. . . . The Japanese sit facing the back of a toilet, whereas we sit facing the front.

4
Their Men

Not long ago a foreign journalist working in Japan reported that while Japanese women were rated Number One in the world, Japanese men were ranked only Twenty-sixth.

This tongue-in-cheek article incurred great wrath from two sources: (a) the Japanese men themselves, who felt that they were being unduly maligned, and (b) many foreign residents, who held that, on the contrary, a ranking of twenty-sixth place was outrageously high and completely unsupportable.

The furor still reverberates today when foreigners—usually males—get together and wonder vocally how one sex of the race can be so pleasing and the other so exasperating. While quite content that the physical distinctions (*Vive la différence!*) should remain just as they are, these foreigners marvel over how far apart the two are in nature, character, and attitudes.

Before discussing such non-physical attributes, however, we should first look briefly at the physical characteristics of Japanese males, who, although they may all look alike to the foreign visitor, can be divided among three broad racial classifications: (a) Mongoloid, (b) Manchu-Korean, and (c) Polynesian-Sumatran. Although the lines have crossed countless times, the majority of Japanese men—perhaps 60 percent —can be loosely considered as members of the Mongoloid group, with 30 percent classifiable as Manchu-Korean. The former generally have short legs, a stocky physique, a large skull, a broad face, high cheekbones, a yellow-tan complexion, little body hair, puffy eyelids, a firm jaw, a flat nose, scanty eyelashes, low stature, small feet, a large mouth, often protruding upper front teeth, the Mongolian fold at the inner corners of the eyes, sinewy, flexible hands, and black, straight, coarse hair. The latter—often members of the elite social class —tend to be taller and have fairer skins, larger eyes, longer and straighter legs, higher noses, smaller mouths, higher foreheads, and more oval faces. Many men—and women, too— have tended in the past toward bowed legs, but these are growing longer and straighter these days, thanks to increased use of chairs, more protein in the diet, and a gradual abandonment of the habit of carrying babies tied to the mothers' backs for long periods. Eighty-two percent of the men are addicted to nicotine, and they have a life expectancy of sixty-nine years.

In *Japan Unmasked,* Japanese author Ichiro Kawasaki wrote that the "Japanese are physically perhaps the least attractive of all races in the world, with the exception of Pygmies and Hottentots." Warming to his work, he went on to describe "their flat expressionless faces" and their "large heads, elongated trunks, and short, often bowed legs." After saying that blacks were at least taller and straighter, he proceeded to make the telling point that Japanese men often have to pay twice as much as other foreigners to buy the time of a prostitute in the major cities of the world. At the time he wrote the book, author Kawasaki was Japan's ambassador to Argentina and considered one of its more brilliant diplomats. Shortly after its publication, however, Kawasaki's career came to an abrupt end for if there is anything the Japanese cannot bear, it is unfavorable comparison of their attributes with those of other races, especially by one who should know.

Spiritually and mentally, the Japanese like to blend in with a crowd, whereas in the United States we would prefer those men who stand out. They are guided by a code of manners instead of an ethical code. They would rather be harmonious than right. They are tolerant of noise and crowds, for these are associated with groups. They seek peace of mind and affirmation of status through ceremonies and rituals. Despite periods of resurgent xenophobia, they are supremely inquisitive and flexible in the face of strange intellectual systems. In their literature and history, they have enshrined as ideals the faithful, competent retainer and the concerned, paternalistic master. As employees, they vastly prefer the hard taskmaster who shows an interest in their personal affairs to the lenient boss who minds his own business. Whereas we are diverse and mobile, they like the congeniality of familiar surroundings. They have tended to punish the group for the individual's indiscretion. In order to maintain social harmony, they eschew the direct negative in their responses. They are lacking in moral courage and civic consciousness. They regard sex as the third most important thing in life, after work and children. They compete better as groups than as individuals. They are fascinated with rank and all its iniquities. They dote on a predictable future and shy away in alarm from the unexpected. They utilize shame rather than guilt as a moral sanction. They accept personal in lieu of legal-rational authority. They are insular and reflective and more concerned with spirit than with matter. For them, loyalty is the beginning and the end of morality. Their *shimaguni konjo* (insular complex) is the result of centuries of self-imposed aloofness. There is a strong undercurrent of irrationality in their nature. They prefer aesthetics, emotion, and intuition to reason and logic. They are much more interested in the position than in the man filling it.

An illustration of the last point is a weekly television play called *"Toyama No Kinsan Torimono-cho,"* in which the hero, one Kinsan, is actually a magistrate or judge in feudal Japan but often poses as an easy-going man-about-town in order to get the goods on doers of evil. The last scene each week never varies: The criminals are arraigned before Kinsan in his court, where they stoutly protest their innocence, although Kinsan—

in his alternate man-about-town role—has witnessed their crimes with his own eyes. What is weird about the drama is that the accused—seated ten feet in front of his bench—never recognize Kinsan, the judge, as the man they knew so well a few days before when he flitted about the edge of their illegalities. Although his outfit as judge differs from his man-about-town costume, no effort at all is made to change his features nor are they masked or shaded in any way. Like all Japanese, the accused have been so intent on the position, the role, the title that they cannot recognize the incumbent—until, in Kinsan's case, he reveals his identity at the last dramatic moment by lowering his garment and showing them the cherry design tattooed on his right shoulder, a unique mark of identification which they have seen the man-about-town display more than once.

Male preferences in clothing are changing so rapidly that it is difficult to generalize about them, but traditionally Japanese men have been indifferent to their attire. To display any interest in one's clothing was regarded as unmanly. Aside from shaving, and knotting one's tie, men thought it shameful to be caught looking at themselves in a mirror. If any article of clothing was dirty or wrinkled, this was blamed on the wife, since it was beneath her husband's dignity and manhood to notice such trivia. (Nor was he in the least interested in his wife's mode of dress on those rare occasions when he was forced to appear in public with her. The American wife likes to believe that her dress is a matter of keen concern to her husband, who supposedly swells with pride when he can sashay forth with a modishly attired female at his side, but it matters not at all to his Japanese counterpart, whose reaction would be, "My wife shouldn't be going anywhere with me in the first place.")

This indifference to apparel was compounded by strange (to us) attitudes toward Western clothing. For instance, in the immediate postwar years, we noticed that many men wore belts so long that they overlapped around to the vicinity of the spine and also trousers that looked like cast-offs from the circus fat man. At the time I figured that these men had all lost much weight due to the hard times at the end of the war, but I later came to realize that this was not the reason at all. The concept of clothing sizes came from their native dress: the kimono was a one-size-fits-all garment, and the Japanese were trying to superimpose this convenience on Western-style apparel. Belts, therefore, were all of one length and had to be long enough to encircle the stoutest man. And while the trousers did come in various sizes, the tendency was to pay little heed to a reasonably close fit but to obtain something plenty large, even though it might envelop the wearer like a tent. I further suspect that there was a soupçon of wishful thinking involved as well, for being fat was a desirable state which all right-thinking men strove to attain.

The typical attitude toward shoes was readily understandable, given the premise that footwear in general was regarded as something filthy to kick off at the door. Accordingly, shoes tended to be dirty, misshapen, ill-fitting, and oddly colored.

But it was in the field of hats that the Japanese man was best able to demonstrate his utter contempt for such sissified nonsense as neat, clean, well-fitted apparel. Almost always of neutral colors, these hats were so crumpled, sweat-stained, and tired-looking that even the most ardent admirers of the Cult of Japan could not escape the conclusion that they had been used for years to swab out toilet bowls, then carelessly tossed into a coal-bin to cure and mold. It was difficult to believe that so many unhappy-looking headpieces could actually be in existence.

Then, as if to crown this caricature, the man wore this name of a name with all the élan of a Neville Chamberlain or a Casper T. Milquetoast. With never so much as a glance at the brim or the crease, he placed it squarely on his head, then pulled it down so far (like other articles, the hats were usually too large) that it caused his ears to fan out and almost cut off his vision.

Indeed so preposterous were these hats that I could not believe that they had reached their nadir simply from neglect. There must have been, I thought, a deliberate attempt made to abuse them. It was then that I learned that this was entirely within the realm of possibility, that there was a hoary tradition among Japanese college youths of preferring filthy, bedraggled school caps and, indeed, of shunning all other. A clean, well-brushed, new-looking *gakubo* was a positive source of shame. When it was first purchased, the student would hurry home with it concealed under his jacket and soak it in salt water, give it to the dog to play with, deliberately tear and cut it for his mother to mend, and place it under his *futon* (comforter) at night to destroy any semblance of shape. Here again was evidence of the cult of manliness. A clean new cap would have exposed a tendency toward effeminate softness, a plain preference for the pretty and prissy. One covered with crud suggested on the other hand the epitome of manhood, of deep voices and pipe-smoking and the lower attributes of a stallion. And doubtless this tradition influenced the attitude toward headgear in later adult years.

The preceding is a reasonably accurate depiction of Japanese male attire during the first five or ten years after the war, but then affluence began to set in and quite a few men determined to spend more money on themselves. Still, they did not want to compromise by buying expensive new wardrobes so they decided to splurge on just a few smaller items.

For instance, I remember when the Mitsukoshi Department Store featured sets of vicuna underwear for men. The demand was so great that they sold out their entire stock in only two days. What's so strange about that? Just that each set cost well over five hundred dollars. (Overcoats made of vicuna were also selling well that year—at about fourteen hundred dollars.)

One of the fads of those days—and one that is still with us to a lesser degree—was the distinct male fondness for alligator leather—in belts, wallets, shoes, briefcases, and cigarette

cases. And another touch of the sybaritic was the large number of gold belt buckles on sale in shops even in the poorer
suburbs. Many of these had a solitary diamond mounted in
the center and cost anywhere from six hundred to two thousand dollars. There was a brisk trade in eight-dollar handker-
chiefs and was—and still is—even a market for gold business
cards costing ¥ 14,800 ($48.00) each.

Today some younger Japanese are becoming quite as pea-
cock-ish as their counterparts in the United States, but while
the older men are spending more money on their dress, they
still cling to many of the traditional habits, such as the white
shirt and the conservative suit colors. (A recent survey, however, revealed that only 13 percent of Japanese men still wear
kimono at home, which is indicative of the degree to which
customs are changing.)

Whatever their attire, the Japanese are traveling to the
United States these days in large numbers, sending, in fact,
more visitors (145,000 during the first six months of 1971)
than any other nation. And herein lies a phenomenon well
worth observation. Namely, the changes in stature (at least,
in his own eyes) of the Japanese male at various stages in his
foreign journey. At the first stage—which is where he is being
given a rousing send-off at the aerodrome by a cheering
claque—he stands about seven feet tall as he sets out to do
high deeds in Hungary to pass all men's believing. After the
jet wheels have left the earth of the Land of the Gods and the
first announcement—in English—is made by a member of
the aircraft's crew, his height drops abruptly to under five feet,
for the disheartening realization has come to him that he is no
longer in Japan, no longer surrounded by all that is familiar
and comfortable and adjusted to his unique convenience and
temperament. The early inklings of future panic wing toward
him. He becomes so tense and preoccupied with envisioned
future encounters (before which his dignity as a representative
of the Japanese race might stumble) that he is hardly aware
of what is happening around him.

When his jet lands in Seattle or San Francisco and when Mr. Japanese Traveler looks into the stern eyes of a U.S. Customs Inspector, his stature shrinks still more. Not because he has any opium in his luggage but because this may be his first encounter with a foreigner on foreign soil, a foreigner who may know little about Japan and care even less, a foreigner who expects this visitor from the Orient to speak fluent English and be perfectly familiar with American ways.

From then on throughout the duration of his journey his stature will continue to diminish centimeter by centimeter (except on those rare occasions when he can replenish his sagging ego at islands of expatriate Japanese) until he becomes a midget in a land of giants. But when at last he boards the homeward-bound jet and is finally told to fasten his seat belt for the imminent landing at Tokyo, he feels a resurgence of physical well-being and quickly regains much of his lost height. The sight of familiar faces beyond the customs barrier restores him completely.

It is only later, however, that he reaches his deserved stature of ten feet, and this comes about soon enough at his first opportunity to strike a pose as the Last of the Great International Travelers. This pose is a prime favorite with Japanese men and is, in fact, a commendable reflection of the importance the Japanese attach to foreign travel and acquaintance with the outside world. The pose is sometimes struck at home but mostly in bars among his peers and hostesses. In his repertoire will be a dozen or more *omiyagebanashi* or travel tales— anecdotes and accounts of what he did and saw, often humorous and designed to spotlight the contrasts between Japanese and foreign manners and mores. His audience usually pays him the courtesy of listening in hushed awe, for he takes care to tell his tales to persons who have never been to the country or countries he has visited. To his credit it should be said that he does not indulge overmuch in plain or fancy boasting, except in the important areas of prowess in amour and of a perhaps pardonable pride in his country's recent economic accomplishments.

This Great International Traveler Pose is actually a subspecies of a larger syndrome known simply as the Expert Pose, which can be observed at almost any hour of the day on television. The pattern followed is for the expert to be interviewed by a stooge, the type to whom you have to say, "Don't-say-yes-until-I-finish-talking." The expert is almost always male and the stooge is usually female, although there are occasional exceptions to the latter. The kind of interviews seen on the late-hours talk or chat shows in the United States and United Kingdom would be unthinkable in Japan. Question the expert about the validity of his statements? Absurd! Challenge this distinguished authority about one of his "facts"? You could be committed for such heresy.

Let's suppose that Dr. Homma has just returned from a trip to Outer Mongolia and is being interviewed on television by a lovely twenty-year-old miss. The beginning of the interview might well go like this:

> Attractive Miss (simpering): "Welcome back to Japan, Dr. Homma."
>
> Dr. Homma, busily posing as an Expert: "Harrumph. Yes, indeed. It's good to be back in civilization again. Can you imagine, I couldn't get salted trout guts for breakfast in that benighted country. Harrumph."
>
> A.M. (paling): "How you must have suffered!"
>
> D.H.: "It was my fourteenth trip to Outer Mongolia, you know."
>
> A.M. (eyes wet with adoration): *"Fourteen?"*
>
> D.H.: "Or maybe it was eighteen. Dammit, girl, how can I be expected to remember such details!"
>
> A.M.: "Of course not, Doctor. I was a fool to have suggested it."
>
> D.H. (extracting a cigarette): "Mad buggers. Can't imagine a country where a man can't get salted trout guts. I'll have to take some with me on my next trip."

> A.M. (fumbling in her haste to light the Expert's cigarette):
> "Oh, you're going to Outer Mongolia *again,* Doctor?
> How perfectly marvelous!"
>
> D.H.: "My lecture schedule is so crowded now that I really
> shouldn't go, but—well—the Mongolians were so dam-
> nably insistent about it. Especially the women. Heh, heh."
>
> A.M. (fluttering eyelashes): "Oh, Doctor, you Lothario,
> you . . ."
>
> D.H.: "Shall I say something for you in Outer Mongolian?"
>
> A.M. (coyly): "Yes, if you'll promise not to say anything
> naughty about *me.* . . ."

And so on.

With their admirable respect for learning, the Japanese
virtually fill the airwaves at certain hours of the day with
these Experts (many of whom, I must admit, are actually
competents or near-competents, unlike the above Dr. Homma)
and their yes-girls.

While Dr. Homma and his nonfictional brothers may entertain their captive audiences back home with audacious
accounts of their amorous accomplishments in foreign parts,
a less partisan observer hesitates to rush to accept these professions of prowess without reservation. Aside from a con-
genital urge on the part of most males in all countries to boast
what bulls they are in bed, one wonders just how much success Japanese men could achieve with foreign—especially
Western—women, given their contemptuous and harsh treatment of their own women at home. And while granting that
they might try not to be quite so fulsomely cave-mannish
while wooing foreigners, I cannot help but believe that enough
of their basic indifference to the niceties of courtship and of
their insistence on absolute male dominance will seep through
to cool the responsive ardor of all but the most desperate females in the West.

At home in Japan this same all-pervasive insistence on
male prerogatives has given birth to a comparatively subservient distaff population—or perhaps the latter brought about

the former. Whichever the cause, the resultant situation has served the Japanese men well in one area of life, which in turn, I think, has aided him in his pursuit of success elsewhere. With sexual satisfaction so comparatively easy to achieve in Japan, the Japanese man does not have to devote so much of his time to its pursuit, leaving him with more time and energy to devote to more profitable, if less pleasant, pastimes. If he is a college student and offers to let a coed accompany him to a movie, she will be less likely to play hard-to-get and may suggest that they go Dutch or even that she pay for his ticket as well. If he doesn't offer to let her share his *futon* that night, he may not even see her home but will leave her instead at a subway or train station. If he is a businessman, he may not hit a homer his first time at bat with a cabaret hostess, but the odds are good that he will succeed the second or third time—and on company funds at that. This convenience in sexual arrangements has probably also resulted in a healthier attitude toward the sport and more sensible marital arrangements (or at least far fewer divorces).

Understandably the Japanese male is disheartened when he fails to find the same degree of sexual compliance during his foreign explorations. He would like nothing better than to tell the boys in Bansuke's Bistro back home in Beppu how he enriched the lives of American women from coast to coast and how in Milwaukee he met this good-looking blond chick who chased him all over the United States because she just couldn't get her fill of him; but even granting him some leeway in which to prevaricate and embroider, he still finds it hard to tell such a story with a straight face when the closest he got to such an adventure was the time in a New York hotel when a fifty-two-year-old charwoman with straggly gray hair fought him off with a wet mop for ten minutes before calling a cop.

The first thing the Japanese man has going against him is his size, for there is little that chills the heart of an American or European woman more thoroughly than the prospect of a

date with a man over whom she towers; and next is his previously mentioned insistence on all-points male superiority,
which slips out in many little ways, such as holding a cigarette
expectantly to his lips while waiting for the woman to light it
for him.

So accustomed are Japanese women to such treatment that
many of them regard it simply as another of those unfortunate
natural phenomena with which the Good Buddha has decided
in his infinite wisdom to saddle them. I had a Japanese secretary once who weighed about ninety-five pounds to my two
hundred or so. When we left the office together one morning,
she picked up a large, heavy package we were going to mail.

"Here, let me have that," I told her.

"I'll carry it, Mr. Seward."

"But it's heavy," I protested.

"That's why *I* should carry it," she explained, as if teaching
something quite basic to a child.

The treatment that Japanese men accord their women is
such that the one quality those women desire in their husbands and lovers above all else is *yasashisa,* or gentle kindness (generally conceded to be a rather forlorn hope). In a
recent year the most frequent cause given for divorce suits
brought by wives was infidelity, followed closely by cruelty. A
very popular TV series these days is called "Playgirl," the
story being built around a group of tough but good-looking
girls who gather to smite the wicked hip and thigh. And
somehow in every show the writers manage to work in two
or three walloping good scenes in which these right-minded
female crime-fighters set upon and chastise any and all men in
league with the powers of darkness. This, of course, is exactly
what battalions of Japanese women have dreamed about for
generations: savage physical punishment of their tormentors.
Otherwise, the series is witless, boring, and absurd. But it
retains its popularity because most women get their kicks from
complete identification with the Playgirls, while more than a
few men like to leer at the generous exposures of flesh that

can be seen when the Playgirls hoist high their mini-skirts to kick the living you-know-what out of male malefactors.

Someday I would like very much to have an American psychiatrist who can read Japanese make a thoroughgoing study of the plethora of magazines on sale here in which the all-consuming passion of the male participants in the stories would appear to be tying up women and tormenting them in wildly imaginative ways. These magazines are so numerous and devote such affectionate attention to these scenes that the layman like myself is forced to suspect that such imaginings must be a major mental activity with many Japanese men of all ages. I have one of these before me now—the August 9, 1971, issue of *Champion* magazine, which carries a finely drawn depiction of a nude woman hanging by her wrists, which are tied to a beam, while a leering man pours a bucket of urine over her. Judging from his expression of ultimate bliss, here is a man who has found his life's work—and he is ineffably content doing it.

It goes without saying that sexual aberrants are to be found in all countries; but if the frequency of such scenes in Japanese books and magazines is any indication, I would say that the Japanese have a catastrophic problem on their hands as well.

While publications overflow with such fun-and-games, Japanese censors are bending their best efforts to prevent certain kinds of foreign lubricity from invading this country. An example is what happened in recent months to *Playboy,* when it began to carry color photographs of naked women in which the pubic hairs are made public.

Now in Japan it is perfectly all right for a magazine to print a drawing of a devoutly degenerate Japanese man pouring a pail of urine over a naked woman hanging by her wrists from an overhead beam *as long as* no pubic hairs can be seen. But let a publication like *Playboy* show the pubic hairs of a happy, good-looking woman, then watch out! Those foreign devils are about to go too far. What happens is that the

Japanese Customs Office requires the importer—a company called Western Publications Distribution Agency—to hire part-time Pubic Hair Expurgators: housewives and college students who industriously ink out every inch of *chimo* (literally, shameful hair) from such photographs in every one of the twenty-five thousand copies of *Playboy* that are imported monthly. And this in a country where pubic hair wigs can be found on sale openly!

With all the mastery that they hold over their womenfolk, one wonders why Japanese men find it necessary to daydream about tormenting them further. One possible explanation is that the Japanese are lacking in sympathy for the underdog. In fact, they often appear to tend in the opposite direction—of bearing down all the harder on someone when they have him down and bleeding. For example, the *Asahi Evening News,* in its issue of July 1, 1971, quoted an ex-colonel in the Japanese army as saying, "With the fortunes of war on our side, it seemed to us at Imperial Headquarters that there was not enough nation-wide hatred for the enemy." What an intriguing comment this is. The ex-colonel seems to be saying that when you're winning, you should hate all the harder, but if you're losing, you should begin to feel affection for your foe.

Another trait of the Japanese male that would fail to endear him to the average Western woman is his inbred vulgarity and uncouthness. Favorably interpreted, this becomes merely a manifestation of his less prudish acceptance of the natural functions, but on another and more disturbing level this preference for crude speech and gestures manifests itself with unsettling frequency before captive female audiences and especially in front of women whom the man feels he must "take down a notch or two."

In the last year on Japanese television, for example, I have seen commercials that would surely raise both spleen and eyebrows in any other civilized country. One of them, a gasoline commercial, showed two happy-go-lucky young Japanese fellows taking a drive in the country in their new convertible. During the course of the commercial they stopped the car, got out, and casually took a leak. Then they got back in and drove off while the announcer continued to extol the glories of rides in the country in cars propelled by that particular brand of gasoline.

While not connected with TV, another recently noted example of the Japanese man's concept of the fitness of things is a sign that I pass every morning walking to work. It stands in front of a small shrine at the side of a road near Naka-no-hashi and has printed on it, *"Tachi-shoben o-kotowari"* or "Do not urinate here." About two weeks ago when I was passing the shrine, I happened to see the priest irately adding to the sign a postscript which read, "Or defecate, either."

A partial explanation for the reputation Japanese men have earned as cold-fish Romeos can be found in their sociological history, where we find that for centuries they could have only the most formal relations with women not in the business of professional entertainment. Their arranged marriages are a custom that still persists, and until 1945 all children from the seventh grade on went to sexually segregated schools, an unromantic arrangement forbidden by MacArthur after the war but now showing clear signs of revival.

Under such conditions the approaches to romance open to the average Japanese were either largely commercial or painfully formal, chaperoned, and noncommunicative, like the oft-heard story of the bridegroom who did not utter his bride's first name until ten days after they were married. With this kind of tradition behind them, it is small wonder that many Japanese men still veer wildly in their courting from sullen silence to immediate attempts to wrestle the woman to the floor.

My wife and I are quite close to an American woman who lives in Tokyo with her Japanese husband. One day we had lunch with her, and my wife asked what she thought of Japanese men in general and then about their attitude toward romance in particular. Our friend's reply to the latter was succinct:

"Well, whatever else Japanese men are," she told us with a wistful sigh, "they certainly aren't lovers."

Another charge often leveled at Japanese men is that they are childish, and it was none other than Douglas MacArthur who once commented—in perhaps his second most often-quoted remark—that the Japanese have the mentality of a twelve-year-old. This childishness is not necessarily of the giggly, asinine variety but rather a longing—in adult years—for the pleasures of childhood (as experienced in Japan), which in turn is largely responsible for the dichotomy in their nature, for their oft-remarked tendency to confuse myth with reality, for their humility and arrogance, for their wishful longing for the unlikely, for their comparative inability to present arguments in logical terms (even when there is a firm basis for the logic), and for their capacity, on occasion, for mass megalomania.

One commentator on this trait in Japanese men has likened their incapacity for logical argument to the haiku, that popular seventeen-syllable poetry form that achieves its effect more from what it leaves unspoken than from what it says—from, in other words, the emotional overtones that flow unseen around the few terse but evocative symbols.

Considered in this light, it is small wonder indeed that more than a few American businessmen in Japan have concluded that some of their commercial counterparts actually have warped minds, so illogical are the positions that they can occasionally take.

For Japanese men, childhood means Days of Glory. Perhaps this is why one hears so little about a Heaven—even a Buddhist Heaven—in Japan, since the Japanese have no need to strain their imaginations to depict such a future existence when all they have to do is cast their minds back to their own childhood, when they were indulgently treated as little gods and allowed to satisfy all—or almost all—of their aggressive urges.

As these boys grow older, society begins to prepare them for a niche in its hierarchy that is often the precise opposite of all that came before. In lieu of braggadocio, they are immured in self-effacement. Instead of aggression, they must practice sacrifice. Where before they were ruggedly individualistic, now they must be concerned first, last, and always with the welfare of the group. Here are the causes that deeply implant dualism in the characters of Japanese men, that cause their pendulumlike shifts in social responses and attitudes.

Childhood also sponsors in Japan what sociologists call a situational ethic, which means that those under the influence of such an ethic generally behave well in familiar situations (e.g., they bow to a teacher on the street because they have been taught to bow to a teacher on the street) but lose control of themselves, often with unhappy results, whenever they enter the realm of the unfamiliar because they lack the more comprehensive guidelines laid down by Western systems of abstract ethics (e.g., "Cultivate politeness as a virtue" is too sweeping, too abstract for the Japanese; it lacks the desirable quality of application to a specific situation).

More evidence of the fondness with which Japanese men recall their childhood is the fact that most really close male friendships in Japan are formed in school days when spontaneity and outgoing individuality and no awareness of the *hombun* (one's proper station in life) concept are the rule of the day.

As boys move further along through the school system, increasingly heavy pressure is brought to bear on them to study diligently and to score high on examinations. Obviously the acquisition of knowledge itself is part of the aim here, but this is dwarfed by the all-consuming desire to ascend the ladder from one school to the next, especially into the senior high schools and universities, e.g., the non-compulsory portion of the educational system.

Despite the Japanese respect for education (*Sensei,* or Teacher, is a title of the highest admiration) and increasing budgetary commitments to its facilities, only one student is able to enter college from among every two and a half who make the attempt each year. In the national universities that are part of the system of what was previously called the Imperial University, the ratio is less: only one in six. And in the case of the Unversity of Tokyo Medical School, only one in forty-two applicants is accepted.

Deluged by so many candidates, school authorities give very stiff entrance examinations and take only the cream from the harvest. This "entrance exam hell," as Japanese students call it, becomes a focal point in the entire educational process beside which much else that may actually be more important pales. Numerous preparatory schools exist for the sole purpose of cramming pre-exam knowledge into weary brains, and pirated copies of tests are perennial best-sellers. Affluent parents think nothing of contributing magnificent sums to college coffers or teachers' pockets to assist their offspring in the acquisition of a degree.

Some parents (*kyoiku mama,* or education-bent mothers, are a phenomenon of recent years) begin this process even before kindergarten. One well-known Tokyo center of learning has a range of affiliated schools that starts with a two-year kindergarten and ends with a graduate school. Once in this pipeline, it is comparatively easy to follow it to the finish, for the Japanese dislike to fail a student or make him repeat a grade. Getting in, however, is the hard part. There is now even a one-year preparatory school to which it is highly advisable to send one's tots if the parents hope for them to enter that particular two-year kindergarten.

Getting into schools, especially colleges, is so difficult that the Japanese seem to compensate for this by slanting the remainder of the process downhill. Most students who enter college are permitted to graduate, the exceptions being mostly those whose health or finances fail them en route. After graduation, the government employs a significant percentage of the students from the University of Tokyo, while large private companies take the rest from that school and many from the three or four other most respected institutions.

These graduates move up through government ranks as they grow older, and either reach the pinnacle in their late forties or fifties or switch over to private industry, where there may be more room for such growth. In any event, matriculation at a good university is much of the struggle and very nearly guarantees job security throughout life.

The dualism of the Japanese male—a longing for the daring independence of childhood while submitting to the conformative necessities of adulthood—is at the bottom of the Great Actor Tradition in this country. Boys grow to men and are taught to conform, but the depth at which these teachings take root must obviously vary with the individual. Stronger-minded men, for instance, may not be so receptive as the meek and malleable. Consequently, those who resist to any extent find themselves, as adults, forced to pay lip service to a social system in which they do not believe or about which they have lingering doubts. To do this successfully—or at least without being pounded into the ground by their peers—calls for considerable play-acting.

It would seem that many Japanese, while being consummate actors in real life, are wretched ones on the stage. While granting that I have witnessed some fine, even inspired, Japanese acting performances in several different entertainment media, I do nevertheless have the strong impression of a generally low level of competence—even lower than in the United States today, if that is possible—in most television and cinema fare. This pervasive incompetence is highlighted by two particular failings: one is The Pause for Breath and the other The Forced Laugh.

In the former, the actor says his lines and pauses for breath at the most unnatural of moments, thus dealing credulity a mortal cut, for all the world like a second-grader in a school play who has just been given his lines and told to read them for the first time. The latter is perhaps the *most* forced of all imaginable forced laughs. It goes, "Ho." (Two-second pause.) "Ho." (Two-second pause.) "Ho." Its only variation is that sometimes there will be four instead of three "Ho's."

It is so artificial and so contrived that the observer is led to conclude that this is another of those situations in Japanese life in which the audience has been conditioned to ignore the obvious, as in the case of the Joruri Theater, those puppet plays in which the puppet-masters and stagehands move openly about the stage among the puppets themselves, without evidently lessening at all any sense of realism which they might have been aiming to impart.

Yet many—I am compellingly tempted to say "most" instead—Japanese are excellent actors in real life. What escapes me is just how conscious and aware other Japanese may be of when and to what extent their confreres are play-acting. Is it possible, I often ask myself, that Mr. Uda over there doesn't realize that this elaborate apology by Mr. Sakuma is all a put-on performance? Is the fact that my non-Japanese eyes have not yet (I hope) been beclouded with the veils formed by just being Japanese a reason that I can discern this more clearly than Mr. Uda? Or is Mr. Uda just as keenly aware of Mr. Sakuma's pretense as I am but blandly accepts it as part of playing the game in Japan? If one chooses the latter, then he should also consider the probability that it is Mr. Sakuma's histrionic skill and dexterity—more than the false substance— which will weigh in favor of Mr. Uda's acceptance of the apology and of his subsequent good will.

This institution of the Heart-felt Apology is deeply ingrained in the Japanese consciousness, and I have often thought that a competent actor in this country could get away with almost anything. In criminal matters, for example, the apparent sincerity of one's apology—and does anyone possess a computer which will accurately measure such sincerity?—is a most vital factor in decisions regarding degree of guilt, severity of punishment, and time of parole or amnesty. Where such sincerity is apparently lacking, the Japanese like to say, *"Hansei no iro ga mienai,"* or "We cannot see any color of self-reflection."

A sincere apology—offered with all the concomitant frills: tearful protestations, deep bows, a wan countenance, gifts, etc.—can soothe even the most outraged and sinned-against pillars of probity in Japan, but no one has ever satisfactorily explained to me how these expressions of regret can be weighed on the scale of sincerity.

Japanese play-acting and dualism come together in one most advantageous area from which to regard the Japanese male character, and this area is the arena of sword duels in the popular *chambara,* the equivalent of our Western gun-fighter movies. The scene is usually the same: one master sword-fighter is shown standing alone, surrounded on all sides by a dozen or even twenty enemy swordsmen, all skilled in cutting their opponents to the ground.

One by one the enemy begin to slash at the single stalwart, who is, of course, the hero of the piece. He cuts back in retaliation, weaving, dodging, and spinning to avoid the opposing thrusts while getting in some telling blows of his own. At length he prevails, either by slaughtering all of his enemies or killing some and driving the others off or, much less often, by jumping lightly over a ten-foot-wall, slapping his hip in defiance (also a custom of some American Indian tribes), and making off into the darkness or the woods.

The point is that he *prevails.* Over absolutely impossible odds, he wins. It simply could not happen in real life, but it takes place with metronomic regularity in samurai movies. And this is advanced even further into the realms of the risible and ridiculous by movies in which the hero conquers not with a sword but with only a wooden staff or a willow switch or even his hands alone. This is far more absurd, immeasurably more impossible than those chase scenes in our cowboy sagas of the Thirties in which a dozen black-hatters grimly pursued

Tom Mix or Tim McCoy across the desert landscape, firing wildly without ever seeming to hit their target. (After all, it *is* difficult to hit anything from the back of a bouncing horse, and most pistols of those days were not made for accuracy at more than fifteen or so yards.) Quite obviously, then, this samurai scene is symbolic, but symbolic . . . of what?

As I read it, the many enemy swordsmen stand for Japanese society, conformity, the jellyfishlike group that engulfs and stifles the individual in its all-enveloping, irresistible, smothering, initiative-slaying, pulpy white mass, while the lone sword-fighting protagonist is individuality, self-reliance, independence, self-fulfillment, innovation, the charismatic trailblazer. In a strictly conformist society the Japanese have permitted this protest, this rebellion, by marking it with the stamp of the patently impossible. It is so ludicrous that they feel it can do little damage. It is a dream of childhood, harmlessly recalled in adult times. It is pure fantasy, and perhaps it even serves as an opiate to otherwise burgeoning restive spirits.

The single sword-fighter in these *chambara* is also acting out another fantasy after which the Japanese long but seldom attain—individually inspired and individually conducted courage.

In certain situations, the courage of the Japanese male is unquestionable. In war they were what one American general called the "fightingest men on earth." At Angaur Island in 1944, there were only 35 survivors out of 1,300 Japanese defenders. At Tarawa there were only 6 left out of 4,000. Their Banzai charges and Kamikaze attacks are legend (which is not, however, the same as saying that there were no cowards among them. Or that they all were eager to die. When I was stationed in Fukuoka just after the war, we were billeted in a commandeered Japanese-style inn where the pilots of the Special Attack Corps [Kamikaze] from nearby Gannosu Air Base were taken for their bon voyage parties. Sumiko, the maid who tended to my needs, had served at many of those parties and told me how little enthusiasm some of those deathcourters displayed for their prospects on the morrow. Mr. Tsugio Iida, who is now Publicity Director for the Japan Broadcasting Corporation, made on-the-spot recordings of last messages from the pilots and tells how he cried to hear them protest that they didn't want to die.)

Japanese masculine fortitude in the face of death or danger, then, is group-oriented, but the Japanese group does not necessarily have to be larger than the enemy group. Nor does the Japanese fighter necessarily have to be *with* his group at his hour of Gethsemane. What is essential, however, is that what he is doing must be group-inspired and group-sanctioned. With this mental—and sometimes material—backing, he can fare forth unafraid. Without it, he tends to quail.

This is why the Japanese have had comparatively few great leaders of the stature and magnetism of Lincoln, Lee, Mac-Arthur, and the Roosevelts, especially in the days since the House of Tokugawa began to stifle personal initiative throughout the land with its blanket of conformity. And when one like Takamori Saigo, a famous Satsuma revolutionary of the early Meiji Era, does rarely emerge, he is given short shrift by history for his failure to follow rather than to lead. Such leadership requires initiative and self-reliance, which in turn is to be shunned because it can give birth to unexpected actions, to the "Terror of the Unexpected."

The Japanese group is like the mythical hydra which can quickly grow new heads if old ones are pinched off. And the inspiration for its leadership may not come from any of its several heads but may develop from somewhere within the body, grow in strength with transfusions of agreement, and reach the stage of action-productive decisiveness when unanimity or near-unanimity is achieved. The heads of the hydra are easily expendable, as evidenced by the readiness with which the body will sacrifice a leader. Even when the body as a whole is wrong, it will let one of its heads—usually the top one—immolate itself on the Altar of Responsibility for the welfare of the group.

When boys and young men with a seeming future potential for leadership and for independent thought and action do emerge, it is the task of the group to halter such tendencies, to redirect them into more group-manipulative channels. In illustration, whereas the task of the American psychoanalyst is normally to assist his patient in identifying and attaining individualistic self-fulfillment, the assignment of his Japanese colleague is to light the way toward self-realization only within the framework—or restraining meshes, as it were—of the group.

Quite possibly, too, the nonexistence of a pure frontier in Japan for nearly one thousand years has played a major role in militating against individualistic leadership. (Was it the need for a frontier to test their mettle that drove the Japanese military to the continent in the Thirties? Is it the absence of a frontier from the American scene today that is pushing us farther and farther down the path to less substantial—than Japanese—types of conformity?) And the cultivation of paddy rice (like cotton-picking in the South) may also have been a contributing factor, for this "stoop labor" fosters back-bent passivity and mind-deadening rhythmical responsiveness as little else can.

Students of *Yamato-damashii* (the spirit or soul of Japan) have been fond of likening this ideal of male courage and aspiration to the cherry blossom, pointing out that the life of the samurai, like that of this blossom, should be brief but glorious. In support, they recite a famous poem which they say was inspired by the ideal of the samurai: *"Shikishima no Yamato-gokoro wo hito towaba, asahi ni niou yamazakura-bana* (Should anyone ask you what then is the Spirit of Japan, bid him look to the mountain cherry blossom casting out its fragrance on the rays of the morning sun)." But unfortunately the author of the poem, Nobunaga Motoori, was not referring to the samurai and their ideals when he penned those beautiful words. Rather, he was talking about a naturally glowing maid of the mountains in contrast to the painted, artificial, conniving court ladies of the day. In Motoori's analogy, the latter represented *Kansai,* the Chinese learning that he feared was overwhelming his country, while the former stood for the native purity of that unsullied era before the induction of Chinese-style knowledge.

Interestingly enough, the symptoms of the manliness syndrome in modern Japan differ rather largely from those in America, where, at least traditionally, we have tended to know the creature when we see it by such signs as hair-on-the-chest, leather goods, deep voice and booming laugh, a predilection for hunting and fishing and the Great Outdoors, familiarity with firearms, an aversion to evident emotion, the firm handclasp, a preference for straight whiskey, raw onions, garlic, and mustard, chivalrous behavior toward women, suspicion of any excessive leaning toward learning, devotion to any activity in which grown men pursue, kick, hit, or otherwise fumble with a ball, a fondness for poker, tools, and big-breasted, blond, wide-hipped women.

In Japan, however, the *otoko-rashii otoko* (the manly man) is known by his previously mentioned complete indifference to matters of dress, his readiness to get staggering drunk at the right times, his loyalty to all of several icons, his sacrifice of self for the welfare of the group, his aversion to personal ambition and material gain, his expression-laden glances in lieu of words (in kabuki theater, actors can express severe inner turmoil by crossing their eyes, which evokes sharp cries of acclaim from their audience), his openly expressed contempt for romance, his Come, no-nonsense-now! approach to sex, his feeding and stabling of one or more mistresses, his unhesitating plunge into the crude and uncouth in front of women in the entertainment trades, his shunning of financial details, his willingness to shoulder responsibility, his concern for those who depend on him, and his grooming of several candidates to succeed him in his work, the weight of his heel on the back of collective womenhood, and his sincerity.

Sincerity is, as I've noted, a key word with all Japanese, and its meaning is different from the one we usually assign to it. Quite a few years ago in Japan I had to discharge a maid who worked for me. She was a good worker and an honest girl, but my household circumstances had changed, and I simply didn't need her any longer. Of course, I gave her some severance pay and helped her look for another job, but even so she was resentful and took me to task by telling me that I wasn't showing *seii,* or sincerity.

But, by our definition of the word, I *was* being sincere. I sincerely wanted to be rid of her and I was sincerely sorry that I had to let her go and I sincerely tried to get her another position (and finally succeeded). Nevertheless, by her lights, I wasn't showing "sincerity," so I began to investigate the Japanese interpretations of this word *seii* (pronounced "say-ee"). I found that it is used to identify a person who is not self-seeking, one who is self-disciplined and free of passion. (My ex-maid must have used it to mean that I was thinking only of my own wishes and not at all of her welfare.) In a broader sense, one could say that *seii* is not a separate virtue or quality in itself but rather is the enthusiasm that a zealot demonstrates on behalf of his own beliefs. It is that quality that sets the "Japanese Spirit" apart. It is behaving the way the Japanese expect a decent man to behave. (Which differs variously and sometimes largely from how *we* would want such a man to behave.)

5

Their Women

Seventy thousand American men have married Japanese
women since the close of World War Two, a number which
would assuredly be much larger if our military authorities,
mindful of racial prejudices back home, had not placed so
many formidable obstacles in the path of such proposed
unions. Furthermore, the number of Japanese women who
have been full-fledged mistresses of Americans living in Japan
is still greater, and those who have associated with Americans,
to varying degrees of intimacy, far exceeds that, of course.
After all, millions of Americans have spent time in Japan since
1945, and the single (as well as more than a few of the married) men among them most probably became acquainted
with, on the average, two or three Japanese women while in
their country.

Physically, they tend to be petite, graceful, energetic, and
fine-skinned. On the minus side, their legs are too often short,
heavy, and slightly bowed, but, as noted in respect to Japanese men, the practice of strapping babies to their mothers'
backs for ease in carrying is diminishing, so that the last de-
fect should become less common in the future. Their noses are
low, while the Mongolian folds at the inner corners make
their eyes appear too far apart to us. Both of these defects,
however, are being corrected in large numbers daily in the
more than three hundred (seventy in Tokyo alone) cosmetic
surgery clinics and hospitals throughout the country, while

improving nutrition together with new concepts of baby care and feeding are giving women taller bodies, longer, slimmer legs, and better vision. (It is common these days for fourteen- or fifteen-year-old children to be taller than their parents.)

Go to the Ginza on a warm Sunday afternoon—the stores are open then—and observe Japanese femininity at large. Stroll along for an hour or so, and you will see some of Japan's loveliest women. Slim, gay, clean, tastefully dressed mostly in Western clothes, and not too heavily made up, they are light years apart from the "beauties" of Japan's past.

A typical beauty of the Heian Period (794–1185), for example, would have worn her hair five yards in length and blackened her teeth; she would have shaved her eyebrows off and coated heavily with white powder that part of her body which aroused her male admirers as erotically and effectively as deep cleavage today excites the breast-minded American male, e.g., the nape of her neck; and she would have walked pigeon-toed with a mincing gait (which is still common in women wearing kimono and zori).

Even today the Japanese man's concept of female attractiveness differs largely from that of his Western counterpart, which is a fortunate circumstance for some of us, for we can often find the most comely girls languishing away for lack of suitors in out-of-the-way Japanese towns: girls who, because of their height or their higher noses or their more-oval-than-round faces, are amenable to sharing their neglected attributes with foreigners, in lieu of local lovers.

In Yokosuka in 1952, I knew an American navy officer who once went boar-hunting in Miyazaki Prefecture down in Kyushu. Instead of boar, he came back with one of the three most stunningly beautiful Japanese girls I have ever seen. She was only seventeen and spoke very little English, but theirs had been a case of intense mutual attraction from the start. With hardly a word to her parents, she had packed a small suitcase and followed the navy officer, who was a tall, clean-cut young man from an old New England family, back to

Yokosuka. Obviously, they were deeply in love with each other and indifferent to much that went on around them, but inability to communicate adequately—at least, in words—forced them to call on me frequently for interpretation. During these meetings, her utter lack of feminine wiles, her naiveté, and her charming, pristine innocence became obvious and incontrovertible. When I learned that she had never before had a date with a boy, I expressed my surprise, so she explained that it was because people thought she looked *okashii* (funny) and *gaikokujin-kusai* (foreign).

I lost track of the couple soon thereafter, but I did hear that he married her and took her home with him.

Much of the controversy about Japanese women spins around the pivotal question: How subservient are they to men? Are they merely child-bearing house-cleaners who are, in the words of Tennyson, "something better than his dog, a little dearer than his horse"? Or, are they, as some would have it, calculating creatures with velvet-covered claws and hearts of steel? And, whichever they are, what made them that way?

The tradition of male dominance did not always obtain in Japan, there having been clear-cut matriarchal overtones at times in the distant past. The highest deity in the Shintoist pantheon of gods was Amaterasu-Omikami, the Sun Goddess, and, going from mythology to ancient Chinese records, one finds such commentaries as, "The Japanese formerly had kings, but after years of civil war, they agreed to set up a woman named Himeko as their sovereign. When Queen Himeko died, a great mound was raised over her and more than a thousand of her attendants followed her in death. Then a king was raised to the throne, but the people would not obey him, and civil war broke out again. A girl of thirteen, a relative of Himeko named Iyo, was then made Queen and order was restored."

About 200 A.D., the Empress Jingo, whose martial ways may have inspired our English word *jingoism,* led Japan to its first successful foreign conquest (of part of Korea), a feat that no Japanese man was to match for seventeen hundred years.

Nor were these instances of female leadership exceptional. The names of such empresses as Koken, Komyo, and Suiko figure largely in the pages of early history. Then, in the late twelfth century, there arose the Lady Masako Hojo, who was surely one of the most competent and strong-minded women of any age or any country. On the night of her wedding to a Taira governor, she eloped with the renowned warrior Yoritomo Minamoto and ruled Japan at his side until his death in 1199. Thereafter, as the *Ama Shogun* (Nun General), she ruled Japan wisely and well, from several stances, until her death in 1225.

(What may well be one of the first recorded examples of the cosmetic urge in women is a painting, more than a thousand years old, that hangs in the Imperial Museum in Nara. It is called "The Goddess of Beauty," and its goddess's lips are painted crimson. Another example of Japanese women leading the way in fashions is to be found in an old photograph in my files: taken in Oiso, south of Tokyo, about the turn of the century, it shows a beach scene with perhaps a hundred men and women in and out of the water, and at least one-third of the women are wearing topless bathing suits.)

At the beginning of the Muromachi Era (1392–1573), Japan entered a period of gradually worsening lawlessness and confusion, a time that contrasted sharply with the previous centuries of comparative order and peace. Divisive currents flowed strongly, old loyalties and ideas were uprooted, relatives battled each other in sporadic but savage outbreaks of violence. When the heads of families and clans died and divided their holdings equally among their sons and daughters or perhaps left the reins of the blood kinship group in the hands of an only female child, this often resulted in the diminution of the property and the dissolution of the unit. The women simply were not strong enough to fend off the physical inroads against them and to hold the unit together. Of necessity, the family heads and clan chieftains came to choose sons to take over and preserve unity. If they had no sons, they adopted them from other families, preferably blood-related but often not—a custom that persists today.

This, then, was the beginning of the downward road for Japanese women, and the slope was made more precipitous by Buddhist precepts that women were fundamentally more prone to sin than men and that their only path to expiation lay in total subservience to the male element.

How far downhill did the Japanese woman ultimately go? To that lower level where, in the traditional ideology, she not only obeyed her husband and master in everything but also "enjoyed" every minute of this subservience. She had no rights, only duties. Her pleasure came not from establishing her own independence and dignity as a human being but from learning to do what she had to do as a woman. In life, she had three masters: her father while young, her husband during the middle years, and her son or sons in old age.

If her husband proved unfaithful to her, she could take no legal action against him, but if she was caught committing adultery, both she and her lover could be literally crucified.

In time, her position became like that of the American Indian squaw in the oft-told anecdote: On a hot summer day, a white man saw an Indian chieftain riding a horse with an Indian woman walking along behind him in the dust.

White man: "Hello, Chief."

Indian: "How."

White man: "She your squaw?"

The Indian nodded affirmatively.

White man: "Why isn't she riding?"

Indian, with a look of long-suffering patience at the manifest stupidity of all white men: "She no got horse."

This is also reminiscent of the story I heard in Korea during the war there: An infantry private fresh from the States said that he had been told that Korean men were very considerate of their womenfolk, that they often permitted the women to walk ahead of them. A sergeant with more experience answered, "Yeah, but only in the minefields."

Proverbs, which are often accurate weathervanes of popular attitudes anywhere, reflect the discredit done Japanese women: *"Onna wa mamono* (Women are demons)"; *"Onna-gokoro to harubiyori* (A woman's mind and spring weather," i.e., both are too changeable); *"Onna no saru-jie* (Woman's monkey-like wit)"; *"Onna-hideri wa nai* (There is never a dearth of women)"; *"Onna sannin yoreba kashimashii* (Three women together make a terrible clatter)"; *"Onna wa sangai ni ie nashi* (A woman has no home in any of the three worlds)." And the most cynical of all: *"Shichinin no ko wo nasu tomo onna ni kokoro wo yurusu na!* (Never trust a woman, even though she has borne you seven children!)"

Her chief aim in life, it was held, was to bring comfort and happiness to her husband, to his parents and other relatives, and to her children. She married at the command of her parents and was ruled by her husband's every wish and whim. She was the first to arise in the morning and the last to go to bed. In the evening, her husband bathed first, the children next, and she last. If some of the more tasty dinner dishes were in short supply, they were distributed in that same order. In olden times, her husband could divorce her simply by giving her a *mikudari-han* (literally, three and a half lines): a letter of notification of intent, only three and a half lines in length. In more recent times, all that was required was a trip to the ward or town office where the family register was kept and the obliteration of her name. Seven reasons were considered acceptable. Among them were talkativeness, a communicable disease (flu or the itch perhaps?), jealousy, and refusal to serve her husband's parents.

She didn't dare dream of going out with her husband for pleasure and if they had to attend a social function (such as the wedding of a relative) together, she was expected to walk three paces behind him, stay clear of him during the reception that followed, and speak only when spoken to in mixed company.

If, despite her best efforts, he nevertheless divorced her, her chance of making another marriage was slim indeed. *Demodori* (girls who have "gone out and come back") were rated only one notch above cripples and the untouchables in order of desirability.

Shortly after the end of the Pacific War, I was invited one evening to have dinner at the home of a professor at Kyushu Imperial University. A woman in a rather shabby kimono answered the door, asked me to come in, took off my shoes for me, and guided me to the room where the professor awaited my arrival. Then she bowed and withdrew, only to appear again from time to time with drinks, ashtrays, peanuts, rice crackers, and other offerings. The professor did not introduce her to me and because his tone when speaking to her was very abrupt—almost angry, in fact—I was half-convinced that she was a maid. (This was one of my first visits to a Japanese home, and I was trying to learn by watching in silence rather than asking questions that might prove embarrassing or inappropriate.) When at length dinner was served, this same woman served us but did not sit with us at the low table on the tatami mats, which persuaded me that she was, after all, a maid.

Thereafter, I'm afraid, I began to talk to her as I would talk to a maid myself. In polite enough language, of course, but not in the words that one should have used to the mistress of the home. And, as you have already guessed, it turned out that she was the professor's wife.

We may wonder why the Japanese woman endured all this, why she did not demonstrate, confront, and even revolt? The answer reflects economic necessity. She could be divorced at almost any time for even whimsical reasons. The word *alimony* was not to be found in the Japanese dictionary. Any money she got from her husband was prompted by his generosity—

again, whimsical—and not by force of law. (And it was almost always comically inadequate.) She seldom had the skills needed for gainful employment, but even if she did, she would most probably have been forced to quit work at the age of thirty or so, to make room for a male employee. (This practice is still common today. Work for a woman is regarded as something to fill the brief time gap between school and marriage, not as a means of supporting herself for more extended periods.) If she was one of the lucky few from affluent homes, she went back to her parents to wait out her years in physical, if not spiritual, comfort. Otherwise, she became a servant, a waitress, or a member of the *mizu shobai:* that nether world of drinking establishments, geisha houses, and restaurants where a man can enjoy food and drink and usually women.

So she "endured the unendurable" and stuck it out with her husband. Of course, such a life was not entirely without its compensations. The husband usually was not an insensate brute. Although he held the whip, he did not always use it, and even though he would have thought it unmanly and degrading to tell her that he loved her, he may have demonstrated sincere affection for her in other ways. The pages of Japanese history and literature are liberally sprinkled with accounts of extreme examples of mutual devotion. And then she had the children to raise, and they were devoted to her in her old age, perhaps even more devoted than their American counterparts would have been. When her eldest son brought a bride back to the family home, the mother's stature grew considerably, for now she too had someone to boss and to scold, someone to serve her and to gratify her ego, even as she had done for her own mother-in-law years before. She found a measure of satisfaction in playing the traditional game of butter up and trample down.

In one sense, this was—and still is—the bad age for Japanese women: their forties and fifties, when they become mothers-in-law. When they pass forty, few of them make any serious effort to retain their attractiveness or to retard the inroads of time. Why should they? It is now, if ever, that their husbands will begin to enjoy enough extra income and influence to acquire mistresses or at least to have occasional extramarital romances. Their husbands are seldom home, and the other children have moved away. Only the eldest son and his bride remain. What better way to spend the now-empty hours of the day than by passing on to her son's wife the same treatment she got from her mother-in-law?

Unkempt and uncaring, her tongue grows sharp, her patience thin, and her temper short. In a word, she becomes a shrew.

But this time, too, passes. Either the daughter-in-law adjusts her ways to those of her husband's mother, the Empress Dowager figure, or she is rejected. Soon the older woman's bile empties itself. Grandchildren come along to divert and amuse her. She mellows. When her husband relinquishes control of family affairs to the eldest son, they both begin to enjoy life. They may move to a smaller house within the same compound, where they relax and drink tea and sun themselves and play with their grandchildren. These are their golden years.

To what extent has all this changed during the postwar period?

First and foremost are the legal changes inspired by the Supreme Commander, Allied Powers. These gave the Japanese woman rights, whereas all she had possessed previously had been duties. She was given an interest in part of her husband's property, whereas before all that she could take out of a marriage was what she had brought to it as property in her own name. (And her husband had the legal right to manage even that during the term of their marriage.) She could not now be cast aside as easily as before. As a popular saying had it, two things became stronger after the war: stockings and women.

She was also given the right to vote. Our Occupation spared her what her American sisters had had to go through to acquire the franchise; Douglas MacArthur handed it to her on a silver *o-bon*. In 1946, thirty-nine women were elected to the national Diet, where there had never been even one before. Nor did the fact that many female voters had mistakenly believed that they could only cast their votes for women diminish her triumph.

The downhill road that had reached its nadir when most women were browbeaten into wearing the wartime *mompe*— drab, baggy trousers that are the most unfeminine and most unfashionable of all conceivable garments for women—was at last beginning to slant upward. The subdued, withdrawn, melancholy women of former days now began to take hope. Little by little, as the wretched years of the early postwar era passed, they began to hold their heads up, to smile, to speak less diffidently, to think that even they themselves might hope for a measure of fulfillment as human beings.

Instead of being urged by their government to produce children every season, like animals in the field, they were pleasantly startled to hear that they should practice birth control. Coeducation was introduced, and more girls began to get higher educations. (At this writing, 18 percent of Japanese college students are female, in comparison to 38 percent in the United States. However, in the leading universities of Japan, the percentage is only five, while in the junior colleges it ranges as high as sixty.)

More women began to take jobs (now one in four, over the age of fifteen), although their pay still averages only 48 percent of that of men. They have begun to organize themselves into political, religious, and economic groupings, while their collective voices are heeded to an extent undreamed of in prewar days. The old saw, *"Fusho fuzui* (When the husband beckons, the wife had better jump),"* has been reversed in meaning by wags because, with fitting coincidence, the combined-form readings of the characters for *husband* and *wife* are both *fu* and can be reversed for the sake of the pun.

One of the most vivid indications of how far things have gone in the other direction is contained in a recent announce-

ment from the Superintendence Bureau of the Japan National
Railways: During the three-month period under report, 53
percent of those persons committing indecent acts on trains
were women. (In Japan, the trains are so crowded—even
standing room is at a premium during rush hours—that some
men get part of their daily erotic satisfaction from pressing
themselves up against the women standing next to them. If
they did not like it, there was little the women could do about
it, since making a scene was out of the question. Now, however, we see some of them becoming the aggressors and re-
paying their tormentors in the same coin.)

Miss Kazuko Shiraishi, who is renowned as the *Dankon wo
utau shijin* (poetess who extols the phallus), may not yet be
typical of Japan's postwar emancipated women, but she is
blazing a broad trail for others to follow in her bold march
toward complete sexual freedom.

Increasingly women are bringing their sexual affairs, questions, and problems (mostly, it seems, of a quantitative nature)
out into the open, which is not, however, to suggest that they
were so well concealed in the past. Magazines that in the
United States would be named *Seventeen* or *Debutante* or
Young Bride print a continual stream of articles and surveys
about sex and the young girl. Although often written in a
lurid style, much of the advice appears to be sound or, at
least, non-toxic.

I have one such article before me now. It concerns a round-
table discussion among five Tokyo girls, ranging in age from
fourteen to nineteen, about female masturbation. The tone
is serious, and the girls discuss the subject frankly. When did
they first masturbate? What was the stimulus? Do they believe
it is harmful? Do their boyfriends, if any, know about it? And
so forth.

Articles and surveys about virginity are also numerous.
Often they use the round-table discussion technique and probe
in depth such questions as the age at which the girls lost their
virginity, the place, the amount of pain or bleeding, and the

identity of their partners. (Among the categories of partners given in one set of answers I found one intriguing group called "old family friends.")

As they began to understand the enlarged dimensions of their freedom, the younger women started to look around and consider what they might do other than get married. (They had a saying: *"Kekkon wa josei no hakaba de aru,"* or "Marriage is a woman's grave.") Jobs as stage and movie actresses had always held their charm, although understandably opposed by concerned parents, but now the most desired professions became those of airline stewardess, fashion model, and ballet dancer.

At the same time, however, the practice of *jinshin baibai* (trafficking in human flesh) remained very much in evidence. Young girls, some mere children, flow into Tokyo and Osaka, the two largest cities, from the country districts during seasons of poor harvests and natural disasters, to be caught on the hooks of the *yakuza* who await them in the railroad stations. The methods of the dealers and the market prices may vary, but the lure of the big city and the desire to leave farm drudgery do not. And only too often the girls' parents give them a nudge in that direction.

The vicissitudes of prostitution (one of the Japanese words for which is *baishun,* or "selling spring") can be regarded as another indicator of the status of women. Japanese farming families have always welcomed the birth of sons more than that of daughters, for sons mean more hands to harvest the rice paddies and garden plots and to care for their parents in old age, while daughters are of more limited usefulness and, in addition, have to be supplied with dowries when they are given in marriage.

In times of poor crops and natural disasters the least useful members of the family unit, namely, the daughters, were sacrificed for the sake of familial survival. (The practice of *mabiki* —"weeding out" children, especially girl children, at birth— was common for hundreds of years and is evidenced in the

Japanese proverb, *"Ko wo suteru yabu ga aredo oya wo suteru yabu wa nai,"* or "Although there is a bamboo grove where you can leave your babies to die, there is none where you can discard your parents.") The daughters chosen to save their families were "sold" to brothel-owners, in whose establishments they were placed under long-term employment contracts and where it was difficult to ever get enough money ahead to redeem their freedom.

Japanese society recognized that these girls were innocent pawns in a struggle for survival. Their quiet acceptance of this fate, in fact, bespoke their willingness to abandon their personal dreams of having their own homes and families in order that their families might live. They were regarded with pity—and respect.

The brothels in which these girls worked were mostly concentrated in regulated areas throughout the country, often surrounded by walls or moats, like Tobita in Osaka and Yoshiwara in Tokyo. The latter became the most famous in Japan, lasting from the early 1600's until its end by government decree on the first day of April, 1958. In its heyday, it was a city within a city, with fine shops and all the sources of supply and service it needed to function as a municipal entity. Called the *Fuyajo* (the castle that knows no night), it closed its gates at midnight, which was the hour of curfew, but the revelers trapped within merely continued their bacchanalia until the gates were opened again at six o'clock the following morning. (The prostitutes themselves could leave the environs of Yoshiwara for only two reasons: to visit dying parents or, in a group, to see the cherry blossoms in Ueno, which betokens the importance of cherry-blossom viewing in the Japanese scheme of things.) Samurai, otherwise not permitted to enter, went there in disguise and in droves, as did merchant princes and artists and poets and writers of stage plays. The leading prostitutes were idolized and glamorized to an extent reminiscent of the nimbus of awe in which American movie queens of the late Twenties and Thirties lived and thrived.

Yoshiwara's slow descent from glory began as far back as 1760, caused by changing social conditions and attitudes, and the rate of descent accelerated during the militaristic regime of the Thirties and early Forties, until it plunged to stagnation as the war neared its end. The advent of red-blooded American boys, however, staved off disaster, at least for a while. In fact, it acted like adrenalin pumped into the main artery. The prostitutes perked up and prospered as American sailors, marines, and soldiers strolled along the streets of Yoshiwara, gaily lit with lanterns and hope again, regarding and then selecting from the merchandise on display.

On January 21, 1946, the office of the Supreme Commander, Allied Powers, dispatched a memorandum to the Japanese government urging that it take steps to abolish legalized prostitution, including, of course, Yoshiwara. This memo shocked Japanese solons. Abolish the gay quarters? What on earth for? What could possibly be wrong with it? What would take its place? They were so astounded and distressed that it took them one full year to respond and to make initial motions in the direction of compliance.

Having pressured Japan's lawmakers into accepting a new Constitution, the officials of the Occupation were then hesitant about forcing a sweeping anti-prostitution edict down their throats. They preferred to let the Japanese adopt the proposal and take the reins themselves.

The Japanese did just that. The Japanese women, that is. The newly elected female members of the Diet called for the cooperation of women's organizations a-borning all over Japan in that early dawn of their emancipation and they made a strong fight of it. Interestingly enough, these women supported the abolition of licensed prostitution not so much from fear that their husbands might wander from the path of virtue and stumble into such lairs of temptation as from concern over the fate of the prostitutes themselves. They held prostitution—and, in particular, enforced prostitution—to be the penultimate indignity a woman might suffer.

It took them eleven years, but at last they won. The quarters in Yoshiwara closed their gates to seekers of carnal pleasures and were converted in time to a district of coffee shops and restaurants, including one youth hostel. Although it became a crime for a woman to "sell spring," it did not become a crime for a man to buy it. In 1966, the women of Japan tried to correct this oversight; they sought the passage of a bill that would make it illegal for a man to buy the services of a prostitute or even to ask anyone to help him find such a woman. The fine would have been ¥10,000 (approximately $33.00).

The bill was defeated, mostly because the male legislators of Japan were in no mood to consider any extension of the Anti-Prostitution Law. A curtailment would have been more to their liking. During those eight years since 1958, strains of syphilis resistant to the new drugs were appearing and proliferating alarmingly. Instead of being rehabilitated, most of the former dwellers of Yoshiwara and other quarters had continued to exercise their talents in the guise of masseuses, girl guides, Turkish bath attendants, waitresses, cabaret hostesses, and models at nude-posing studios. Those who worked with pimps (who often doubled as gangsters) found themselves slaves to masters more heartless and demanding than any Yoshiwara brothel-keeper. Sex crimes, which had always been few in Japan, were growing in number, and this, suggested Justice Minister Okinoro Kaya, might be traced to the closing of the gay quarters.

No, indeed. The legislators might not yet have the ammunition they needed to justify reopening the quarters, but they most assuredly were not going to try to arrest and fine every man who asked the whereabouts of a whore. "Let's defeat this ridiculous proposal," they agreed. "After that, we'll bide our time for a while longer. Then we'll see."

As for the less controversial professions, city maids are still working fifteen hours a day, on the average. In the field of education, some middle schools that had been opened to both sexes are now reverting to all-boy or all-girl status. Most marriages are still arranged by parents, while many fall into the category of delayed-registration marriages.

Most husbands still do not tell their wives when they think they may come home late. (According to a recent survey, 64 percent of Japanese husbands stop off "somewhere" on the way home, and within the ambiguous limits of that one word *somewhere* is contained another many-chaptered story, which may or may not have something to do with the fact that Japanese women commit suicide more often than any other national group in the world.) Although her husband may call her by her first name (without the polite ending *-san,* of course) the wife cannot reciprocate but must use the polite form of you (*anata*) when addressing him. When his guests come to the home (this is seldom), she is more servant than companion.

While this chapter was being written, I came across a news report that says a good deal about the present situation of Japanese women. The *Shukan Asahi,* one of the most prestigious of Japan's many weekly magazines, carried an interview with Mrs. Hiroko Sato, wife of Premier Eisaku Sato. In essence, Mrs. Sato said that her husband had been a rake in his younger days, that he never consulted her about anything, and that he beat her to boot. (That such an interview appeared at all, however, argues for considerable emancipation of Japanese women.)

Shortly thereafter, reporters cornered Premier Sato and asked him if it was true that he used to beat his wife.

Certainly it was true, he answered. Do you still beat her? they asked. No, he replied. Times have changed, they said. He nodded.

Then, in a moment of mutual candor, he asked them, "How many of you beat *your* wives nowadays?"

Fully one-half of them answered—sheepishly—that they do.

This chapter will close with a brief note about one of

Japan's best-known women, Mrs. Fuji Murayama. Her father was co-founder of the *Asahi Shimbun,* one of the two most influential newspapers in Japan and one of the largest-circulation dailies in the world. Having no son to whom he could leave his fortune, Mr. Murayama adopted one, who then married his daughter and took the family name. Perhaps with an early inkling of his daughter's spirit of independence, however, Mr. Murayama took steps before he died to place safeguards around the editorial policies of his newspaper so that his heirs could not inject too much personal opinion and individual fancy into its pages.

Nevertheless, his daughter was strong-minded enough to try to do just that in later years, and this led to a series of disputes with the editors that culminated in a court battle.

About this time, the nation was watching with half-held breath the progress of the *Asahi*-sponsored Japanese Antarctic Expedition, and everyone was extremely concerned when the expedition radioed back to Japan that its advance party was in trouble and might have to abandon its dogs in order to get the men back safely. (The dogs eventually *were* abandoned, and when the expedition returned to the Antarctic the following season, they found one of the animals still living. Evidently it had kept itself alive by eating the others.)

In a memorable effort—and one that will always endear her to me—to save those dogs in a civilization in which animals generally get very poor treatment, Mrs. Murayama commanded the editors of the *Asahi* to radio orders to the expedition to save the dogs and, if necessary, abandon the men.

6

Their Homes and Home Life

There has been a marked tendency in recent years for foreigners to gush over Japanese living space ("An enchanted house built by fairies in a perfect and exquisitely beautiful garden" is but one of many examples), but the truth is that even in this age of increasing modernization the typical Japanese house palls as the acquaintance deepens. It is fine for foreign visitors to pass a few hours or even several days in such surroundings and exult over the marvelous woodwork, the tasteful simplicity, the refined bareness, and the spiritually serene atmosphere, but when they extend their stays into months and years, a certain weariness, a decidedly testy and bleak outlook may take the place of their previous enthusiasm.

For the short and straight of it is that there are few, if any, Americans who have long lived in a typical Japanese house —and liked it. Such a house is itself an anachronism, as much out of date today as a prairie sodhouse would be on San Francisco's Nob Hill. It is hard to heat, hard to cool, hard to keep clean, and easy to burn down. It is small, cramped, dimly lighted, unsanitary, lacking in privacy, insect-prone, and downright dangerous. (It will collapse—in typhoons—as quickly as it will burn; because it has no yard, its children play in the streets.) Its bathing arrangements are outrageous, and its kitchen would be an American housewife's nightmare. Since it has no screens, insects vie with humans for occupancy rights and seem to divide their time between the open-pit toilet and the dining table. Having no bookcases and few general utility shelves, it offers infinite possibilities for disarray. With tatami that should be replaced every two or three years and with shoji (sliding panel doors) that children, pets, and wayward broom handles delight in poking holes through, it readily lends itself to the appearance of squalor. It is uncomfortable, unhealthful, and undeserving of the better connotations of the word *home*. (The fact that the Japanese tolerate their own houses I can only attribute to ignorance, sheer necessity, or the binding, blinding restrictions of traditionalism and conformity.)

When one sets out—should he be so ill-advised—to construct one of these houses for himself, the first skull-binding trauma to distract him is the cost of land. Especially in Tokyo and the other major cities. From 1955 to 1965 Japan's urban-land price index rose 670 percent and since then it has continued to average a 10 percent increase yearly, making it the most expensive real estate in the world. Choice land along the Ginza in Tokyo costs about twice what Manhattan's best would cost, thrice San Francisco's, and five times that on the French Riviera. Even an hour and a half from downtown Tokyo the going rate is nearly $50,000 an acre.

Tokyo land is so valuable that the worth of the structure standing on it usually fades into insignificance. For example, an acquaintance of mine recently bought a place in suburban Omori; the land (3,500 square feet) cost $30,000 while the fifteen-year-old, two-bedroom house standing on it was valued at $3,600.

The reader may wonder how the average Japanese, whose income is still only one-fourth of that of his American counterpart, can afford to build a home in Tokyo, especially when most builders require payment of one-third of the total cost at the time the construction contract is signed, one-third when the roof-beam is raised, and the remainder when the house is ready for occupancy. The answer is easy: he can't.

Instead, he may have one of several choices: moving into

company housing, living with parents or other relatives, renting one or two rooms, or applying for a government-owned apartment. (These are inexpensive but eagerly sought after and in such short supply that they are assigned only by lottery to a fortunate few.) All of these may be unhappy substitutes for one's own residence, but what can Mr. Hashimoto do when he has to work six and a half years to earn enough to buy the same amount of land that an American could buy with the product of only forty-five days of employment?

Even so, these structures, standing on land that costs so much to acquire, have a kind of built-in impermanence about them, most not being constructed to last as long as in the West. Over the years, fires and natural disasters have destroyed homes with such appalling frequency that their builders understandably opted for inexpensive, readily available materials and fast, almost temporary construction methods.

The Japanese have also to make another choice: heavy construction for warmth in winter or light construction for coolness in summer? Considering their preference for accommodation with or a graceful yielding to nature, it should not be surprising that they selected the latter. Wanting to live in intimacy and close harmony with the elements, they built for themselves houses that could be easily thrown wide open to air and breeze and sun and light. Given a degree of indifference to stinging insects, this made for not-intolerable living conditions during the summer, but paper doors and balsa wood and feathery construction do not keep out the wintry winds that originate in Siberia and pick up more chill as they sweep across the Japan Alps en route to Tokyo and the other heavily populated regions along the eastern coast.

So over the years the Japanese improvised. Rather than heat all the interior space of a dwelling, they decided to warm the individual himself. Thus the long soaking in the piping hot bath. The frequent cups of hot, weak tea. The long winter underwear worn from September through May. The *futon,* or sleeping comforters, so bulky that their weight has been authoritatively listed as a contributory cause of several serious ailments. And the *kotatsu,* that cunning well in the floor with a hibachi at the bottom and a low table and heat-holding quilt over it.

In appearance, the Japanese house is not at all prepossessing. It is never painted, inside or out, and while the interior woodwork may be polished to a fine natural glow, the exterior becomes weatherbeaten. This unpainted drabness used to be enhanced by the thatch roof, which, for reasons of flammability, largely gave way to the dark gray tile roof (glazed blue or reddish brown in some instances). But tile is expensive and the structure must be strong to support its weight, so nowadays rust-proof tin of varied hues is becoming popular, lending touches of color to a scene that had been uniformly and uninspiringly neutral (but which reflects the Japanese preference for the natural characteristics of the materials with which they build).

Those who possess the means will surround their homes with walls, solid evidence of the Japanese desire to isolate their private lives from the outside world. (These walls are often topped by ugly and formidable arrays of broken glass and barbed wire, for the most part installed in the immediate postwar years when many relied on burglary for livelihood.) Within such walls may lie Japanese gardens with stone lanterns and teahouses of the picture postcard variety, but these are adjuncts only to affluent homes.

The typical residence will not have a true garden, although most will install a few rocks and a bit of greenery in a corner, perhaps against a bamboo fence. There are, of course, no lawns as such, and the Japanese thus fortunately avoid that curse of American suburbia (the maintenance of which costs us untold billions of dollars and billions of hours of totally unproductive labor). Proper garages are largely unknown, although the terrifying increase in the number of those lethal weapons—automobiles—is bringing the problem of parking space more and more to the fore these days. For several years

Tokyo residents have not been able to buy a car unless they could prove that they had a place to park it. Before that they merely left their vehicles on the already too-narrow, over-crowded streets.

The floor plan of an average Japanese house will generally include an entranceway, or *genkan,* where shoes are exchanged for slippers, two all-purpose (for eating, sleeping, and receiving guests) tatami rooms, a kitchen, a toilet, and a bathroom. These will be connected by a hallway. (Slippers should be removed when one enters the tatami-floored rooms but may be worn wherever there is board flooring. The tile-floored toilet will have a special set of slippers, often *waraji,* or straw, sandals, for its exclusive use.) The two tatami rooms will be side by side and are separated by paper and wood doors. By sliding these doors open or removing them entirely, the two rooms can be converted into a larger space for social gatherings. *Futon* are folded and stored in a closet in one of these tatami rooms and can be easily brought out to provide sleeping arrangements for as many as the space will accommodate.

Along one side of these two tatami rooms will usually run a veranda, which may be an extension of the hallway. This will be separated from the tatami rooms by *fusuma,* sliding doors made of wood and heavy paper, and from the garden or outdoors by sliding glass doors and (at night) by heavy sliding wooden shutters. On the veranda may be placed a small table and two chairs, a minor concession to Western ways. Here the head of the household may occasionally sit to read, smoke, or brood.

One of the tatami rooms will be used more for the formal reception of guests than the other. It will contain an alcove called the tokonoma in which a scroll hangs (and is changed with the season or felicitous event) and in which is usually placed a floral arrangement, perhaps in an old valuable vase, or figurine. On one side of this tokonoma stands the *toko-bashira,* a natural wood pillar that may cost hundreds of dollars. The most honored guest is seated with his back to this tokonoma.

While the *tokobashira* may be of especially fine wood, the lumber used in the construction of Japanese house is usually a combination of cypress, cryptomeria, pine, and *rawan* (lauan).

The typical family of four lives in only three rooms, while near the center of Tokyo the majority of private homes average less than two hundred square feet. This shortage of living space was dramatically illustrated by the recent case of a taxi driver who was arrested while having conjugal relations with his wife in the back seat of his taxi parked in the plaza in front of the Imperial Palace. The authorities were prepared to deal harshly with this blatant disregard of the Imperial Presence, until the driver humbly explained to the judge that his family of six all lived and slept together in a 9 foot by 9 foot room and that he had existed without the benefits of his wife's embraces for several long months. (Whereas the American family tends to commune at the dinner table, the Japanese family satisfies its need for physical and spiritual proximity by sleeping together . . . and, to a lesser extent . . . by bathing together.)

While the kitchen may be many an American housewife's pride and joy ("My Guests Like My Kitchen Best"), in Japan it comes closer to being her counterpart's shame and disillusion. It tends to be dark, dingy, and inconvenient. Even in this day of rising affluence, its appliances will usually be limited to a two-burner gas stove, a *denki-gama* (electric rice-cooker), and perhaps a small refrigerator. Unless she has some Western orientation, the Japanese housewife will never show her kitchen to formal guests, although a neighbor may join her for a cup of tea in that room if she happens to be occupied there.

Because the Japanese dislike to connect the two functions, they will have kept the toilet and the bathroom separate. Most toilets will provide both a urinal and a toilet bowl, the latter being the kind that the user squats over. (The Japanese are revolted by the thought of bringing the skin of their buttocks into contact with a toilet seat on which many others may have sat and performed a necessary if unpleasant function. They vastly prefer their own tiled version of the G.I. slit trench.)

Unfortunately for those with sensitive noses and a concern for hygienic living arrangements, most toilets do not flush. The waste is dropped directly into a pit which can be reached from outside the house and which is emptied periodically in the cities by vacuum-hose trucks. Only about 20 percent of Japanese homes enjoy the benefits of modern sewerage, compared to 90 percent in the United States and 93 percent in England.

Guests in Japanese homes are generally limited to relatives, close neighbors, old family friends, and persons having specific business there, such as a teacher of one of the children. The Japanese vastly prefer to entertain other friends and business acquaintances in public establishments. They would think it rude to invite a guest to a house unworthy of him, and to assume that one's own home *is* worthy would be impertinent. (Showing a guest through one's home and proudly exhibiting one's possessions in the American manner is considered insufferably boorish.) Sometimes an American couple will have the opportunity to entertain a Japanese in their home in the United States and if they later visit Japan, they look forward to a chance to see an example of Japanese home life. Depending on his degree of Westernization and on the quality of his residence, the Japanese friend may or may not invite them to his home. If not, the American couple is sorely puzzled and not necessarily placated by a sumptuous dinner at a fine restaurant. Often the Americans will tell their Japanese host straight out that they want to see his home and meet his wife, thereby sorely puzzling *him*. If they are invited to his home, they go with the expectation of seeing Japanese home life as it is really lived, but more often than not the host and hostess will have bent every possible effort toward making their home, food, drinks, and apparel as American as possible for the occasion.

Because the Japanese prefer to entertain away from home and because the husband enjoys doing the town without the style-cramping company of his wife as often as he can, husband-and-wife togetherness is much less in evidence than in the United States. (One concession to the modern world is a growing tendency on the part of the male to take his wife and children or sometimes only his children on Sunday outings.) To be in love with one's wife was considered demeaning, according to the code of the samurai, and many Japanese men still hark back to the glorious, swashbuckling days of Bushido even as American men watch Marshal Matt Dillon on *Gunsmoke* with more than a trace of national nostalgia. For the husband and wife to go out in public together was shameful, and to give the appearance of being at all concerned about her pleasure or comfort was a sign of weakness. (An indicator of the woman's place was the fact that traditionally a man mourned the death of either parent for thirteen months but that of his wife only eight.)

These days many persons, both foreign and Japanese, point with satisfaction to the growing evidence of female liberation in Japan, and more than a few young women scoff at arranged marriages and chafe at male supremacy, but the cautious observer wonders how deep these apparent changes go. The man who is a militant democrat in public but an arrogant despot at home has become a standing joke by reason of his frequent intrusion on the scene, while the flaming angry youth who later becomes a hidebound traditionalist is so commonplace as to be nearly standard.

Although the Japanese housewife is left at home more often than her American counterpart, her life—even among the less privileged—is not quite the unceasing round of drudgery that one might otherwise imagine it to be. (According to a 1970 survey by Video Research, housewives have an average of five hours of leisure time daily.) Several factors alleviate her situation: Because her house is small, she has less space to clean. In the morning, she opens all doors and windows and, if the sun is shining, she airs the bedding. Then, with a stick that has several strips of light silk cloth fastened to one end, she goes through the house flailing away at dust-covered surfaces. Unlike an oil cloth, the dust does not adhere to these strips of silk but rises into the air. Part of the idea behind the open windows is the hope that a passing breeze will blow through the dwelling and carry off the offending particles, but more often than not the breeze fails to oblige and the dust slowly settles back approximately to its previous place of rest. This takes a few minutes, however, and provides the housewife with the illusion that she has thoroughly dusted the area.

Furthermore, stowing the *futon* away in a closet is a much less time-consuming task than making the equivalent number of beds. I have seen Japanese women put away the bedding for six people in less than two minutes. How long would it take to properly make three to six Western beds, even without changing the sheets?

The yard, if any, takes but little of the housewife's time. She may pick up a few leaves and scraps of paper and occasionally sprinkle water about to lay the dust. The almost universal electric washing machine has greatly reduced the physical effort involved in laundering. In homes without gas-operated hot-water heaters, the housewife may have to spend thirty minutes or so in the early evening heating the bath, but she can tend to other chores while occasionally testing the temperature of the water and tossing in another handful of wood or coal. Even if her kitchen is equipped with a refrigerator, she will nevertheless fare forth on her shopping rounds late every afternoon, because this offers a not-to-be-relinquished opportunity to gossip with neighbors as she goes from greengrocer to butcher to fruit-store to fishmonger, all usually within a few minutes' walking distance.

The attention required by her children will vary with their number and ages, but otherwise her principal task of the day will be the preparation and serving of food, and here also her work is less onerous than that of the American wife, even given the latter's edge in labor-saving appliances. For one thing, the housewife in Japan will not have an oven and so is never expected to attempt such time-consuming dishes as roasts, broiled fowl, casseroles, cakes, and pies. Rice comprises by far the largest part of a Japanese family's daily food intake and its preparation, never difficult, has been made laughably easy by the electric rice-cooker, which well over 90 percent of all Japanese homes own. Some vegetables—such as cucumbers, radishes, eggplants, Chinese cabbage, and gourds—are purchased pickled and ready to serve or are pickled at home in large quantities in vats of brine. Other vegetables are short-cooked in the Chinese tradition, only a minute or two in oil over a very hot fire. Complicated vegetable dishes are seldom attempted.

Fish are eaten raw, sun-dried, fried, broiled on a metal net over a gas burner, or lightly cooked in a clear soup. (Meat and fish shops deep-fry and sell fish, hamburger balls, potato croquettes, and beef and pork cutlets, and these make frequent appearances on the table.) Japan's most popular soup is *miso-shiru,* which is standard breakfast fare. Its preparation requires nothing more than boiling water, a few *niboshi* (small dried sardines) for stock, and a half-cup or so of bean paste. Itinerant vendors still come to most neighborhoods, selling such comestibles as sweet potatoes, kept warm among heated rocks, and noodles. (Instant noodles and instant dehydrated stew have become prime favorites in the past few years.) Fresh fruit or even a bowl of rice with hot tea poured over it takes the place of fancier desserts.

And the Japanese housewife has two more factors militating on her behalf: One is that with her kitchen equipment she is not expected to serve a meal with all dishes invitingly warm. Most Japanese, in fact, are content if only their rice and their tea are hot. The other is that the Japanese have no tradition of adventuresome eating. The cook does not experiment or extemporize. Rather she sticks to simple traditional dishes and does not try to concoct anything new. One never hears of "Mrs. Kase's award-winning rice crackers" or "Mrs. Iwao's secret recipe for venison sukiyaki." Even tempura and suki-yaki (which are somewhat more popular in foreigners' imagi-nations than in fact) are prepared simply and quickly in comparison to a several-course, Western-style meal.

7

Their Love Life

My introduction to love and romance in the Japanese manner came in 1943, when we were studying Japanese at the University of Michigan. We students were being shown weekly movies obtained from Japan before Pearl Harbor, and one particular screen gem depicted the adventures of a samurai who, Ulysses-like, had fought and loved over much of Japan's real estate before at last returning to his home and faithful wife for the first time in years.

Conditioned as we were then to straightforward, American-style connubial bliss, all of us fully expected this samurai to clasp his beloved wife passionately to his scarred chest and tell her, straight out, how much he had missed her. Instead, he quietly got off his horse and sat down on the porch. Leaning back, he heaved a sigh and looked out over his holdings with the air of a man wondering if the rice had been planted at the right time.

After a few minutes, the long-suffering wife happened to come out on the porch. Seeing her husband, she brushed a strand of now-graying hair out of her misting eyes, got down on her knees, and bowed until her forehead almost touched the floor.

"Okaeri-nasai" was all that she said.

We were soon to learn that *"Okaeri-nasai"* meant "Welcome home," but at the time we heard it in the movie, we had progressed in our studies only far enough to know that *kaeru* was the verb meaning to return or to go back and that the addition of *-nasai* to its infinitive stem (*kaeri-*) resulted in a polite imperative form (the initial *O* is honorific) meaning "Please go back." Confused, many of us took this to mean that the wife was saying to her wandering samurai husband, "Please go back to wherever you came from," nor did this seem so strange to us when we considered that he had left home without telling her where he was going and that he had never deigned to communicate with her over the years.

The teachers seated among us in the theater, however, soon corrected this misunderstanding. In the meantime, the samurai uttered to his wife the one laconic word, *"Tadaima,"* which meant simply "I'm home."

Still kneeling behind him, the wife chose her next words with care: *"Ocha wo agemasho ka?* (Shall I bring you a cup of tea?)"

Tearing himself away from such important considerations as the rice crop, the samurai replied, *"Morao,"* or "I'll have (a cup)."

That was the end of the movie. After it was over, the lights in the student theater came on, and our teachers answered a few questions. (Most of us, however, just sat there, lost in the wonder of it.) Finally one of the teachers announced that the movie for the following week would be *Bokuseki,* the story of a Japanese nurse. *Bokuseki,* the teacher explained, was written with the two characters for wood and stone and meant "Lacking in human feelings" or "Frigid." Inasmuch as the movie we had just seen had been heralded as "the drama of a samurai tossed on seas of passion (*bonno no umi ni tadayou samurai no monogatari*)," we left the theater wondering how a nurse frankly proclaimed to be frigid would act—or fail to act.

If the above gallant samurai was that reticent about showing affection for his wife when he was alone with her, the mind boggles at trying to imagine how much more undemonstrative he would have become in a crowd. In her book *The Chrysanthemum and the Sword,* Ruth Benedict mentioned the scandal that took place in the nineteen-thirties when a well-known liberal, upon returning to Japan, told the press that he was pleased to be back in his own country and then gave reunion with his wife as one of the reasons for that pleasure. A storm of public disapproval ensued. Imagine saying such a thing and in public, at that! But had he given instead Japanese food or the neighborhood bathhouse or his coworkers at the office as reasons for his homecoming joy, not the slightest murmur of protest would have been heard.

Nor does one need to go back to the nineteen-thirties for examples. They exist abundantly now. I would not try to count the number of times in more recent years that I have gone to the Tokyo International Airport at Haneda to see Japanese friends off on trips or greet them upon their return (meeting the jets at Haneda is akin to going down to the depot to see who was coming in on the afternoon train in our small towns in America eighty and ninety years ago) and watched them ignore their wives completely while they gave their undivided attention to mere friends and coworkers.

The traditional attitude of the Japanese male is that love, in the romantic sense, weakens a man. The more he indulges in it or talks about it or displays symptoms of it, the weaker he becomes. Sex, he wants. Marriage, he accepts—for the sake of children and the continuation of the family name. But love? He tends to fight shy of it.

While Japanese literature teems with Great Love Stories, they are for the greater part ghastly tragedies in which the leading actors are laid low by love. For them, love conquers nothing, it solves nothing. It brings only suffering and heartbreak. And in these stories, it is usually the female who gives in to love first and sets out to pursue the male, to break down his barriers of cautious good sense.

To me, one of the best avenues—aside from direct personal experience, of course—to comprehension of romance, Japan-style, is daily reading of the Advice to the Troubled and Love-lorn columns (*Minoue Sodan* or *Jinsei Sodan*). I believe that all the newspapers carry them under these or similar titles, as do many of the forty or more *shukanshi* (weekly magazines) on the newsstands.

For some years, an American friend of mine and I were in the habit of meeting after work every day to regale ourselves with that day's Advice to the Troubled columns in the several newspapers and magazines we picked up en route to the bar. Many of the letters were sad, some were preposterous, and a few hilarious. (I fondly remember one that began, *"Watakushi wa munage de nayande iru juroku-sai no musume desu,"* or "I am a sixteen-year-old girl who is troubled by chest hair.") But all were revealing to us of Japanese romantic attitudes.

Even granting that those who took this trouble to expose their problems to the public in such columns may have been exceptional, the answers and recommended solutions, usually written by well-known social critics and commentators, reflected, I believe, accepted Japanese attitudes and values.

I have before me such a letter that I have kept in my files because it comes closer than any other I have ever read to compressing the panorama of Japanese love and marriage into one tidy package. Translated into English, this is the letter in its entirety:

> I am a twenty-one-year-old woman who was married only three months ago. After the one arranged premarriage meeting, my husband and I did not see each other socially even once. I thought that this was just like all other old-fashioned marriages, and I did not feel much inclined to go through with it, but my mother was ailing, so I decided to get married quickly while she was still alive. For that reason, I did not look closely at my future husband's face and did not notice it then, but his lips are much bigger and thicker than those of most people, and I can't bring myself to think about kissing him, to say nothing of living my whole life with him.
>
> My husband's elder brother and his wife live near us. When my mother suddenly became sick, I went to Nagoya

to pay her a sick visit. Upon my return, my brother-in-law scolded me, saying, "You shouldn't go home every time your mother gets sick. You should think only of your husband."

I did not think that my brother-in-law had any right to say that to me, so I determined to get a divorce. I was two months pregnant and my husband knew it, but I had an abortion without telling him. Since we did not register our marriage, we can get a "divorce" at any time. Now I shudder every time I look at my husband's lips.

The only thing not typical about this letter is that the writer has shown the courage to defy her brother-in-law and has decided to leave her husband. The rest says a great deal about traditional marital concepts in Japan.

In the first place, the marriage was arranged, that is, it was not a love match, and the couple did not have any dates with each other before getting married. During their one brief formal meeting, the woman evidently kept her eyes glued to the floor and did not see her husband-to-be's "repulsive" lips. In the second place, she agreed to get married just so that her mother could go to her grave happy in the knowledge that her daughter was safely married. Next, the husband's elder brother, as titular head of the family, was trying to boss his younger brother's wife as if she were a servant, to which the younger brother was apparently not protesting. And finally, the couple was not really married at all. Their union was one of those "trial," or delayed-registration, marriages popular in Japan. It probably would not have been registered—and thus legalized—until a normal child was born, or until everyone concerned, including the husband's elder brother, declared himself satisfied with the match.

Although *renai kekkon* (love marriages) are gaining in popularity, most marriages in Japan are still of the *miai,* or arranged, variety. Parents with a nubile child ask a respected relative or acquaintance to seek out a suitable mate. The advantage of working through this go-between or *nakoodo* is that he or she can praise the candidate to an extent the parents could not, ask delicate questions bluntly, and take rebuffs that would be insulting or at least ego-damaging.

Since the Japanese feel that love comes after the marriage —and is often found outside it—the institution of the go-between is still acceptable to the majority of young people. Nowadays, however, most parents do not present their child with only one incontrovertible selection as they did in the past. Instead, they offer a list of carefully screened candidates, all suitable to them, from which he or she can make a choice.

Lest we be too hasty in deploring this system, I should point out that it seems to work better than ours. At least, only one in twenty-five Japanese marriages ends in divorce, in comparison with one in four of ours. (How much genuine happiness is to be found within each marriage is another matter.)

Once the go-between obtains the approval of all concerned and the amount of the bride's dowry, if any, is agreed upon, the date of the wedding ceremony is set. Actually, this ceremony is not legally essential. In my own case, I remember that my wife and I walked into the Minato Ward Office in Tokyo, filled out and signed a short form and paid a small fee, and so got ourselves legally married. (The ward office in Tokyo notified the ward office in her home town in Shikoku so that an appropriate entry could be made in her *koseki,* or family register, and later I took a copy of our marriage form to the U.S. Embassy so that it could be registered there.)

Most Japanese, however, are married in a ceremony that is performed in the traditional Shinto manner, then register and thus legalize the marriage the same day—or months later, as strikes their fancy. The high point of this ceremony is the *sansankudo,* in which the bride and bridegroom both take three sips each from three shallow cups of sake. Both wear formal Japanese attire at this time, and on the bride's head is a white headdress called a *tsuno-kakushi,* or horn-hider. This serves to conceal her proverbial female horns of jealousy and signifies that she should not be jealous of her husband, no matter what he does, even on their wedding day.

A wedding reception and feast follow the ceremony, during which numerous toasts are drunk and the guests approach the newlyweds one by one, bow, and offer congratulations and wishes for future harmony, fertility, and prosperity. When leaving, each guest is given a present to take home with him, usually a box of food or a piece of lacquerware or a *furoshiki* (a scarflike cloth in which articles are carried).

Although a few more weddings now take place in April, which is the end of the school year, the fall—traditionally regarded as the season for marriage vows—is still popular. The heat of summer is past, the harvest is over, and the cold of winter is yet to come. In October and November, the autumn colors tinge the mountain foliage, which newlyweds can enjoy from the balconies of inns that perch on the banks of sparkling streams.

No rice is thrown at the couple; to waste rice is considered almost criminal. No old shoes can be tied to the bumpers of their car since most honeymooners travel by train. In the fall of the year, Tokyo and Osaka Stations are scenes of nearly unending honeymoon departures. The bride and bridegroom, who have by now changed to street clothes, get aboard an express bound for Hakone or Nikko or Shirahama and begin to bow to all their friends and relatives as the departure bell starts to ring. The well-wishers shout *"Banzai! Banzai! Banzai!"* while the bride's younger sisters and friends run along beside the moving coach for a way, waving and crying.

In the sudden silence that follows within the coach, however, the fixed smiles fade from the faces of the bride and her new husband, and they cast an uneasy glance or two at each other. The excitement is over, the crowd is gone, and a moment of truth has arrived.

I have witnessed what usually happens next many times: The bridegroom, who has shown commendable foresight in buying a great quantity of magazines, newspapers, peanuts, tangerines, beer, and assorted soft drinks on the station platform before departure, now takes off his shoes and coat and hands the latter to his bride to fold neatly and place on the baggage rack above them. If the day is unseasonably hot, he may also take off his trousers, but not with any impatient thoughts of romance in mind.

From his pocket he takes a transistor radio, switches it on, and inserts the earplug. Next he opens a package of peanuts. If he is a kind soul, he may remember to offer some to his bride. Or he may hand her a tangerine—to peel for him. When at last he believes that he is as comfortable as he can reasonably get, he buries his nose in a magazine and reads until he gets sleepy. When they reach the resort town where their marriage, born of passion, is to be consummated, he stands up and lets his wife help him on with his coat, then precedes her out of the coach. She meekly follows after him, carrying most of their luggage.

This luggage may or may not contain *makura-e,* which were once very popular gifts to brides. *Makura-e* are wedding charts or pillow pictures, the latter name being derived from the fact that these pictures were placed under the pillows of newlyweds on their wedding night as a kind of felicitous and informative surprise.

In the form of a scroll, the *makura-e* depicted for the presumably ignorant all the things the honeymooners might conceivably do to and for each other on that and subsequent nights. Judging from candid accounts of sex life in days when pillow-pictures were in greater vogue, however, I suspect that the purpose of the *makura-e* was not so much to inform as merely to serve as a checklist, lest one of the newlyweds overlook, in his or her excitement, one or two of the forty-eight standard positions.

While the *makura-e* presented the fundamentals, the finer points were often conveyed directly by fond mothers and doting aunts to brides or young nubile females. Brief hours before killing herself, Lady Nogi thoughtfully took time out to pen a lengthy, specific letter to her favorite niece, telling her of the many things she should and should not do on her wedding night. One of the noble Lady's prime points of caution concerned the paper with which the bride was expected to wipe away the traces of the encounter. Extreme care should be taken, Lady Nogi stressed, not to let the paper crackle, for that could offend the sensitive ears of her consort, who would doubtless be relaxing in that delicate state of post-coital trance.

Just as soon after marriage as they can afford to do so, a great many Japanese husbands begin looking around for a true love away from home. Fortunately (or otherwise, depending on the point of view) for the wife, this blessed day of affluence usually does not come until the man is well along in his forties, or even later. (This in turn gives rise to another heartwarming aspect of Japanese romance: the old man-young girl syndrome, which will be taken up directly.)

A survey of 9,500 men and women undertaken by the weekly magazine *Shukan Yomiuri* found that 60 percent of the men interviewed said that they would have an affair with another woman if they had the chance (meaning when they could afford it). Thirty percent more felt (note this wording) that they absolutely *had* to have such an affair. The remaining 10 percent were noncommittal, probably not wanting to expose their hands to anyone at all.

Fifty-five percent of the wives interviewed in the same survey said that they would forgive their husbands if they found out about such extramarital adventures. Most of the others were uncertain whether they would or not (meaning that eventually they would manage to overlook such missteps, after the situation had been milked of certain distaff advantages).

In the dim past, this Oriental practice of keeping mistresses or concubines had its roots in the overwhelming desire to perpetuate the family through the bearing of sons. If the legal wife could not provide male heirs, then let another woman try her hand, they said. Although the Japanese device of adopting sons (*yoshi*) from the families of relatives or respected friends answers this need at least in one sense, mistress-keeping is by no means on the wane.

For one thing, women outnumber men by two million. Denied the likelihood of legal union, many of these women are willing to accept mistress-status as better than spinsterhood. For another, Japan's miraculous economic boom is enabling more and more men to maintain two households. (Recently a domestic airline in Japan offered special low fares to wives in Tokyo who wanted to visit husbands who had been temporarily transferred to other cities, but the airline was quickly flooded with complaints from the husbands, who explained, off-the-record, that such visits would prove most embarrassing.)

For a successful Japanese businessman, keeping one or more mistresses is as effective a symbol of conspicuous consumption as the long black company car he rides in, or his seaside or mountain villa. I know one rich, reputable Osaka banker who, because of his Christian upbringing and Western education, resists all temptations to philander, but he told me that his business suffers because the Japanese with whom he must associate look down on him. Since he does not keep even one mistress, they say that he has a small stomach (*hara ga chiisai*) and does not live up to the responsibilities of his position.

A recent investigation conducted by the Women's and Minors' Bureau of the Ministry of Labor revealed that of 2,900 persons polled, 53 percent believed that the number of men keeping mistresses would not decrease in the near future. And I have read estimates by reputable authorities that as many as nine out of ten successful businessmen have *nigo-san*, or Miss (Mrs.?) Number Two's, as the Japanese call mistresses. About the only thing that has changed since the war is that they don't talk about it in front of their wives as openly as they did before.

Although the ties that bind the couple together are not legal, it is not as easy to break up housekeeping with a mistress in Japan as one might otherwise suppose. Unless she is young and beautiful and deluged with better offers, the mistress opposes the divisive effort with tearful entreaties, threats of suicide, and attempts to embarrass or otherwise inconvenience her patron by the exposure of whatever dark secrets she has gained knowledge of during their time together. After convincing him that he cannot throw her callously aside like a worn-out *fundoshi* (loin-cloth), she sits down at the bargaining table with all the cold skill and singular dedication of a Walter Reuther facing up to General Motors.

What she demands is *isha-ryo* (consolation or heart-balm money) in often quite preposterous amounts. If her patron has five million yen in the bank, she may demand of him thirty million. If his monthly income is ¥100,000, she asks for twenty times that amount. Now that she has lost her lover, she will explain, she needs that much to "guarantee her livelihood" (a favorite expression). With it, she will buy a tea shop or build a small apartment building or open a bar.

As an example of the singlemindedness with which many Japanese mistresses pursue their objectives, monetary or otherwise, I recall what happened to a Japanese friend of mine, a Mr. Ikeda, one quiet Sunday afternoon in Tokyo.

This Mr. Ikeda kept a mistress named Hisako, an ex-acrobat, and was in the habit of spending two nights each week in her apartment. Mrs. Ikeda, who naively believed her husband's fabrication about all-night *go* (Japanese chess) games, knew nothing about Hisako. This was an affair in which the mistress was much more knowledgeable, possessive, and demanding than the wife.

When Ikeda and I got together one Saturday night for a session of Ginza bar-hopping, he chanced to mention that Hisako was in a state of near-hysteria because he had not been to see her at all that week and that she had been bombarding him at his office with frequent calls and supplications.

The next day, a Sunday, I left my home in Omori, which was within six or seven blocks of Ikeda's place, for a walk and decided to drop by to say hello to my friend and his wife.

Relatives of theirs from the country, however, were already there, so I started to leave, but Ikeda insisted that I stay for at least one cup of tea. After I had been introduced, we all sat in the Ikedas' Western-style living room and talked until we heard a knock on the door. Ikeda left the room to see who it was, and in a moment we heard the sound of a scuffle.

Just as I started up to see if I could be of any assistance, the living-room door burst open and in flew Ikeda's mistress, Hisako. Wild-eyed, she looked around at all of us, then plumped herself down horizontally on the floor in the center of the room, facing upward. There was a look of grim determination in the set of her mouth, and Ikeda's relatives eyed her in much the same manner that one would regard a rudely awakened wolverine.

"*Hisako desu* (It's Hisako)," Ikeda, a sickly grin on his face, said weakly to no one in particular.

"I'm not going to move an inch until you say you will come home with me," Hisako announced, staring fixedly at the ceiling.

At that moment, Mrs. Ikeda entered from the kitchen to find all of us frozen into our individual poses like figures in a wax museum. She had been busy preparing a tray of tea and cakes for us and knew nothing of the arrival of the latest guest. Although Mrs. Ikeda had no idea who Hisako was, she rose magnificently to the occasion, and I shall never forget her sangfroid that day.

With all the composure of a great lady, she served us men first, as was only proper, then knelt on the floor beside Hisako. Bowing, she said, "*Irasshaimase* (Welcome)." Placing a cup of tea and a small cake beside this unknown supine guest, she invited her to partake of them. Then, after serving the other women, Mrs. Ikeda retired gracefully and silently to her kitchen.

I muttered something about its being late and started to put on my coat. Ikeda's relatives took the cue and said that they would have to hurry to get home before dark. We all departed together, leaving Hisako still lying there staring stubbornly at the ceiling and Ikeda looking forlorn and distressed in a chair in the corner.

(He told me the next day that he had, perforce, accompanied the victorious Hisako to her apartment soon after we left.)

As mentioned earlier, affairs between old men and young women are common in Japan. Called *oiraku no koi* by the Japanese, such unions are within the pale of approved social relationships, and no one looks askance at them for reasons of age only or makes cutting remarks about *baka na hihi jijii* (foolish old goats). (Aristotle wrote that an eighteen-year-old woman was ideal for a man of thirty-seven, which accords with the traditional Chinese dictum that a husband should be twice his wife's age, plus one.) Since, as already noted, Japanese men generally cannot afford to keep mistresses until their forties or fifties, if then, while most available attractive women are in their twenties or younger, the frequency of such matches is not at all unreasonable. You can go to any nightclub, where such affairs usually begin, and see that the hostesses normally range from eighteen to thirty in age, while almost all of the male guests are over thirty and at least two-thirds are over forty.

This being the situation, older American men visiting Japan for the first time, without their wives, find themselves suddenly rejuvenated. Very young women become available to them, perhaps for the first time in many years. In bars and nightclubs, as many as four or five provocative girls will shower one man with attention and, as often as not, unmistakable invitations. Nor are these petitioners for his favors limited to the women of the *mizu-shobai* (roughly, anywhere you can get a drink). Many young girls who work as clerks or waitresses or secretaries appear willing, even eager, to date Americans as much as thirty years older than they without apparent qualms. If pressed, they will explain that they welcome the chance to practice their English, but one gets the distinct impression that they are often quite willing to reimburse the teacher for their lessons. To such men, Japan represents a Fountain of Youth, an earthly paradise, and they find themselves extending the length of their planned visit and coming back time and time again after that.

Each Japanese girl who associates with foreign men has her own reasons for doing so, and casual observers who say that all of them are hot on the trail of the almighty dollar or that they are all oversexed or that they are really nothing more than Girl Scouts at heart are not even getting close to the answer. Simply because there is no single explanation. Obviously, many of them are after money. Many want fun in bed. Others pine for platonic love. Some, indeed, wish to practice their English. And more than a few merely want to take a peek at a foreign land—almost all Japanese being intensely interested in foreign countries and peoples—through the eyes of a foreign visitor. Others cannot abide the arrogance of their own men. Still others—and the number of these might amaze you—allow themselves to be drawn into affairs with foreign men simply because they have trouble saying No, especially after the foreigner has done them some favor, even a trifling one. (I knew one American man who first came to Japan in his early sixties and remained there until his death ten years later. Although he did not speak a word of Japanese, he had astounding success with Japanese women because he quickly learned and utilized the fact of their difficulty in bringing themselves to say No to any man who had been even slightly kind and thoughtful to them. Once they become accustomed to Americans, however, I notice that they quickly get over this, doubtless as a matter of necessity for simple survival.) And many, many more are motivated by infinite combinations of the above.

Whatever the reasons, altogether too many of the affairs that Japanese women have with foreign men end in heartbreak. (It was recently estimated by officials of the Oriental Service Center that 2,000 Japanese "war brides" have been abandoned by their American husbands in the Los Angeles area alone.) Before me I have an advertisement clipped from the March, 1967, issue of a Japanese magazine called *Shufu to Seikatsu* (The Housewife and Her Life). The magazine was asking its readers to enter a contest to see who could submit the most touching true confession of a love affair with a foreigner. This is how the ad read, translated into English:

MY CONFESSION: HOW I SUCCUMBED TO A PASSIONATE AFFAIR WITH A FOREIGNER!

Sweet whispers, gentle treatment, his white skin—things not seen in Japanese men. Is this how he cast a spell over you? Oh, but that joy! That ecstasy! How did it end? Regret, sadness, the pain of a never-to-be-forgotten love affair? Send in your true confession. We will not reveal your name.

First prize: TEN THOUSAND YEN!

I remember one Japanese girl, however, who took a perhaps unique form of revenge on her American lover when he tried to cast her aside.

The American's wife was expected to arrive from the United States the next morning, so he had gone to pay his Japanese girl friend one last visit the night before. The Japanese girl had protested and cried and begged, but he had taken refuge in whiskey and stubborn silence. It was very late when he finally went to sleep, fully clothed and stoned with alcohol, on the tatami.

When he began to snore, the girl made ready to wreak her vengeance on what he probably regarded as his single most prized possession. But instead of amputating the member, as the famous Miss Sada Abe had shocked all of Japan by doing to her own lover ten years before, this girl merely painted it with red fingernail polish.

The next morning she deliberately let him sleep until the last minute, then awakened him brusquely and told him that he had only a few minutes to get out to Haneda to meet his wife's plane. Still only half awake, he splashed water on his face and staggered out of her room. When he got to Haneda, his wife was already there waiting for him, so he wasted no time putting her in his car and driving to the hotel where they would stay until permanent quarters could be assigned to them.

As he told the story a few weeks later, he was in no mood for romance that morning but he realized that if he didn't pretend to be bursting with sexual desire, his wife would, quite reasonably, want to know into what other avenues of release he had been channeling all that energy during their separation.

Summoning his wilted forces, he manfully escorted her forthwith to the bed in their hotel room and prepared to do the best he could under the circumstances. But as he disrobed, his wife instantly spied the splash of color—he later learned that the shade of the fingernail polish was "Flaming Glory"—with which he had been adorned.

Even more astounded than his wife, he was utterly unable to think of any explanation at all. Stunned, he could only slump down in a chair and stare in open disbelief.

His wife returned to the United States on the next available flight, and he and the Japanese girl were soon reunited.

Given the Japanese male tradition of seeking true love outside marriage, it is not surprising to find those female entertainers called the geisha (pronounced *gay-sha* and literally meaning "a person of the arts") figuring largely in many classic romances, both fictional and real.

Doubtless the geisha best known to the Western world is the heroine of *Madama Butterfly,* that beautiful opera by

Giacomo Puccini, an Italian who wrote the opera in French about an Oriental country of which he was almost totally ignorant. In the final scene Butterfly commits hara-kiri (which no Japanese woman has ever been known to do) because her American lover, the navy officer Pinkerton, has returned to the scene of their mad passion with American wife and child in tow. For many years the Japanese stiffly regarded the opera as an affront to their national dignity and refused to allow it to be performed within their borders.

But while poor Butterfly was fictional—and a trifle ridiculous—there have been plenty of real-life geisha whose lives were far more colorful, adventure-filled, and, in some instances, tragic.

Tsuma-kichi, for example, was a geisha who danced so well that she received her dancing teacher's certificate at the age of fourteen. In time she was sent to the Mountain Plum Tree, a geisha house in Osaka's gay quarters, where the master—a man named Manjiro Nakagawa—became her guardian. There were six women in Manjiro's house: five geisha and his termagant of a wife, O-Ai, a vigorously obscene woman whose wild drunken escapades eventually pushed Manjiro to the verge of insanity. One night after O-Ai had been on a tear a blackness came over Manjiro, so he tanked up and went out to see a play called *The Murder of Ten*. Returning home late, Manjiro got out a sword and killed five of the six females in his house while they were sleeping. The sixth was Tsuma-kichi, who woke up as Manjiro (who was later hanged for his crimes) came staggering into her room, bloody sword in hand. Tsuma-kichi lay paralyzed with fright, praying that he would go away or be distracted, but unfortunately he was not to be denied his alcohol-inspired vengeance on all womankind. He gave Tsuma-kichi three mighty whacks, the first of which completely severed one arm, the second cut off the other arm except for about two inches of flesh, and the third dealt the geisha a powerful slash across the face, knocking out most of her teeth. Manjiro then left the house of death to spend the night supine in an alley.

The next morning a neighbor, puzzled by the unnatural stillness of the Mountain Plum Tree, went into investigate. What she found brought her back out screaming. When the police and a doctor arrived, they were surprised to find Tsuma-kichi still alive, despite the loss of quantities of blood. Despairing of her chances, the doctor shook his head negatively at the ambulance attendants who came to carry her away. Tsuma-kichi was blessed, however, with one characteristic that was also to stand her in good stead later: tenacity. She clung to life . . . and survived, although her other arm had to be amputated as well.

After recovering her strength, she enjoyed considerable popularity for a while as the Armless Geisha, but when the geisha-oriented public's curiosity had been satisfied on this score, she taught herself to use a brush with her teeth—and with her toes. She became quite adept at calligraphy, painting, and poetry composition. In the meantime, she had married a painter and had borne him two sons, but her husband abandoned her and she had to rely on her brushwork to support the children and see them through school. In 1956, at the age of sixty-seven, she became a Buddhist nun in Kyoto.

(It is interesting to note how many geisha shaved their heads and became nuns in their declining years, the number being entirely out of proportion to that of the rest of the female population. Gio and Shizuka Gozen—both twelfth century *shira-byoshi*—may have set this fashion: The former fled from the palace of Kiyomori, head of the Taira clan, but was forced to take refuge and spend her remaining years in a nunnery. The latter became well known as the inseparable companion of Yoshitsune, Japan's most famous warrior, and donned the cloth only after his death.)

Then, there was Hatsuyuki (First Snow). In 1903 the geisha quarters of Kyoto—called the Gion—buzzed with excitement when this twenty-year-old geisha of stunning beauty appeared on the scene. Her name was later shortened and changed to Oyuki (Honorable Snow). It was rumored that many tried to win her heart or, more importantly, her body, but the geisha did not avail herself of these opportunities to take a patron.

Two years after her debut in the Gion, one George D. Morgan, nephew of millionaire-financier James Pierpont Morgan, visited Kyoto on his way around the world, apparently determined to taste all the wine and try all the geisha while there. Oyuki, however, bedazzled him. Her beauty shocked him into a state of motionless wonderment. More than any of the others, he *had* to have her for his own.

Eventually he was successful in his suit, after spending the unheard-of sum of $50,000 to gain her freedom. (One story has it that Oyuki was secretly in love with a university student and would have spurned the Morgan fortune for his sake, but the student's parents opposed the union and forced their son into a "proper marriage." The annals of geisha, by the way, are filled with stories of their deathless love affairs with college students, leading one to wonder how so many geisha got together with so many students in the first place.)

In 1905, young Morgan took Oyuki, now his legal wife, to the United States and then to France, where they settled and where Morgan died eight years later, in 1913. The Morgan family took warm care of her for many years, but in 1938 Oyuki decided to return to Kyoto, where she lived a not-so-happy life—pestered by many who falsely believed her possessed of a Morgan-size fortune—until her death at the age of eighty-two.

The forerunners of the modern geisha were *shira-byoshi* (meaning "white beaters of rhythm") of the late twelfth century—female troubadours who traveled from fief to fief, castle to castle, market town to market town. They dressed all in white with long, voluminous sleeves. Their performances included epic ballads, ancient poems, and dramatized accounts of tribal conflicts and high deeds. These women committed their entire repertoire to memory, many of them being descendants of the minstrels who in earlier times had preserved in the repositories of their memories the myths and legends of ancestral adventures.

By the mid-sixteenth century, the word *geisha* began to appear in the records, most frequently as *machi-geisha,* or geisha of the town or streets. These women were in truth streetwalkers and were considered even lower than bathhouse prostitutes.

In the seventeenth century, the geisha took a long stride forward toward their present image by becoming the performers whose job it was to keep the customers content while waiting for the *oiran* of the Yoshiwara to appear and take over. Because the *oiran* would brook no competition, the geisha were compelled to place less and less emphasis on sex and more on music and dancing. But as the popularity of the *oiran* declined, that of the geisha rose—until it reached the peak mentioned above, when geisha became symbols of status who could marry even prime ministers and members of the nobility.

From the time of the Meiji Restoration until the close of the war in the Pacific, the geisha were beset by few of the vicissitudes and abrupt changes in status and reputation that had characterized their development theretofore. The downfall of the Tokugawa, the concentration of diverse political forces in the capital, the widening distribution of affluence, the modernization of the nation, and the deterioration of the elaborate licensed quarters combined to form the backdrop against which the geisha could act out their moments and hours on the stage—as the playthings—and sometimes as the manipulators—of rich, famous, and powerful men.

During this period of three-quarters of a century, the selection, training, and utilization of geisha reached a degree of standardization never before realized. While there were always exceptions, the typical geisha was the offspring of a poor farming family, of another geisha and her lover, or of casual couples in the lower levels of the *mizu-shobai,* or entertainment world. She was sold into apprenticeship at a *geisha-ya* at an early age, often as young as five or six. (In part, this explains the comparative dearth of beauties among geisha: most were tapped for candidacy at an undeveloped age when it was still difficult to predict how their features would appear years later.)

The training lasted from five to ten years, depending on when the apprentice began. Often it included attendance at a neighborhood school; otherwise, tutors were called in, for it was vital that the geisha be able to read and write as well as know something of history, literature, and current events. More than a few of them would be expected in later years to speak intelligently and entertainingly to some of the sharper minds in the country, many of whom chose the geisha to grace their parties as carefully as a bon vivant selects his wines. Even so, lessons in singing (they were once commonly called "singing girls"), dancing, and the samisen took priority, for these were the basic tools of the trade. Housed in the *geisha-ya* under the supervision of the manageress who held their contracts, they led simple—but not necessarily Spartan—lives. Contrary to what more lurid imaginations might expect, a deliberate effort was made to protect these young girls from foreknowledge of the seamier side of geisha existence—simply because apparent naiveté in geisha-to-be was highly prized and because such manifest pristine innocence at the time of the girl's "debut" could enable the manageress to significantly recoup her investment.

In time, each apprentice was assigned to a full-fledged geisha of the house, partly to run errands for her and assist in her time-consuming daily ritual of bathing and dressing and partly to enable the apprentice to absorb knowledge by watching and listening. When she was judged ready, she became a *hangyoku* (half-jewel) or *maiko* (as they were called in Kyoto). These young geisha-to-be dress more elaborately and colorfully than their "elder sisters" and are more demure and retiring. Usually they make their appearance early in a party, pour a few rounds of sake, answer questions with downcast eyes, and then retire with a graceful bow amidst the tinkling of tiny bells (part of their coiffure).

At about the age of seventeen, the *hangyoku*'s moment-of-truth arrives. She first decides what she will call herself for the remainder of her professional life and chooses the name from among such as *Kosode* (Little Sleeve), *Osome* (Honorable Dyeing), *Ponta* (phonetic; no particular meaning), and *Kosen* (Little Hermit). Armed with her new name, she and her manageress set out on her *o-hirome,* or debut. They call at each of the restaurants that might eventually avail themselves of her services, to introduce her and leave small presents. Shortly thereafter comes the *mizuage-shiki* or the defloration ceremony itself, which is quite important for the geisha's future welfare and prosperity. The more influential and affluent her despoiler, the better this augurs for her later popularity. Like the number of mistresses he keeps, the number of geisha he has deflowered is an important ingredient in one's reputation for "masculinity" in Japan. Furthermore, as a general rule, to become known as a man about town in the world of geisha, one must spend at least ten evenings every month for one year in a restaurant with geisha in attendance and must run up a monthly bill from such activities of at least one million yen (approximately $3,300) for the same length of time. . . .

After defloration, the geisha adopts more conservative (but nonetheless expensive) attire and more mature hairstylings, then settles down to her life's work. She may have several patrons at the same time, she may become attached early to one patron who will sooner or later take her out of the world of the *mizu-shobai,* or she may go through extended periods without any patrons at all. And she may have isolated sexual encounters without any regard to the existence of a patron.

Perhaps in reaction to the life she leads, she may enter into a relationship (which probably is—but need not be—sexual) with a man entirely unrelated to her way of life: a cook perhaps—or a teacher.

For reasons of convenience and economy, she will continue to live under the roof of her "house mother," at least as long as she is in her debt. Because most geisha parties are over by ten or so, she is able to bed down—alone or in company—comparatively early and thus rise in the mornings long before her spiritual sisters of the cabaret, bar, and nightclub circuit. Her mornings are filled with lessons: flower arrangement, tea ceremony, dancing, samisen and so forth. After a simple lunch —usually brought in from a nearby *"demae"* (home delivery) restaurant, she relaxes and chatters with other geisha until about three o'clock, when she begins to beautify herself for the evening: facials with rice bran (nightingale dung is said to be the best but is quite costly), light hair shaved from wherever it is excessive or unsightly, skin bracing with dried gourds, hard skin removed from the feet with pumice, the public bath, milk lotion for the face and neck, hair styling, the application of white powder to the nape of the neck, and finally the donning of the kimono and the tying of the obi (sash).

Until quite recently, the financial affairs of the geisha were strictly controlled, mostly by persons other than herself and generally to her disadvantage. It was her custom to go from her quarters in the early evening to the *kemban,* or agency, where she received her assignment slip. From there she rode in a rickshaw to her first *o-zashiki* of the evening. (The few rickshaw still in business in Japan are those that specialize in carrying geisha. It is an eye-catching contrast to see those two-wheeled, coolie-drawn conveyances of bygone days pull up to the fashionable *o-zashiki* of Shimbashi and Akasaka to mingle with the long black limousines of conservative politicians and stalwarts of the commercial and financial communities.) After leaving the party, the geisha got someone in the *o-zashiki* to sign her slip testifying to the length of time she shared her wit and charm with the guests. At the end of the month, the *kemban* billed the restaurant, that in turn billed the host of the party. Upon receipt of the payment, the *kemban* deducted its fee as agent and forwarded the rest to the person responsible for the geisha's finances. Depending on her age, experience, popularity, extent of indebtedness, and other factors, each geisha made her own arrangements with her manageress. The so-called *maru-kake* geisha, for instance, was entirely dependent on her manageress, who accepted her earnings, paid her expenses, and doled out spending money. A *shichi-san* (literally, seven-three) geisha was one who had reached that stage of semi-independence in which she bought her own (murderously expensive) kimono and gave three-sevenths of her earnings to her manageress for other expenses. A *wake* (from *yama-wake* or dividing in half) geisha paid one-half of her earnings for room and board and bore half the cost of her own kimono, of which she would have to buy ten to thirty yearly, each costing as much as ￥ 200,000 (approximately $660) or more.

Nowadays the geisha is considered an independent business woman. She is fully protected from exploitation by labor regulations and must be eighteen years old in order to become a full-fledged entertainer (and fifteen to become an apprentice). While the older women may still ride to work in rickshaw, the younger ones may go on scooters—or even drive their own cars. (Of the 402 geisha in the Shimbashi district, over 100 now have driver's licenses.) Instead of devoting their mornings to lessons in the tea ceremony or floral arrangement, many may practice golf or visit their stockbroker. In lieu of four or five years of arduous training, a woman may decide that she wants to be an "instant geisha," register herself with a *kemban* for ￥ 20,000—and lo! be established in business. Of course, the higher-class districts will insist on some proof of ability in the traditional geisha arts, but others may be satisfied with

only her physical presence (especially if she is attractive)—
and initiation fee.

Estimates of the number of geisha presently working in
Tokyo range from 3,500 to more than 5,000, with 35,000
being the figure most often given for all of Japan. The number
of young women interested in becoming career geisha is decreasing, and the postwar years have witnessed a general falling off in demands for geisha services. Recently in Niigata, for
example, geisha-house operators reminded themselves that the
number of registered geisha in their city had fallen from four
hundred to just over one hundred during the 1950–70 period.
Desperate for new talent, they took the unheard-of step of
advertising for apprentices in a local newspaper, promising a
minimum monthly income of three hundred dollars (twice
what factory and office girls would earn), free kimono, and
no compulsory training.

Only three girls answered the ad, and twelve geisha-house
operators competed anxiously against each other to see who
would be the lucky employers. Of the three, however, two
were found to be entirely unusable on closer examination,
while the third quit in dismay after only a week of indoctri-
nation.

Niigata's experience is typical, leading many observers to
predict the expiration of the geisha as an institution by the end
of this century, if not sooner.

To a very large extent, hostesses have already taken over
the role played by geisha in Japan's night life. They number
more than one million, and foreign visitors—male, at least—
may well have more meaningful contact with them than with
any other segment of the population of Japan. An American
businessman who stays in Tokyo for three weeks may confer
with eight or twelve or fifteen counterparts in the Japanese
business world, but except in rare instances these meetings
tend to be superficial and stereotyped. Nor can he expect too

much from the usual run of drivers, bartenders, maids, and guides. But if he finds an appealing hostess and spends eight or ten evenings in her bar and maybe five or six nights—and a weekend—with her, there is likely to be more uninhibited pouring forth of opinions, exchange of insights into social attitudes, and general heightening of mutual cultural awareness than with anyone else he meets in Japan.

The particular hostess may have been young, shallow, banal, poorly educated, and meanly motivated, but no matter. She could turn out to be the one and only Japanese whom he feels he came really close to getting to know and understand while in Japan. If he never visits Japan again but should be reminded of the country five or so years hence, the odds are good that he will recall the hostess before he remembers the president of the large corporation with whom he negotiated important business deals. Unless he is an unusually acute man, he may—consciously or unconsciously—base most of his interpretations of Japan and its people on her comments and attitudes.

So it is that while most foreign visitors seldom see a genuine geisha of the traditional variety, a great many of the men do achieve the most intimate of relationships with their successors, the hostesses—the so-called "modern geisha."

8

Their Food and Drink

While I was vacationing in Hawaii in 1956, two Japanese friends of mine left Tokyo on a round-the-world trip, with their first stopover in Honolulu. One was the editor-in-chief of a women's magazine; the other, his photographer. After two days of sightseeing in the islands, I took them to the Honolulu airport for departure on the next leg of their journey.

I helped the two men carry their suspiciously heavy luggage to the weigh-in counter, where they were told by a surprised clerk that it greatly exceeded the weight limitation, and I wondered if the airline that had carried them from Japan to Honolulu had looked the other way when their bags were placed on the scales in Tokyo. Whatever the case, having now no choice but to lighten their luggage, they opened their bags on the floor in front of the counter and began jettisoning provisions. They handed me packages of rice, tins of tea, plastic bags filled with pickled vegetables, cans of bamboo shoots, and bottles of sake. When I could hold no more, I stacked it all in a pile off to one side and then turned back to be given dried fish, jars of salted plums, boxes of seaweed, bags of rice crackers, cans of fish, hard rice cakes, bottles of soy sauce, and containers of various indescribables. The pile grew alarmingly while their luggage shrank.

At length, the weight of their impedimenta dropped to an acceptable figure, and my two visitors hurried off to board their waiting plane, looking sadly over their shoulders at the small mountain of Japanese comestibles beside me. Hastily waving good-bye, I commandeered a baggage cart and fled from the quizzical stares of bystanders with my curious windfall.

Later I weighed it all on the bathroom scales at home and found that my two Japanese friends had left me with more than eighty pounds of their native food that they had intended to carry with them on their trip to such impoverished and benighted towns as San Francisco, New York, London, Paris, and Rome. For all I knew, they may have had still more of these field rations among what they were at last allowed to take with them.

I happened to be back in Japan myself when these same two men returned to their home base two months later. My wife, who modeled for their magazine, wanted us to meet them at Haneda International Airport and drive them to their homes. En route, the editor-in-chief turned to me and said, "Mr. Seward, I wonder if you'd be kind enough to stop at a restaurant I know in Gotanda?"

I had thought that both of the men would be eager to get home to their wives and children, whom they hadn't seen in two months, but I agreed to take them wherever they wanted to go. In the Gotanda restaurant, one of them explained to me why they had wanted to come there:

"We haven't eaten real Japanese food in such a long time that we just couldn't wait. . . ."

Again, while I was working for the GHQ Censorship Detachment in Osaka (1947–1949), our U.S. Army-operated dining room served the best American-style meals that I had eaten anywhere during my years of military service. All the dining-room waitresses were Japanese women, and I called them together one day to announce some new regulation or other. Afterwards, I opened the meeting to general discussion, to give the waitresses a chance to offer suggestions or register complaints. When we got around to the subject of their recreational time and facilities, I casually asked them how they spent their days off and was somewhat surprised to learn that nearly all of them made trips back into the country districts to visit relatives or friends.

In those days trains were more crowded than they are now, though this hardly seems possible, and our waitresses' salaries were not really adequate for such weekly excursions. Had they remained in Osaka, they would have been able to stay in comfortable rooms in their dormitory, see the movies our unit showed, and eat the American-style meals provided by our mess. Instead, they chose to stand long hours on incredibly crowded trains in order that they might spend their free time in distant, probably uncomfortable homes.

I asked why, but none of the waitresses was willing at first to give me a clear-cut answer. Curiosity, however, made me press the question, and at last one of them spoke up to explain:

"Washoku ga hoshii kara desu ga. . . . (It's because we want Japanese food. . . .)"

Amazed, I blurted out, "But we give you your meals here! Don't you get enough to eat?"

Oh, yes, they agreed. We gave them plenty to eat. So much, in fact, that they were all getting fat, they said, laughing in feminine concern. But they craved *Japanese* food.

Well, I had not been so naive as to expect that the girls would renounce Japanese food and happily eat nothing but our American food for the rest of their lives; but after all, I reasoned, our food was by their own admission nourishing, and it was free and, most important, it was right there with them in Osaka. No need to spend their scarce money to travel many miles to get their native victuals from people who probably did not have any to spare. Nor was it a matter of their getting accustomed to our fare, because most of them had been with us since 1945—more than three years.

It was simply that the waitresses, as well as the two men who visited me in Honolulu, were *addicted* to Japanese food. The Japanese diet, having changed very little over many hundreds of years, has instilled in the average Japanese an advanced degree of both psychological and physical dependence upon it.

This fanatic addiction is the most salient fact about the eating habits of the Japanese. Among the major civilized nations of the world, it is unlikely that any other people crave their own food to the extent that the Japanese crave theirs, or that there are any whose food differs as distinctly from ours as theirs most decidedly does.

The reaction of American visitors to this food ranges from straightforward revulsion to ecstatic paeans of praise. (The Food Editor of *House Beautiful* made a careful study of Japanese cuisine and declared it the best of the twenty-nine countries she had surveyed. She rated it even above that of the French, which had until then been Number One on her list.)

This food editor was referring to the kind of Japanese food served in first-class restaurants in the large cities, where meals can cost the customer dear. (The most expensive dinner in Japan may well be one offered by a dining room in Tokyo's Hotel Okura. Prepared only for parties of ten or more, it comes to nearly ninety dollars a person. In contrast, consider that you can buy a filling, nourishing meal for thirteen cents in a street stall in Nishinari in Osaka.)

Who are the customers who keep Tokyo's 33,000 restaurants in business? Answer: businessmen and, to a lesser degree, officials with expense-account privileges. As a fringe benefit that the employee does not have to report as income, Japanese companies let their upper ranks spend a great deal of money in bars and restaurants entertaining government officials, distributors, joint-venture partners, competitors, and customers. Moreover, this febrile passion for feasting and amusing others is considered essential to the Japanese way of doing business. In a recent year, the Tax Administration Agency announced that Japanese firms spend one-fifth of their total income in providing *osake, onna,* and *ongaku* (wine, women, and music) for those persons whose good will they seek.

Aside from the sick feeling one may get together with the bill, the revulsion felt by many American visitors upon coming to grips with Japanese food is caused by such dishes as vinegared sparrows of Wakayama, salad made with raw cartilage of pig's ear, sweet and sour sexual organs of ox, and turtle-blood-and-sake cocktails. Or crimpled snake meat, vinegared grasshoppers of Akita, fried bee grubs, pickled cherry blossoms, and sliced ovary of pig with mushrooms. Or fried red ants dipped in chocolate, smoked frogs, cooked newt with vegetables, and oiled cockscombs.

The above outré dishes are admittedly favored more by those whom the Japanese call *getemono-gui:* people who hanker after such bizarre foods. But even among the more common foods we can readily find items that serve the purpose nearly as well: fish-eye soup (the Emperor likes this), broiled sparrows, raw fish, dried squid (which the Japanese chew as we would gum), pickled seaweed, octopus, loach marinated in sake, fern fiddleheads, salted trout guts, and sweet-bean jelly laced with snake blood.

Part of the problem of presentation, however, is in translation, and an imaginative translator working with a competent public relations expert could greatly increase the degree of foreign acceptance of Japanese food. Because the lower-echelon Japanese who write menus in English are generally limited to straight dictionary (meaning uninspired) translations, they come forth with mouth-watering items like "dried gourd shavings" and "strips of fish skin and guts prescalded in boiling water" and "hot turtle soup including little eggs from the womb."

These menu-writers might well borrow a page from the notebook of the American advertiser who suggested that the poisonous puffer or globe fish be marketed under the name "sea squab." Surely someone could, for example, find a more palatable description for the tasty vegetation of the ocean bottom than just plain "seaweed."

While some visitors are nauseated and a few wax lyrical, the average foreign reaction to Japanese food is hesitation and doubt: a total lack of enthusiasm. To us, the Japanese diet is bland, low in fat and sugar, and deficient in protein. They take their green tea without sweetening and their rice without sugar or butter or milk. They prefer fruit or a bowl of plain rice with hot tea poured over it to a sweet dessert. Upon coming home from school in the afternoon, their children ask for tangerines, rice crackers, or a handful of vinegared rice instead of a candy bar, dish of ice cream, or slice of bread with jam and peanut butter on it.

For breakfast, the Japanese usually eat steamed white rice, seaweed, a pickled vegetable (such as radish, eggplant, turnip, cucumber, spinach, or Chinese cabbage), and perhaps a small slice of grilled fish or fried egg. For lunch, rice again predominates: a bowl of it topped with curry or in a lunch box with a few bites of vegetables and fish tucked away in one corner or in a *domburi:* a deep bowl in which the rice is covered with a stewlike mixture. For dinner, they may enjoy more variety, but rice will again prevail, together with one or two pickled or short-cooked vegetables, seaweed, a clear soup (clear so that the diner can see the artistic offerings therein, such as a tiny whole shrimp floating free or vegetables cut in the shape of flowers), and possibly a slice of grilled fish.

This menu may err on the generous side. After all, the national daily caloric intake in Japan still hovers around 2,300 units, in comparison to 3,000 in the United States and 3,300 in Denmark. Despite this scantiness, Japanese food must benefit its devotees in some ways: Their incidence of coronary disease is about half of ours, and their blood-cholesterol level averages 150 in comparison to 225 for us.

It follows that not many Japanese get fat (with the notable exception of sumo wrestlers, who become obese deliberately). Short and stocky, yes. But very few really fat people. So few, in fact, that the fleshy ones are nearly always congratulated. They are regarded as persons who must be financially successful. (Or else how could they afford to eat that much and work so little?) A large stomach, for example, is called a *juyaku-bara:* the stomach of a company director.

For several of my years in Japan, I was considerably overweight, and I can tell you that it was a long time before I could pretend indifference to having Japanese constantly say to me, *"Suwado-san wa jitsu ni futotte imasu, ne!* (You certainly are fat, aren't you, Mr. Seward!)" A very long time, indeed.

Why is Japanese food so different from any other? In addition to being dominated by rice, it is a cuisine in which the appearance of the food as it is served ranks in importance with its taste and nutritive value, a standard which probably evolved over the centuries in compensation for the unending sameness of the diet. Designed to please the eye and the aesthetic sense, food is artistically laid out on exquisite china and colorful lacquerware that may be polygonal, triangular, square, or shaped like leaves or fans. The color scheme, the arrangement, and the seasonal significance of certain foods stimulate Japanese appetites. Tiny boats, for example, are fashioned with their hulls made of bamboo sprouts and their sails of thin cucumber slices and with toothpicks for masts. Hard-boiled eggs are tinged pink or green to blend or contrast with the colors of other foods. Bits of greenery, such as parsley and maidenhair, are adroitly mounted here and there with a fine eye.

Another feature of Japanese food is the extensive use that the people have made of the available materials. During the thousand years that the meat of four-legged animals was denied them, the Japanese learned to harvest the sea of an incredible variety of fish as well as plants. Also, while using their prime bottom land for rice and vegetables and the fields on the lower slopes for fruit and tea, they turned to their mountains to discover an extensive and edible array of leaves (such as maple and chrysanthemum), sprouts (such as bamboo and ginger), roots (such as lotus), bulbs (such as lily), fungoid growths (such as mushrooms), pepper tree buds, fern fronds, and so forth.

Still another characteristic is the care given by the farmer to raising his produce. I have seen hundreds of pear, peach, and apple orchards in which each piece of fruit is painstakingly wrapped in paper to prevent blemish and to ward off insects. Also slope after slope of strawberry plants which are covered at night and uncovered in the morning only after the sun is high enough to warm them. And fields of watermelons with forests of stakes giving the approximate date when each melon should be picked. After harvesting, the farmer continues to exercise the same assiduous care in packing his yield for shipment to market so that there is as little bruising weight on top of each piece as possible.

Other features of their cuisine include the prevalent use of vegetable oils instead of animal fats in cooking, the exotic soup stocks (made from dried bonito, kelp, and laver), the unusual dipping sauces (such as soy sauce with grated fresh ginger or soy sauce and lemon juice garnished with finely chopped scallions), the almost complete absence of oven-baked foods in the home, the comparative lack of frozen and canned items, the short cooking time of vegetables, and the effort that is made to preserve and keep distinct the intrinsic qualities of each food (whereas the Chinese and the French, for example, mix and blend a great deal).

More than seven hundred varieties of rice are cultivated in the world, of which the Japanese raise forty-four, although they vastly prefer just one, *mochi-gome* (a glutinous, short-grain rice). They raise 4,220 pounds of rice per acre of paddy land, which is the world's highest rate of production. The average American eats 7 pounds of rice a year in comparison with 184 for the Japanese.

Rice is, in fact, the national delicacy of Japan, one of whose names (*Mizuho-no-kuni*), means the Land of the Ripe Rice Ears. The first lesson in Japanese etiquette is to treat rice with veneration, and a man who is forgiven for squandering money will be condemned for wasting rice. It is much more to the Japanese than what bread and potatoes combined are to us. Rice means to them what reindeer mean to the Lapps and the coconut palm to the natives of certain South Pacific islands. It provides them with food in variegated forms, drink (rice wine), wearing apparel (sandals and rain capes and rain hats) made of rice straw, and elements of building materials (thatched roofs, matting, clay-and-straw mortar).

Note what Japanese of the past have said about rice: In *Bosho,* Hikomaro Saito wrote, "The most important panacea for long life is rice. . . . Rice is the miraculous medicine of life." In *Jinyaku Shinran,* Tsurushiro Sato wrote, ". . . rice is the foundation for the existence of the [Japanese] people given to them by the Sun Goddess, from her love of mankind." In *Tamakatsuma,* Norinaga Motoori wrote, "There is nothing that can be placed above the value of rice, and so it can be called either god or Buddha." In *Daido Ruishuho,* Shinchoku Abe wrote, "In this universe rice is the most important thing for the survival of mankind."

Rice provides half of the Japanese caloric intake, even more in terms of bulk. After sweet potatoes, it is the cheapest food they raise. It is so important in their scheme of things that the pages of their history are studded with accounts of "rice riots," in which the normally docile peasantry rebelled against rice prices or rice taxes. In more recent years, when a group of Japanese fishermen were released after long months in Korean prisons where they had been confined for crossing the Rhee Line, their first comment on being handed over to Japanese officials was a complaint about the quality of the rice they had been fed. In fact, the Japanese word for rice (*gohan*) is synonymous with food.

Most Japanese will insist on having at least two and often three rice meals daily. This devotion to the white grain, which is 100 percent digestible, may have been occasioned by economic necessity, for it has doubtless saved the Japanese people from many severe famines. An underlying principle of

Japanese food consumption is to cram as much rice into the stomach as possible, and to make this unseasoned white manna somewhat more palatable, they take a nibble of salted or pickled vegetable with every one or two large mouthfuls of rice. Many, however, eat the rice with almost no side dishes. A favorite lunch, especially in hard times, is called the *Hinomaru-bento,* or Rising Sun, lunch box. In the middle of a bed of plain white rice is placed one small red pickled plum. This plum is all that is eaten with the entire box of rice. The spot of red on the white rectangular background resembles the national flag, hence the name.

This passionate adherence to rice takes its toll of the nation's health. Always insistent that the hull and embryo bud be removed from their rice, the Japanese display a syndrome of troubles that point to a chronic deficiency of B complex vitamins. This results in such ailments as beriberi, nutritional edema, pellagra, keratitis, anemia, hindered secretion of hormones from the ovaries, and various disorders of the nervous system and brain. Because they must eat so much rice to feel satisfied and to maintain strength, their stomachs become distended and so are positioned comparatively lower than ours.

Although the Japanese enjoy eating as much as the next fellow, there is a male tradition of pretended indifference to food. Seldom if ever will a Japanese husband discuss what to have for dinner that night with his wife, and I have even dined with men who returned the menu to the waiter without glancing at it, saying, *"Nan de mo ii* (Anything will do)." Furthermore, I have known many Japanese hosts who have reserved a room in advance in a Japanese-style restaurant and ordered dinner for their guests without making any mention of the menu and not knowing what will be served until the food itself is actually set before them on the appointed date.

Another facet of the same syndrome is what the Japanese call the custom of *"Migi e narae!"* or "Eyes right!" The idea is that the guests should let the host order first (in Western-style restaurants) in order not to appear self-assertive, not to inconvenience the host by selecting dishes beyond his budgetary means, and—at least in some instances—not to reveal one's ignorance of the cuisine and of whatever non-Japanese language the menu may be written in. Should the foreign visitor happen to be the host, he is placed in the unfortunate position of feeling obliged to order the more expensive items on the menu if he really wants his guests to choose the best for themselves, without any reserve.

The Japanese do two things while eating that repel and even nauseate most Westerners: They slurp with unstinted enthusiasm while partaking of such dishes as noodles, and they lift bowls to their mouths and literally shovel food in. I shall try neither to defend nor to decry. It is their country, so let them behave as they see fit. Be thankful that it is no worse. (Go to a workingman's restaurant in Taiwan or Hong Kong and observe the diners spit bones and other inedible odds and ends on the floor in their unrestrained appreciation of the quality of the cooking.)

Noteworthy Japanese dishes include *sushi,* a popular and comparatively expensive food, which consists of vinegared rice topped with thin slices of raw fish and hand-rolled into two-bite size. Originally, *sushi* meant merely pickled fish, and it was not until the Tokugawa era that a man named Yohei began to sell it in its present form. A dab of tart green Japanese horseradish (*wasabi*) is placed between the rice and the fish. The fish utilized cover a wide range including shrimp, bluefin tuna, sea bream, squid, abalone, and octopus. Soy sauce, fresh ginger root, and tea or beer are served with *sushi.*

Sashimi, or raw fish, has doubtless done more than any other single food to turn Westerners against Japanese cuisine, but we need not be quite that finicky. After all, we eat much more raw shellfish, in the form of oysters, than the Japanese do, while the Dutch and the Germans relish raw tunny (as well as raw beef). And the Italians and the Greeks dote on raw octopus and squid. Moreover, the Japanese do not eat just any finny creature raw. Only selected parts of certain prime fish are eaten uncooked, and then they must be extremely fresh and dipped in soy sauce mixed, usually, with horseradish. In this condition, *sashimi* doesn't have what we would characterize as a "fishy" smell or taste.

Tempura is any kind of fish, meat, or vegetable dipped in batter and fried in deep grease. Contrary to prevailing foreign opinion, it is by no means limited to shrimp, although shrimp is doubtless the culmination of the tempura chef's art.

The classic tempura restaurants seat customers at a round table with the chef sitting in the open center. The restaurant is so constructed that fresh supplies can be passed up to the chef from below. He cooks the tempura before the eyes of the guests and serves it to them one or two pieces at a time. Before eating, the guests touches his tempura with lemon juice and salt or dips it into a mixture of soy sauce and grated radish. Such restaurants in Tokyo pay three to four dollars a pound for the fresh shrimp that they have flown in from the Inland Sea daily.

Fugu is variously translated as blowfish, globefish, puffer fish, balloon fish, and moon fish. It is a small creature that inflates itself into a balloonlike shape when caught. It is eaten both raw and cooked, has a delicate, elusive flavor, and leaves the lips numb, as after eating a green persimmon.

Its ovaries and liver contain a deadly, hard-to-isolate poison called tetrodotoxin which kills two hundred Japanese in an average year. (In 1947, the peak postwar year, the number of deaths reached 470.) Skilled cooks, who are specially licensed, cut out the poisonous parts under running water, so *fugu* eaten in reputable restaurants is almost (an uneasy word) always safe; most deaths occur in fishermen's families, who prepare their own *fugu*.

The *sashimi* of one valued species, the tiger *fugu,* costs four dollars an ounce. *Fugu* testis mixed with hot sake is drunk by eager seekers after lost virility.

Of all Japanese dishes, eel was one taste that I acquired

almost at first meeting. After the head is removed, the eel is split open and the bones taken out. It is then skewered, steamed, and barbecued over charcoal. While barbecuing, the cook takes it off the grill repeatedly to dip it in a marinade of soy sauce and sweetened sake. The eel may be eaten alone or on a bed of white rice. Its aroma is ambrosial.

Reference to eels as food is found in a poem written by Yakamochi Otomo 1,200 years ago. Although rivers are their natural habitat, most eels in Japan today are raised in lakes or ponds, Lake Hamana being the best known and the largest source.

It is estimated that thirty million eels are eaten in Japan annually. In the town of Kamaishi in Iwate Prefecture, an annual memorial service is held to pray for the peaceful repose of the souls of eels sacrificed to man's hunger.

Such diverse personalities as the food editor of *The New York Times,* the Governor of Kansas, the managing editor of the *Dallas Morning News,* and the author of the James Bond books have acclaimed Japanese beef as the world's best. Yet for a thousand years, until after the Meiji Restoration in 1868, the Japanese ate almost no beef because Buddhism forbade the consumption of the flesh of four-legged animals and because most Japanese farmers felt kindly disposed toward the working cattle that shared their labors in the fields. (When Commodore Perry first came to Japan in 1853, he asked that the Japanese sell his fleet sixty head of cattle. Puzzled, the Japanese asked what on earth he intended to do with them. Why, eat them, of course, Perry explained. Astounded and horrified, the Japanese at first replied, "We can never comply with your cruel wishes to kill and eat such animals.") Later, in 1856, when Townsend Harris was installed as U.S. Consul in Shimoda, he partially satisfied his desires for meat with the flesh of wild boar, deer, golden pheasant, and rabbit, until he was at last able to prevail upon the Japanese to butcher a cow for him. The place is marked today by a monument erected by "the butchers of Tokyo" and reads in part, ". . . marks the spot on which the first cow in Japan was slaughtered for human consumption."

Even stranger, the visitor sees no herds of beef cattle anywhere in Japan. Why? Because each farmer in the beef-raising districts owns only one or two head, which he keeps penned up or has staked out grazing in the wooded hills.

Japan has three centers of beef production: Matsuzaka, Omi, and an area near Kobe. The practice in each varies somewhat, but generally two-year-old calves are bought in other prefectures and shipped to one of these three areas, where they are worked on farms for two years. At the age of four, they retire and enter a six months' fattening-up period.

During this time they are fed the best fodder: rice, rice bran, and beans. If their appetites fall off, they are given beer or distillery slops to drink as appetizers. In hot weather, electric fans keep them cool. In cold weather they are covered with blankets or padded quilts, and farmers have been known to take covering off their daughters' (but not their sons') beds for the sake of a high-living bovine. Daily massage works the fat into the lean meat, resulting in well-marbled beef or what the Japanese call *shimofuri gyuniku* (fallen-frost beef).

Whereas every American, on the average, eats one hundred pounds of beef yearly, a Japanese eats only ten. As it works out, the poorer farming families seldom taste beef.

Japan may be reaching a crisis in its beef production. In recent years, the number of cattle has been decreasing while the rate of consumption, as well as the price, has been going up.

Doubtless sukiyaki is the Japanese dish best known to foreigners, although it is not that often eaten by the Japanese, for reasons mentioned above. Thin strips of beef are short-cooked in a heavy iron pan together with such vegetables as onions, mushrooms, bamboo shoots, and trefoil and with bean curd. In place of beef, sometimes pork, chicken, fish or even boar may be used. The dish is prepared in front of the diner, who dips each bite in a mixture of raw egg and soy sauce.

Sukiyaki originated in Japan some ninety years ago. Perhaps the most convincing version of the etymology of the word is that laborers working out in the fields away from home cooked (*yaku* or *yaki*) their meat and vegetables on a spade (*suki*) over an open fire.

In lieu of salt and pepper on the table of the average Japanese home, you will find soy sauce (which Japanese housewives buy in two-quart bottles and replenish frequently) and monosodium glutamate or glutamic acid soda (sold under such brand names as Ajinomoto and Asahi-Aji). More than a seasoning, the latter is really a chemical that makes the taste buds more sensitive to the taste of the food.

A most exotic seasoning or stock is *katsuobushi,* which is made by steaming bonito, a fish found in abundance off the coasts of Japan. It is then dried and a green mold is allowed to form. When ready for market, the mold is brushed off, leaving a dark brown slab of fish that is as hard as rock. Every housewife owns a box with a blade, like a carpenter's plane, mounted in it, which she uses to strip thin shavings from the adamantine *katsuobushi,* and with them she makes the stock for soups and seasoning for certain dipping sauces.

What passes for the sandwich in Japan is surely worth mention in passing, for here one is forced to suspect the existence of an insidious movement to stamp out this Western import by inspiring in all a natural revulsion against it. First of all, the Japanese do not appear to be acquainted with the basic premise that a sandwich is, or should be, meat between two slices of bread. One keeps coming across such wonders as spaghetti sandwiches and potato sandwiches. Nor would it be surprising to learn that a rice sandwich is being readied for the market.

The prime motivator of this movement is, I believe, a small shop in Toriizaka in the Minato Ward of Tokyo. It stands on a corner near the Toyo Eiwa Girls' School, and on every school day it offers an imposing array of sandwiches, already made up, for the schoolgirls' lunches. I have at last succeeded in erasing most of their monstrous and grotesque concoctions from my memory, but three of the more formidable will remain, I fear, forever: 1) the tangerine slices-and-whipped-cream sandwich, 2) the strawberry-and-whipped-cream sandwich, and 3) the boiled carrots-and-yoghurt-sauce sandwich.

The Japanese have a penchant for devising out-of-the-ordinary settings in which one can get unusual dishes. Perhaps this is competitively necessary in a city like Tokyo that offers seventy styles of cooking in, as noted before, thirty-three thousand restaurants. There are restaurants, for example, that serve lobsters only. And others that serve only sardines. Or tortoise or crab or loach. Or horse meat, which the Japanese euphemistically call *sakura-niku* (literally, cherry meat). There are revolving restaurants and restaurants where the band goes up and down on an elevatorlike stage. There are underground restaurants and restaurants (*okonomi-yaki ryoriya*) where you can cook the food yourself. Restaurants aboard barges on canals in downtown Tokyo and Osaka, and restaurants perched above lonely coasts, where the spray beats against the dining-room windows when the sea is running high. And restaurants in conjunction with inns back in the hills where only game—boar, deer, pheasant, bear—is served.

I think that the one that will remain most firmly fixed in my memory, however, is a restaurant on the bank of a river near Tokyo where I went once to sample its tempura. As is customary, I took off my shoes at the entrance and was escorted to a tatami room with a low table in its center. It was *kotatsu*-style, with an open space under the table so that the diner could ease his legs by letting them dangle. In cold weather a hibachi is placed in the bottom of this space to warm the feet and legs of the guest. It was in August, however, when I went there and stifling hot. Even so, I could not understand why the waitress insisted that I remove my socks as well as roll up the legs of my trousers, although it admittedly felt good to place my hot, aching feet on the cool concrete at the bottom of the space under the table.

About the time my beer was served, I thought I felt a dampness around my feet, and this dampness quickly grew until it became an undeniable flow of water. Puzzled but by no means displeased, I looked under the table and then asked for confirmation of what my eyes had told me.

It was, the waitress explained, an arrangement whereby the feet of the guest are bathed in cool, running water throughout his meal.

According to Shinto mythology, the gods who created Japan were exceedingly fond of drink, and the Japanese have never found any reason not to follow this divine example.

During the Han and Wei dynasties, Chinese historians who visited Japan (before the Japanese had a written language of their own) recorded that "the people of Wa [Japan] are much given to strong drink." But it is recorded elsewhere that until the beginning of the Nara Era in the early 700's, sake (pronounced like *blasé*) was supposedly drunk, because of the influence of its first godly imbibers, only at religious rituals. Either there must have been a surfeit of such rituals or else the Japanese had found something besides rice from which to brew intoxicants.

In Japan's two oldest books, the *Kojiki* (A.D. 712) and *Nihon Shoki* (A.D. 720), mention is made of *Yashiori-no-sake,* which was made from several kinds of fruit, and *Amano-tama-sake,* which was made from rice. During the Heian Period (A.D. 794–1191), the Japanese were already beginning to drink warmed sake, at least from September until March. Probably someone discovered that heating this intoxicant enhanced the delicate aroma and warmed the body of the consumer on chilly nights. This was when the *sakazuki,* or sake cups, began to come in smaller sizes; in larger cups, the liquid too often cooled before it could be consumed.

Although cold sake is now enjoying a revival of popularity, most Japanese drink their sake warm. It is poured into 180-cc. porcelain bottles called *tokkuri* and heated in a pan of hot water on the stove. (U.S.-made baby-bottle warmers sold briskly in Japan for several years after someone found that they were ideal for this purpose.) Individual tastes vary, but 110°–120° Fahrenheit is the preferred range of temperature. The sake is poured from the *tokkuri* into the *sakazuki*—the 18-cc. cup not much larger than a thimble, the bottom of which is placed on the tips of the forefinger and middle finger of the left hand and held in place there with the thumb and same two fingers of the right hand. The drinker should not fill his own cup but only those of others, who will in turn fill his for him, and no one's cup should be filled to the brim.

Exchanging cups is a sake-drinking ritual in which one man first hands his empty cup to another, then fills it for him from a *tokkuri*. The second man immediately drains the cup, rinses it out in a bowl of water provided for that purpose, and returns it to its owner with a bow of his head and then fills it for him. It is the social inferior (in the Japanese sense) who usually initiates this exchange. When one has had enough sake, he may indicate this by turning his cup upside down on the table. Sake is drunk throughout the meal until the rice is served.

Sake is most often given in English as rice wine, and it is true that it is similar to wine in alcoholic content (15–20 percent), in the enjoyment of its bouquet, and in the sipping method by which it should be consumed. On the other hand, the process by which it is brewed more nearly resembles that of beer, and it bears further similarity to that drink in that it is generally not aged.

Japan has 3,870 sake breweries that produce 350 million gallons of this derivative of rice annually in 5,000 brands. Although the breweries are located throughout Japan, Nada (producing 24 percent of the total) and Fushimi (9 percent) are the two areas whose rice wines are considered best. Nada, which is a suburb of Kobe, began producing sake in 1331, but it did not gain national fame until 1840 when it began to use *Miya-mizu*, a kind of water found in underground rivers in the city of Nishinomiya just north of Nada. Fushimi's sake dates back even farther, to the Heian Period, which began in A.D. 794. Nada's sake is generally dry (*kara-kuchi*), while Fushimi's is sweet (*ama-kuchi*).

Sake comes in three grades: special (*tokkyu*), first (*ikkyu*), and second (*nikyu*). One quart of the best (special) grade may cost about $1.50, of which nearly one-half will go to the national treasury. The tax on sake and other spirits ranks third in national importance, after corporation and individual income taxes.

Although the production of sake continues to increase, the Japanese are drinking less of it in comparison to whiskey and beer. In 1937, sake accounted for 68 percent of the country's total liquor consumption, whereas it is now only 30 percent. Several years ago, beer production and consumption passed sake for the first time.

One of the strange misconceptions we Americans hold about sake concerns its potency. According to this popular fallacy, sake packs the wallop of the 151-proof Demerara rum that the British navy uses, diluted copiously with water, to make grog.

Obviously, this is not so. As noted above, sake varies, with the grade, from 15 to 20 percent in alcoholic content, making it only slightly stronger than wine and not nearly so strong as gin. Nor does the warmth of the sake matter much since the liquid adjusts to body temperature shortly after entering the stomach.

As well as I can determine, this fallacy has its roots in the islands of the Pacific, where American troops found bottles of clear alcoholic liquid among supplies they captured from the Japanese. Some of this was no doubt sake, but most of it was probably *shochu*, a much stronger drink (to be described later), which would have looked like sake to anyone unable to read the Japanese writing on the label. If it was *shochu*, and if our soldiers drank it as quickly as I have often seen them swallow such windfalls of liquor (that is, before an officer could "confiscate" it), then it is little wonder that sake earned for itself an undeserved reputation for potency.

Although sake is very mild, I usually awaken the next morning with a slight hangover after drinking it. At many Japanese-style dinners, the host, in his expansive generosity, will have sake, beer, and Scotch placed on the table so that each guest can have his preference, but the trouble comes with the cup-exchanging ritual. The man on your right may offer you the Scotch he has been drinking, after which the man on your left may offer you beer. And then a geisha refills your *sakazuki* with sake. It is difficult, if not downright rude, to refuse these offerings, and after a few such rounds, you don't much care, anyway—at least, not until the next morning.

Synthetic sake, which was developed during the Pacific War, still accounts for about one-tenth of all the sake consumed. *Mamushizake* (the *mamushi* is Japan's only poisonous snake) is sake in which this serpent has been embalmed and is taken as a restorative. In Hawaii, one can buy carbonated sake, which is faintly—but only faintly—reminiscent of dry champagne.

The Japanese drink 3½ gallons of sake per person every year, or slightly over a quart a month. In 1968, the average American drank just under 1½ gallons of distilled spirits. (Criers of doom who are forever telling us that Americans are drinking more and more should note these comparisons: In 1960, the average per capita consumption of distilled spirits in the United States was 1.2 gallons. One hundred years before that, in 1860, the figure was 3.3 gallons, nearly three times as much.)

To draw a conclusion, however, from such a comparison of sake and whiskey consumption would be meaningless. If we calculate the alcohol actually contained in various drinks, our intake is about twice that of the Japanese.

Shochu, the drink referred to above, is written with characters meaning "the strong drink that burns." Its alcoholic content varies from 45 to 60 percent, and it is distilled from the dregs of sake or from sweet potatoes. Kagoshima, Japan's southernmost prefecture, has 141 distilleries that produce four and a half million gallons of this drink yearly, which is also known as "Satsuma vodka," Satsuma being the old feudal name of that region.

As might be expected, the problem of drunkenness in Japan is different from that in the United States in several aspects. For one thing, there are not nearly so many genuine alcoholics in Japan, with the exception of the prefecture of Kagoshima mentioned above. Alcohol inebriates the Japanese more quickly because of their smaller consumption of animal fats and flesh and because of the binding behavioral restrictions of their society, which produce a compensating need for release. Given lesser actual consumption of alcohol and faster reactions to it, their bodies seldom reach the point where they require continuing infusions of spirits. (Many Japanese react so quickly to alcohol that only two swallows of a Martini will cause a speedy dilation of the capillary veins and a resulting feverishly red coloration of the skin. This reaction is so severe that many refuse to drink at all because of it.) Another differing aspect is that the Japanese have always been notoriously lenient and forgiving toward the inebriated, and it has only been in recent years that a few faltering steps have been taken toward correction of this attitude.

Note what the Japanese themselves say about their country being a "drunkards' paradise":

". . . The first step toward the extermination of this nuisance is to train the public to believe that irresponsible conduct by drunkards must not be tolerated." (Mr. Kondo, Chief of the Crime Prevention Department of the Tokyo Metropolitan Police Department)

". . . the ordinary Japanese believes that the best policy is to endure everything and do nothing when the other party is drunk." (*Mainichi Daily News*)

"In Japan, the drunkard's Eden, you may drink like a baboon and not lose an iota of respectability in the eyes of the

people, be you a Lord Abbot or a Minister of Education."
(Santaro's column in the *Asahi Evening News*)

"Japan is a paradise for drunken men. Intoxicated behavior
is dismissed lightly, even in criminal cases." (Mrs. T. Tazaki,
vice-president of the Tokyo Federation of Women's Organizations)

Pfc. Adolph W. Merten, an American marine, was acquitted
and released by a Japanese court after he had shot to death
nineteen-year-old Shiro Takawa in a bar in Yokosuka some
years ago. The Japanese judge explained that Merten had
been drinking and so was non compos mentis at the time of
the killing. (Clause No. 39 of the Penal Code reads, "Acts
committed while of unsound mind shall not be punished," and
drunkenness is equated with temporary mental incompetence.)

That Merten's case is not so unusual is supported by this
comment from the "Vox Populi, Vox Dei" column of the
Asahi Shimbun: "There have been many cases in the past of
murderers being acquitted or getting off with incredibly light
sentences on the grounds that they were drunk and non compos mentis at the time of the crime. One judge has been moved
to complain with a heavy sigh, 'Japan is a paradise for drunkards.' "

To try to correct this situation, however, by legislating more
severe penalties for public inebriation may result in serious
trouble in other quarters. As suggested earlier, drunkenness is
a major safety valve on the pressure chamber of the society.
Clamping it shut could cause the excess pressure to seek release through even less desirable avenues.

The tremendous pressures that build up internally characterize Japan's social structure, and any student who fails to
take them into account will not succeed in understanding the
Japanese and their culture. In their vertical social arrangement, few are equal, and the Japanese spend a good part of
their days calculating how much higher or lower they stand
than the next fellow. And these precise distances govern the
degree of respect or disrespect, the depth of the bow, the kind

of language, the frequency of the smile, the willingness to oblige, and the extent of compliance that one Japanese must extend and show to another. The gauging of these distances and reactions alone is a time-consuming and often frustrating job. The negation of individuality and the repression of personal choice in which they result would be stultifying to anyone, even people born in such surroundings and aware of no other system.

Sometimes individual Japanese can endure it no longer. A trigger will release their pent-up resentment, anger, and frustration, and explosions of varying intensity follow. Until now, drunkenness, quickly achieved and publicly flaunted, has been the major channel through which these explosive emotions have spent themselves. Of course not everyone takes advantage of this form of release, which at least partially accounts for other excessive behavior (suicides, riots, and crimes of violence) in Japan.

Realizing this, the Japanese have tended to be lenient, if not sympathetic, toward men in their cups. Since it was a condoned activity, many Japanese came to take advantage of its pressure-reducing benefits. Indeed, things came to such a pass that failure to get looped when the opportunity presented itself was viewed with suspicion and distaste.

Santaro, the *Asahi Evening News* columnist mentioned above, wrote in his column of August 19, 1957: "If a respected foreigner in this country wishes to gain the good opinion of his Japanese friends, he could do no better than to be their guest—or victim—at a Japanese dinner and get as drunk as a lord so that he had to be shoved into his car and taken home and had to tell his host on the morrow that he remembered nothing of the evening before. *It would elevate his credit in their eyes as nothing else could.*" (Italics mine.)

So commendable has inebriation become at most parties that some Japanese will pretend to be half-seas over when in reality they have had only a very small quantity of liquor. I was drinking on the Ginza with a Japanese friend one night when he received momentous news of changes in regulations that would permit his company to import a certain locally scarce raw material in unlimited quantities. He happened to know that the president of his company was disporting himself that same evening in a restaurant in Shimbashi, so he and I hurried over there by taxi. A maid escorted us to the door of the large tatami room where an uninhibited bacchanalia was in full swing. My friend at last caught the eye of his company's president, who was down on all fours with his shirttail out, letting a geisha ride him around the room like a horse. In the few seconds it took him to get to his feet and reach us at the door, he had recovered much of his equanimity, and by the time he heard my friend report the news, he was stone-cold sober. Without hesitation, he issued comprehensive instructions covering quantities, shippers, dates, and terms of payment in fine detail and told my companion to cable the orders that same night.

We then watched him as he returned to the party. Before he had got halfway to his geisha's side, he had already begun to stagger again and, as we were closing the door, he was getting down on his hands and knees, urging the geisha to mount him once more.

The Japanese were first exposed to the American and European disapproval of getting falling-down drunk at formal social gatherings with the influx of foreign teachers and advisers in the 1880's. Thereafter, some Japanese attempted to restrain their alcoholic exuberance in the presence of foreigners, but most of them dismissed such niceties with contempt. They called it "killing the sake" (*sake wo korosu koto*).

Every year the Japanese drink some 36,000,000 gallons (one-third of a gallon each) of foreign-style hard liquors, both imported and distilled at home. Among the imported spirits, Scotch and gin are favorites, with little attention being given to American bourbon. The domestically produced liquors cover a wide range of variety and quality, including one lavender-colored concoction bottled in a glass replica of Tokyo

Tower that may have no equivalent in foreign lands. (At least, I hope not.) Imported spirits can be painfully expensive (fine French brandies selling for $12 a bottle in Hong Kong will fetch as much as $100 on Japan's retail market) with the exception of gin, which falls into a different classification for customs purposes and so is usually cheaper than in the United States.

Foreign-style liquors have had a hard time getting off the ground in Japan, although Japanese living in Tokyo, Yokohama, and Kobe were exposed to them a hundred and more years ago. In one famous case, a liquor salesman tried to sell foreign whiskey to a kimono dealer in Hiroshima and ended by being arrested and charged with vending poison without a pharmaceutical license.

Suntory, Ltd.—Japan's oldest and largest producer of foreign-style liquors (Suntory, Torys, Hermes, etc.)—tried to overcome public indifference in 1922 with a poster showing a "half-nude girl" drinking its Akadama Port Wine. Although the picture would be considered tame by today's standards, it created a scandalous sensation in the Japan of forty-seven years ago. As a result, the company was swamped with orders for, not the wine, but copies of the poster. (Much Japanese wine is sweet and is still considered more a tonic than a pleasure-producing potation.)

A team of twenty Japanese distillation experts has been hard at work for some years now trying to develop the techniques needed to produce high-quality Scotch-type liquor in Japan. Considering the success the Japanese have had in producing the "three B's" (beer, bread, and beef, none of which was consumed in Japan until after 1853), it would not be at all surprising if they eventually succeed admirably.

Qualified judges of beer hold that the Japanese product is one of the very best in the world, if not the best, and I would be among the last to disagree. Although I like the Kirin brand myself, it would seem that many foreigners, perhaps a majority, prefer Sapporo. The average per capita consumption of beer in Japan is about six gallons a year in comparison to seventeen gallons in the United States (and thirty-two gallons in Belgium).

My introduction to Japanese tea drinking was instructive— and very filling. It came just after the war in Fukuoka, when I became the Liaison Officer for the Civil Censorship Detachment and was meeting the various Japanese officials, companies, and individuals with whom I would be doing business. Since we were to censor everything from stage plays to radio broadcasts, from personal letters to newspapers, it took more than a week for me to see all these people in the city of Fukuoka only, to say nothing of the island of Kyushu, and I had at least one cup of tea with each. I estimate the total consumption for the first week at seventy-five cups. Fortunately for me, the cups were small, and the Japanese consider it impolite to fill a teacup more than two-thirds full.

Even more than sake, tea is vital to the Japanese way of life and must be ranked after rice in importance. (Witness the Japanese expression for an everyday happening: *"nichijo sahanji,"* or "a usual tea-and-rice thing.")

Tea first appears in Japanese historical records in the year A.D. 729, when the Emperor Shomu invited one hundred Buddhist monks to join him for tea. This Imperial supply, however, may have been imported from China because the first tea shrubs were reportedly grown from seeds brought back from China in 805 by a monk named Saicho.

Buddhist monks were the first to make significant use of tea, because it helped to keep them awake during long, motionless hours of contemplation. They in turn recommended it for its medicinal properties to the Imperial court. For centuries thereafter tea was the drink of the aristocrats, samurai, and religious classes, and it was not until 1737, when a man named Nagatani of the Yamashiro district, near Kyoto, succeeded in making an unfermented tea called *sencha,* that the popularization of tea among all classes began.

The Japanese word for tea is *cha* or, with the honorific prefix, *ocha,* while in Mandarin Chinese it is pronounced *ch'a.* As early as 1696, the British were using the Chinese word for tea, and even today it is common to hear British workmen talk about a "cup of *char*." (And in Russian the word for tea-house is *chaihana.*)

The best tea comes from Uji, near Kyoto, while the most comes from Shizuoka (50 percent), but production is by no means limited to these areas. The tea shrubs are grown mostly on terraces but many can be raised on level ground as well, if it is well drained. The first harvest comes when the shrub is three years old, but the shrub produces its best tea between its fifth and ninth years. The infinite variety of tea proceeds not only from the location, kind, and age of the shrub but also from the time of the harvest, the location of the leaf on the branch, and, of course, the method of preparation.

Only one percent of Japan's annual tea production (totaling 80,000 tons) is black (*kocha*), while the rest is green. The Japanese drink black tea as we do, with combinations of sugar, lemon, and milk, but green tea is always taken without any additives. Whereas Americans average $\frac{7}{10}$ of a pound of tea yearly (much of which is wasted in tea-bag form), Japanese consumption is nearly two pounds. (If two pounds a year does not sound like much tea drinking, you should consider that a pinch of tea leaves will produce much more of this liquid refreshment than the equivalent weight, for example, of coffee.)

The genuine teahouse (*chaya*) is fast disappearing from the Japanese scene. In *Things Japanese* Basil Hall Chamberlain wrote, "The tea-house is a thing by itself—in the country, an open shed, in the towns, often a pretty, but always open, house, sometimes with a garden, where people sit down and rest for a short time, and are served with tea and light refreshments only. . . ."

In place of the teahouse, we now find in towns *kissaten* (tea and coffee shops), where music may be the most impor-

tant offering, and in rural areas *o-zashiki* (Japanese-style restaurants), where tea is assuredly served but is not the focal
point of the guest's visit (which may be food, carousing, or
dalliance).

When I was living in Tantakabayashi near Kobe in 1948
and 1949, my landlord was in the habit of inviting me to his
home next door to attend the tea ceremonies (*chanoyu*) that
he held every Saturday afternoon. Because he was the retired
president of a large steel-manufacturing company, his other
guests were often men of equal prominence, so I usually accepted his invitations for the opportunity they presented to
exchange views with Japanese of distinction, although I had
little real interest in the ceremony itself, which is surely one of
the most esoteric aspects of Japanese culture.

Little by little—by a process of sheer osmosis, I suppose—
I developed a tolerance, if not fondness, for the ceremony,
which was first codified by the Buddhist abbot Eisai and later
more rigidly by Sen-no-Rikyu, whose descendants still operate
one of Japan's best-known schools of the tea cult.

The origin of the tea ceremony as we know it today is to be
found in gatherings of Buddhist monks in front of an image
of Bodhindharma to drink tea from a single bowl with all the
formality of a holy sacrament. After this religious stage, the
tea ceremony moved on to a second sybaritic stage, in which
the guests and host reclined, like ancient Romans, on fine furs
and studied costly finery and works of art. Guests were invited to participate in such games as guessing where the tea
being served was raised or where the teacups were made.
For correct guesses, they were given the right to take their
choice of any of the gold and silver vessels or brocades or
swords arrayed before them. And it was the custom for these
guests to pass on their prizes to the serving girls in attendance.

It was during this stage, in 1587, that the de facto ruler of
Japan, Hideyoshi, gave what is most likely the largest tea
party ever held. Hideyoshi invited every devotee of the tea
ceremony in all of Japan to attend and warned that any who

failed to come would be barred from ever participating in the ceremony again. The party was held in Kitano, near Kyoto, and lasted ten days. Estimates of the number of attendees range as high as 16,000.

One of the men who attended this party, the same Sen-no-Rikyu mentioned earlier, is the person most responsible for introducing the third and present stage of the tea ceremony, in which stark simplicity is the keynote. Exhausted as their country was from long years of internal warfare, the life of the average Japanese had become increasingly difficult. The utmost frugality and plainness were in order. Reflecting the needs of the country, Sen-no-Rikyu took simplicity and restraint as his themes and around him built the tea ceremony as we know it: "a worship of simplicity and of antique objects of art, together with the observance of an elaborate code of etiquette." He aimed at making it a cult of aestheticism and discipline designed to promote mental composure, internal peace, and enlightenment. Through it, he taught his disciples to be keenly aware, to sharpen their senses to discover depths of beauty that might not otherwise be apparent.

A typical tea ceremony lasts two or three hours and is attended by the host or a tea-master (who may or may not be the same person), his assistant, and five guests. It is held in a small separate building in the garden. Although the English translation is the same (teahouse), this building is called a *sukiya* in Japanese and is different from the larger commercial teahouse mentioned earlier. The door through which one enters is small and cramped, this to inculcate humility. Once inside, there is a set order in which the guests examine and praise the seemingly plain implements of the ceremony and other decorative objects. Some of the teacups, which to the untutored may look like unglazed, chipped rejects from a cheap porcelain factory, are often worth hundreds of dollars, if not more.

I found a cracked teacup at one of the first tea ceremonies I attended and lost no time in pointing the crack out to the host, thinking that he did not know about it and that he would not want to expose his guests to possible injury from swallowing a chip or sliver of porcelain. He and his other guests smiled to cover their embarrassment, but later, when we were alone, my host explained to me that the misshapen, cracked, crudely colored teacup had been made that way two hundred years before. Seeing my amazement, he went on to point out that the forms of nature are always imperfect, that nothing in nature is symmetrical, and that the tea ceremony, held as it is in the garden and at appropriate seasons of the year, is a reflection of nature; that a perfectly shaped, perfectly painted teacup would be entirely out of place. (Evidently this principle does not, however, apply to *all* the implements of the ceremony.)

The tea served at this ceremony (*matcha*) is made from a light green powder mixed with hot water and swished around in the bottom of the cup with a *chasen,* or bamboo tea-whisk. Each guest takes three sips of this bitter, foamy mixture and follows an elaborate ritual of when to bow, when to praise the quality of the tea, how to hold the cup, how to pass it on to the next guest, and so forth. It is a geometric progression in manners.

Although the guests may talk, the emphasis is on contemplative quietness and peace and the achievement of a silent symphony of graceful but restrained motion.

Today more than two million Japanese consider themselves full-fledged devotees of the tea ceremony.

9

Their Language

After long, arduous efforts to master the language of the "heathen Japanee," Saint Francis Xavier reported to the headquarters of his Jesuit order in Europe that it must have been devised by Satan to prevent the teaching of the Gospel to the natives of that island empire. (Saint Francis first came to Japan in 1549. Four hundred years later, his withered arm made the trip again in a glass case as a Holy Relic sent by Mother Church to be venerated.)

The Jesuits being missionaries of wide experience in learning foreign tongues and converting their speakers to the True Faith, one is led to wonder what it was about this particular language that so exasperated and thwarted the normally patient and kindly Saint Francis.

Japanese, which is kin to both the Ural-Altaic and the Polynesian lingual families, existed only as a spoken language until about A.D. 400, when Chinese books began to arrive in the land of Wa, as the Chinese then called Japan. (They also called it *Ehr-Ban,* which was written with two characters meaning the "source of the sun." In Japanese, the same two characters were pronounced Nihon or Nippon.) Showing evidence of their admirable adaptability even then, the Japanese decided that China's was a superior culture and that in order to profit from it and in order to retain the knowledge to which they were being exposed, they would have to possess means of recording it. Also, they were beginning to realize that their *kataribe* system was not the most efficient method for retaining memory of historical events, familial lineages, and so forth. (The *kataribe* were a class of professional memorizers who were trained from childhood to learn by rote the names, dates, places, and events in Japan's history.)

Short of adopting Chinese in its entirety and abandoning their own tongue, the best way that the Japanese could see to provide themselves with a written language was to fit the Chinese hieroglyphics or ideographic characters to their native speech, and this they set about to do with enthusiasm. But to comprehend what happened and why Japanese became what Professor Ivan Morris has called "one of the most effective barriers to mutual understanding that the mind of man has devised," the reader must realize that this process of assimilation was at best haphazard, often indirect, long drawnout, and riddled with inconsistencies. It was not, after all, as if there had been in the Chinese capital a Central Bureau for the Transmission of the Chinese Written Language to the Land of Wa or, in Japan, an Imperial Agency for the Reception, Codification, and Dissemination of Chinese Characters.

More than three hundred years passed from the adoption of the first character until the Japanese possessed a proper vehicle for recording words. Wars, natural disasters, and internal strife had made traffic between the two countries intermittent and, at times, nonexistent. Often the knowledge came slowly through Korea and was altered along the way. The Japanese scholars who were undertaking to learn Chinese writing and to select portions of it to fit to their native words were not restricted to one area but were scattered throughout Kyushu and southwestern Honshu, while some had gone to China itself to begin the process there. Chinese priests, scholars, and officials, too, came to the numerous centers in Japan from various parts of China, when China's spoken language was made up of more than two hundred recognizable dialects. As a result, a Chinese from the old southern province of Go might tell the Japanese that a certain ideographic character was read or pronounced one way, while a Chinese from Kan in the north would read it with a different pronunciation and a man from To would enunciate it in a manner that bore little or no similiarity to either of the first two.

If, of course, there had been a centralized, coordinated effort to absorb the Chinese characters, then a person at a suitable level of authority would simply have made the decision to use one or another of the several readings and to disregard the others. Unfortunately for us today, there was no such effort. While the Chinese from To may have been teaching Japanese Buddhist priests in the vicinity of present-day Kyoto his pronunciation of the character for, say, *tide,* another Chinese from Kan may have been teaching Japanese scholars in Dazaifu in Kyushu his differing pronunciation for the same character. And so on.

To make the situation even more complex, Chinese pronunciations themselves changed during those three hundred years or so, as one emperor sought to standardize the language and another neglected linguistic affairs entirely, so that a reading taught the Japanese in Dazaifu in A.D. 450 by a Chinese from To province might differ from the reading taught them in A.D. 650 by another Chinese from the same province.

This brings us up to the stage in Japan where we have one Chinese character that may have two or three Chinese pronunciations or readings and one native Japanese reading. For further confusion, now add two more ingredients: The Japanese version of the Chinese pronunciation was seldom perfect. What was said as *"shan"* by the Chinese might, for example, have been said as *"san"* by the Japanese, because the Japanese were incapable, without years of effort or childhood acquaintance, of accurately reproducing many Chinese sounds, and vice versa. Also, the Japanese sometimes decided to add a second or even a third reading of their own to the character. They might have been groping for a way to write a certain verb, and, with no Chinese scholar handy to provide a new character for them, they may have decided to tack this verb onto a character they already knew, like an extra tail, because of a connection, perhaps only tenuous, between the two meanings.

As one consequence of all this, the Japanese of today must work with characters like 明 , which has three Chinese readings (*mei, myo,* and *min*) and five Japanese readings (*akarui* —bright, *akeru*—to open, *akasu*—to publish, *akiraka*—distinct, and *akari*—light), and like 生 , which has two Chinese readings (*sei, sho*) and a whole raft of Japanese readings (*iki*—freshness, *hayasu*—to grow, as a beard, *fu*—a grassy place, *ki*—undiluted, *nama*—raw, impertinent, *nasu*—to bear, as a child, *shozuru*—to produce, *ikiru*—to live, *umareru*—to be born, *haeru*—to sprout, *ikeru*—to arrange flowers, and *umi*—childbirth).

You may reasonably wonder how the Japanese reader knows which reading he should use. The general rule is to take the Japanese or native reading when the character stands alone and the Chinese reading when it stands together with one or more other characters to form a compound word. If there is more than one Japanese reading (as in the examples above), the reader can usually tell which to use by the *kana* (see below) modifications that are suffixed to it. A frequent difficulty comes in deciding how to read a compound word of two or three characters when one or two or all of them have more than one Chinese reading.

Take, for instance, the above character 明 for "bright," and so forth, with its three Chinese readings: *mei, myo,* and *min*. Then make a compound word by adding a second character 星 which has two Chinese readings, *sei* and *jo,* and which means "star." Such a compound would have six conceivable readings: *meisei, meijo, myosei, myojo, minsei,* and *minjo*.

The correct one happens to be *Myojo,* which means the planet Venus. (Literally, "bright star.") This the foreign student must learn by rote, but for the Japanese child it is less difficult because he will already know the spoken word

Myojo by the time he is old enough to have to learn its Chinese characters in school and so will not be tempted to read them as *meisei, meijo,* or what have you.

But this account of Oriental linguistic madness does not end here. The Japanese were finding that they had words for which there could be no Chinese characters: persons' and place names, for example, as well as objects and concepts that were uniquely Japanese. They considered tacking these, like still more extra tails, haphazardly onto the Chinese characters, as they had already done with entirely too many. But at last good sense prevailed. Enough was enough. There had to be another way.

It was then that someone suggested that they take about fifty Chinese characters, discard their meanings, and retain only the sounds. Then, when they came upon a native word (for example, *nichi*) that was in need of a way to be written, they could record its sound with two of the new characters-without-meaning: in this case, the one for *ni* and the one for *chi.*

Someone else protested, however, that each of these proposed phonetic characters contained, on the average, eight strokes, so that it would require forty or more strokes to write, for example, the five characters needed to represent the five syllables in the one word *Shimonoseki* (Shi-mo-no-se-ki). Thereupon another scholar proposed a sweeping simplification in the writing of each phonetic character to reduce the number of strokes from six or eight or ten to only one or two. For example, the character 利 (for the sound *ri*) was reduced to り.

The Japanese now had fifty phonetic characters (later reduced to forty-eight) with which they could write all the sounds in their language. They called this syllabary *hiragana,* and not long thereafter they devised a second syllabary, which was even simpler but stiffer in stroke appearance and which they were eventually to use for foreign words, emphatics, and colloquialisms. This they called *katakana,* and they began to use both it and *hiragana* in the eighth and ninth centuries to write words for which they had no Chinese characters, to modify verbs, and to represent what might be called particles and prepositions.

A page taken at random from a present-day Japanese magazine, for example, will carry two or three times more *kana* (either *hiragana* or *katakana* or both) than Chinese characters. The characters represent the main ideas, actions, or objects, while the *kana* form the siding, shingles, fixtures, flooring, window glass, paint, and shrubbery.

To illustrate an approximation of this in English, take the sentence, "The man walked to town." The ideas of *man, walking,* and *town* would be shown in Japanese with three characters, while the particle "the," the preposition "to," and the past tense ending "ed" suffixed to the verb "walk" would be shown in *kana.*

Of the two *kana* syllabaries, the *hiragana* is the more cursive or flowing, while the *katakana* is more like printing. The Chinese characters, too, are written in gradations between stiff and cursive, the principal among these being *kaisho, gyosho,* and *sosho.* Going from the almost-printed style of *kaisho* to the so-called grass-writing or scribbled style of *sosho* is somewhat akin to going into still another language.

With this the foundation of the Japanese language was formed, but Satan's work was not yet finished. There remained much addition, ramification, elaboration, and mystification to be added. The Japanese had only begun to build their society into the exquisitely formalized, pyramidal structure that it was to become, and the language had to be adapted to this structure—and, in turn, to assist in its control as a manifest gauge of degree of compliance and humility.

Spoken Japanese became not one language but several. Superiors used one set of pronouns, verbs, prefixes, suffixes, and verb-endings in speaking to inferiors, while inferiors replied in a different set. Words spoken between approximate equals differed from both of these, while words spoken to or about the Imperial family differed from them all. Male speech could be readily distinguished from female speech not only by a generally rougher tone and fewer polite forms but also by certain distinctive sentence endings, exclamations, and pronouns. Educated speech varied from the speech of the streets not so much in the absence of solecisms and mispronunciations (as is the case in the United States today) as in choice of vocabulary (staid and Chinese-y for one, racy and native for the other). Dialects developed, some for reasons to be expected in the natural growth of living language and others for political reasons. (For example, the spread and use of the dread dialect of Satsuma, or present-day Kagoshima, were encouraged by clan chieftains to enable their border guards to detect Shogunate or Imperial spies from the north.)

Although continuing efforts were made in the written language to codify the Chinese characters, no one, it seems, ever objected to the adoption of more. Attempts to reduce the number in use were almost unheard-of until modern times. As Western scholars today might flaunt their erudition through the use of French phrases or Latin derivatives in place of plain but effective Anglo-Saxon, the Japanese educated classes learned and used more and more Chinese characters as proof patent of their presumed superiority. This resulted in a written language that bore little more similarity to the spoken language than Latin does to modern Italian. With each new wave of Chinese learning (it ebbed and flowed) from the continent, more characters were adopted. And when Western knowledge poured into Japan after the Meiji Restoration, the Japanese had to dip again into their stock of Chinese characters to confect compound words (using the so-called Chinese readings) to describe Western ideas and objects that were new to them. (A telegram was called a *dempo,* or "electricity report"; a train became a *kisha,* or "steam cart.")

Many foreign words, however, were adopted as they were, and it was not until the xenophobic ultra-nationalism of the Thirties and early Forties that these were at last converted to

Chinese compounds. To illustrate, the English word *elevator,* which had been *erebeta,* became *shokoki* or "ascending-descending machine," and a pitcher of the baseball variety, which had been a *pitcha,* turned into a *toshu,* or "throwing hand."

The actual brush-writing of the Chinese characters—and of the *kana*—became a highly respected art form. The more the writer was able to *kuzusu* (to break down, to write in a running hand) his characters, the harder his writing was to read and the more he was seemingly respected. Even today one frequently finds hanging scrolls on which famous calligraphists penned (or brushed) epigrammatic jewels that are illegible to the average Japanese and sometimes even to the owner of the scroll himself.

There remains one final ingredient that we must add to this mishmash before we can definitively depict Japanese as the thorny, difficult vehicle that it is: namely, the vagueness of the Japanese people themselves. Obviously, this is not the fault of the language. I can be just as exact in speaking Japanese as in speaking English, and I can be just as vague in English, if I choose, as most Japanese are in their own tongue. In fact, the few Americans who speak truly fluent Japanese may be more effective in that language than native speakers are, in the sense that they can avoid the burden of vagueness that the Japanese deliberately use to weight down their own vehicle of communication.

To the Japanese, vagueness is a virtue. To be exact is to be impertinent and arrogant, in that it assumes superior knowledge. To be vague is to be courteous and humble. Directness, especially abrupt directness, confuses the Japanese and causes them to *men kurau,* or "eat their faces" in consternation. To quote writer Sumie Mishima, "In the Japanese language exactness is purposely avoided."

This fondness for indirection is sublimated in the small poetic package earlier referred to called the haiku. English translations of two well-known examples:

1. "The world of dew
   Is but a world of dew
   And yet, and yet. . . ."

2. "Matsushima!
   Ah, Matsushima, ah!
   Matsushima, ah!"

Just as the best novels are those that, by not telling all, invite the reader to participate imaginatively in the building of the tale, so the charm of haiku lies in what they leave unsaid. In the words of famed Japan publicist Inazo Nitobe, "To give in so many articulate words one's innermost thoughts and feelings is taken among us as an unmistakable sign that they are neither profound nor very sincere."

This then is the final ingredient in the formation of the modern Japanese tongue: this preference for the vague, this fondness for indirection, this avoidance of the open declaration. Although more the fault of its speakers than of the language itself, the result remains the same.

Before the postwar language reform, the large Tokyo daily newspapers stocked between 7,500 and 8,000 Chinese characters in their type, and even the Rose-Innes dictionary with its 5,000 characters called itself a "beginners' dictionary." The first effort to reduce the number of characters in everyday use came in 1872, when it was proposed that they be limited to 3,167 specific characters. (The list of these characters was destroyed in a fire, and the proposal came to naught.) Four subsequent attempts were made in 1900, 1923, 1928, and 1939, when it was recommended by the Ministry of Education that the number of characters in common use be limited to 2,000, 1,962, 1,858, and 2,669 respectively. Nor did these efforts meet with any more success.

But in 1946, with the prompting of the Occupation Forces, language reform was again proposed by the Ministry of Education, whose list of 1,850 characters recommended for common use was approved by the National Diet the following year.

This more successful attempt not only limited the number of common characters but also simplified the writing of many of them. Furthermore, it aimed at making the written language more closely resemble the spoken language, rationalizing the *kana* system (so that the sound *cho,* for instance, would be written with the *kana* for *chi, yo,* and *u,* instead of the *kana* for *te* and *fu*), gradually shifting the presentation of a written page from the old vertical format to the Western horizontal, and popularizing the use of Romanized Japanese, with its resultant wedge into English familiarity.

At the date of this writing, the goals of this reform program have been achieved with varying degrees of success. The lesser success is to be seen in the efforts to popularize Romanized Japanese and to shift the format of the written page from vertical to horizontal writing, the greater in the rationalizations of the *kana* syllabaries and the reduction of the *Toyo Kanji,* or the Chinese Characters in Common Use, although indubitably many people must continue to read books written before the language reform of 1947.

Foreign words continue to enter the language (examples: *appakatto* for uppercut, *wan-suteppu* for one-step, *raito ranchi* for light lunch, and *kuraimakkusu* for climax), but twisted as they are by Japanese tongues, they are not much easier for the foreigner to understand than their purely Japanese equivalents would have been.

Standard Japanese is taken to be that of the educated class of Tokyoites, and though rural dialects are far from being extinct, increased social mobility, expanding education, and growth in the communication media have long since made Standard Japanese understood in the most remote corners of the archipelago without noticeable difficulty.

One area, however, in which little progress has been realized is that of typing. The Japanese typewriter, another of Satan's works, is a monstrous device of pedals, arms, levers, and sighting-holes which is used, if at all, more as a symbol of conspicuous consumption than as a popular, labor-saving instrument. It is faster to write by hand, and most business communications are still recorded that way.

Japanese today is a language spoken by the one hundred million citizens of Japan and understood, if not much spoken, by many persons over thirty or so in such Far Eastern areas as Korea, Taiwan, Hong Kong, Saipan, and Guam, as well as in Brazil and our fiftieth state, Hawaii. In its spoken form, it bears absolutely no similarity to any of the dialects of Chinese (in answer to an oft-asked question).

Its sentence order (again different from the Chinese—and from English) is subject—object—verb, and the qualifying words generally precede the word they qualify. It builds up its words and grammatical forms with suffixes tied to the invariable stem or root. It avoids personification, and its elaborate system of honorifics often obviates the need for personal pronouns and for person in the verb. Its nouns have no number or gender, its verbs have no person, and its adjectives no degree of comparison. It is relatively easy to pronounce (its three mildly difficult sounds are the *r,* the *tsu,* and the double consonant, such as *kk* and *nn*) and has little tonal pitch and less syllable stress than, for example, English.

Granting that all the above combine to make, even after the language reforms noted, present-day Japanese one of the world's most difficult tongues for us to learn, the language is nonetheless done several injustices by foreigners with little or no acquaintance with it.

The first of these injustices is that visitors to Japan often assume, after brief experience, that it takes much longer to say anything in Japanese than it does in English. They may ask one short question in English and then be dismayed to hear their interpreter use five or six or even more Japanese sentences (or what sound to them like sentences) to transmit that one question to a non-English-speaking Japanese.

But what is usually happening in such instances is that the interpreter is using the additional verbiage to explain differences in customs and outlook. Let us say you visit Japan for the first time with a letter of introduction to a non-English-speaking Japanese businessman and that you call on him at his office with an interpreter. After several minutes of introductory conversation, you have the interpreter say to him, "I'd like to take you and your wife out to dinner tonight."

In Japanese that sentence should be no longer than it is in English, if as long: *"Komban anata to okusama o yushoku ni oyobi shitai ndesu."* With only those words, however, the Japanese businessman may be puzzled. Why should this American visitor want to ask his *wife* out to dinner? That is unheard of. So the interpreter may have decided to offer the additional explanation that such an invitation is the custom in the United States—to forestall any puzzlement.

This agreed on, you may say through your interpreter, "I'll meet you at seven." In polite Japanese, this need be only three words: *"Shichiji ni aimasho,"* but again the interpreter may have decided, with mutual harmony in mind, to add that "when an American says seven, he generally means seven—and not seven-twenty or so."

Even if you instructed your interpreter to translate only your exact words and nothing else (which, by the way, is not recommended), you might still have this apparently excessive verbiage. Suppose, at the restaurant you go to, you ask the Japanese businessman's wife if she likes, say, cottage cheese. The interpreter would say *koteji chiizu* for cottage cheese, but he still might have to explain what it is, just as the Japanese might have to explain to you what bean curd (English for *tofu*) is.

Nor is it necessarily true that it takes longer to write anything in Japanese than in English. For instance, it takes us thirteen strokes to print "person," while it takes the Japanese only two to print their equivalent: 人. It takes four for "go" and six for 行, which means "go". Ten for "town" and seven for 町 Sixteen for "bridge" and sixteen for 橋. They average out to be about even.

Many foreigners throw up their hands in horror at the idea of learning the Chinese characters, which are admittedly formidable, but a recent study revealed that between 7 and 11 percent of American school children experience significant difficulty in learning to read, whereas the comparable figure for Japan is less than one percent. The cause for our poor showing is attributed to the abstract nature of our alphabet, in contrast to the pictorial nature of theirs. Our children simply have to learn, for example, that the letter *A* represents certain sounds, although they can see no apparent connection between the letter and the sound. We also have confusing "mirror-image" letters such as *q* and *g*, *b* and *d*, while such words as *no* and *on*, *was* and *saw* look somewhat alike but are in no way related.

In Japanese, the Chinese characters are direct descendants of pictures of the objects themselves. Notice how these pictograms evolved: from 山 to 山 to 山 , which means mountain. From ☉ to ⊖ to ⊖ to 日 , which means sun. From 子 to 子 to 子 to 子 , which means child. From 木 to 木 to 木 ,which means tree.

Two or more of these pictograms could be fused to represent an abstract idea (or ideogram): Take a man (亻 in radical form) and lean him against a tree (木) and we get the ideogram (休) meaning *yasumu,* or to rest. Take a person (人) and put him in a box (囗) and we get (囚), meaning *shujin,* or prisoner. Take one woman (女), add two more (女女), and we have the ideogram (姦) for *kashimashii,* or noisy.

Initially the Chinese characters may look like a wild jumble of strokes, dots, squares, and circles; nevertheless there is method in this madness, and it comes from what is called the radical system. The characters are made up of one or more of 214 elements, which are also called radicals. The radicals often, but not always, serve to identify the character, at least in general terms. 木 is the radical for tree or wood, and any character containing this radical is likely to represent an object made of wood or a variety of tree. For example, 梯 means ladder, 板 means board, 櫻 means cherry tree, and 槍 means spear.

Knowing the characters in Japanese can be compared to

knowing the root-languages of English (Greek, Latin, and so forth), for then one has little trouble comprehending otherwise difficult vocabulary. I remember, for instance, that I was well along in my study of Chinese characters in school when we were given the compound word *nomakuen* and its English equivalent *encephalitis*. Although I had never met the word *encephalitis* in English, I understood the meaning immediately because I knew the meaning of the three individual characters for *no-maku-en:* brain-membrane-inflammation. And during the many intervening years, I have often been able to understand the meaning of an unfamiliar word in English from its equivalent in Japanese, when the two were given side by side.

Lastly, I would call into question the ridicule that we sometimes aim at Japanese honorifics in cartoons ("Oh, honorable sir, so sorry, please!") and in books (like *The Honorable Picnic,* in which altogether too many things were called "honorable this" and "honorable that"). The Japanese honorific prefixes are *o-*, *go-* and, rarely, *on-*. Only one or two letters, and just one syllable. Even if two or three of them are used in a sentence, they are hardly noticeable. But translate one of these short honorifics into the nine-letter word *honorable* and cram three of them into one sentence ("Shall I ask your honorable wife to bring you some honorable tea and honorable rice?") —and the result is ridiculous.

Furthermore, the use of these honorifics often actually makes it possible to omit other words. If we are talking about hats (the word for *hat* is *boshi*), you will know that by saying *oboshi* ("honorable hat," as it were), I mean *your* hat and that by saying *boshi* without the initial *o*, I mean *my* hat. Without this device, I would have to say *anata no boshi* to mean *your hat,* which is longer by six letters (or two characters) than *oboshi,* and *watakushi no boshi* to mean *my hat.*

Because both English and Japanese are such difficult languages, with entirely different historical, social, and cultural backgrounds, it should come as no surprise to learn that more than a few truly awesome mistakes have been made in converting one into the other; mistakes that have caused incalculable damage or misunderstanding.

For instance, shortly before Japan's formal surrender, Prime Minister Kantaro Suzuki used the word *mokusatsu* when speaking of the Potsdam Declaration, which Cabinet Secretary Sakomizu took to mean "No comment." The Domei News Agency, however, translated the word as "ignore," and foreign newspapers went a step further and reported it as "reject," thus probably lengthening the war.

Shortly after the war, Prince Konoye called on General Douglas MacArthur to discuss the organization or make-up of Japan's postwar government. For "organization," Konoye had used the word *kosei,* which dictionaries usually translate into English as *organization, composition,* or *constitution.* Unfortunately, the interpreter chose *constitution* to convey the meaning of *kosei,* and MacArthur took this to mean that Konoye was proposing a new constitution for Japan: a possibility which instantly caught the imagination of the U.S. Supreme Commander. Perhaps he envisioned himself as going down in history's pages as the "Father of the New Constitution." No matter that the Japanese already had the Meiji Constitution. No matter that Konoye had not for a moment intended to suggest its replacement. MacArthur swept ahead to embrace the idea enthusiastically and push it through to reality. A nation's principal document of purpose, authority, and organization was thus born from an interpreter's mistaken nuance.

More recently, when Nixon and Prime Minister Sato were discussing the thorny textile problem, Sato told the U.S. President, "I'll take care of it." Rightly or wrongly, Nixon took this as a promise by Sato that he would resolve the textile issue by appropriate action in Japan. When this didn't happen, Nixon was wrathful, concluding that he could not trust the Prime Minister—and perhaps by extension, any Japanese.

Sato, on the other hand, felt that he was misinterpreted, that all he had said in Japanese was that he would try his best to find a solution.

No matter how difficult it may be, the Japanese language is the one essential tool that the foreigner must possess to understand the Japanese people and their culture. About this there can be no question. Becoming fluent in spoken and written Japanese does not necessarily guarantee such understanding (although very few foreigners have learned the language well without having a great deal of knowledge about the customs and social attitudes of the people rub off on them), but it is the initial step—or mighty hurdle, if you prefer—that one must take if he is to travel the road that leads ultimately to significant comprehension. With the language as a tool, the student of Japanese affairs must go on to absorb as much as he can, through both formal schooling and firsthand experience or observation, of Japan's culture, politics, economy, geography, education, and society. Although his individual career plans will cause him to eventually emphasize one or two disciplines at the expense of others, he must nevertheless persist in a well-balanced multidisciplinary approach to Japan, at least until a firm foundation has been constructed.

The number of Caucasian Americans who have become such "Japan Specialists" or who have become genuinely fluent in Japanese remains pitifully small, despite the several million Americans who have spent time in that country since 1945. (Of more than one thousand U.S. businessmen in Tokyo, perhaps three are fluent enough to make an impromptu speech in Japanese.) Here, as elsewhere, "language difficulty is at the root of more problems than man dreams."

Oddly enough, however, the first-time visitor to Japan may meet there an impressive number of Americans who are introduced to him as being "fluent in Japanese." Not long ago an American businessman came to see me in Japan with a letter of introduction, and I met him at his hotel one day for lunch. While we were eating, he told me what he had had been doing since his arrival and happened to mention that he had been invited to dinner the previous night at the home of an American, whom I shall call Mr. Leonard, and his Japanese wife. I knew the couple quite well and listened with interest while the visitor told me about his evening there.

"I enjoyed myself very much," the visitor told me. "Say, Leonard speaks Japanese like a native, doesn't he?"

"Oh? I didn't know that," I said. (The Leonard I knew didn't speak much Japanese at all.)

"Sure he does. Wait now, are you sure we're talking about the same man: tall, about thirty-five, with a scar over his left eye?"

I nodded.

"Well, *that* Leonard knows Japanese, let me tell you. Why, he talked Japanese to his wife all evening."

"Oh?"

"Sure, he has to. She doesn't speak a word of English."

With that, I changed the subject, but the point of the story is that Leonard's wife had graduated with honors from the English Literature Course at the Sacred Heart School, had won first prize in an English speech contest held among all college women in the Tokyo area, and had worked as a ticket saleswoman at the counter of an American airline. She knew a hundred, maybe even a thousand times more English than her husband knew Japanese.

What had happened, it later developed, was that Leonard was looking for a better job, and he and his wife were inviting every visiting American they met who might conceivably want to establish a branch office in Japan to their home for a carefully staged performance designed to demonstrate a highly exaggerated version of Leonard's ability in Japanese.

If you meet ten Americans in Japan who are described to you as being "fluent in Japanese," you will be fortunate if even one of them approaches actually being so. The remaining nine will range from having almost no knowledge at all to a vocabulary of two or three hundred words in Japanese, often misused and mispronounced. The reason why such false reputations gain and retain currency is twofold. One, it is the nature of the Japanese themselves to say that any foreigner who can ask for a drink of water in Japanese is very good in their language (*taihen ojozu desu, ne*). In fact, in all my years in Japan, I can seldom remember hearing any Japanese make of an American such judgments as "his Japanese is poor," "he doesn't speak much Japanese," or "her Japanese is elementary." It seems that it is almost never in them to make such criticisms about individual foreigners. (Recently a Japanese friend and I were discussing a mutual American acquaintance who has a smattering of "kitchen Japanese," and this Japanese friend remarked, "Tom? Yes, I know him. He speaks very good Japanese, doesn't he?" He paused for a moment to reflect, then added, "But I understand very little of what he says.") Two, the Americans in Japan who make or pass on such judgments seldom know enough Japanese to have any idea at all how much any other American knows about the language.

I myself know only five Caucasian Americans (I keep using the word *Caucasian* to distinguish them from Americans of Japanese ancestry who, for several reasons, are in a class by themselves) whom I consider to be well-qualified Japan Specialists or, if you prefer, Japan Area and Language Experts. (Genuine fluency in Japanese is implicit in both titles.) For the past thirty years I have had a deep interest in American students of things Japanese and have met many of them in the six Japanese language schools that I attended. Later, in Japan, I met or heard of others in my work and in my social contacts, but I believe that the five mentioned above must constitute a large percentage of the genuine experts to be found in either the United States or Japan.

There are several cogent reasons why so few Americans have mastered the Japanese tongue:

1) The language is admittedly formidable. Not impossible, but definitely very difficult.

2) Since World War Two, we have had no training program, civilian or military, capable of producing such linguists. (The Defense Language Institute's full forty-seven-week course is grossly inadequate; two and a half years of exclusive study should be considered the absolute minimum.)

3) During World War Two several military language schools started at least two thousand Americans on the road to such linguistic ability, but very few of these students followed through on the start they had been given. For those who wanted to make a career of what we then called Japan Area and Language work, not enough rewarding jobs existed to justify their sustained interest, especially after the end of the Occupation. There were some jobs for historians, economists, sociologists, geographers, and what not—to which the desirability of Japanese-language ability was added, like an afterthought, but almost none for Japan Specialists as such. With few such jobs, there were few such Specialists. Or perhaps it was the other way around, like the question of the egg or the chicken. In either case, the result did not vary.

4) As a people, we take the learning of a foreign culture and language (except perhaps the familiar European ones) far too lightly. We simply have no concept of what is involved. Our national temperament is such that we cannot commit ourselves to the many years of study and mind-bending effort required to cope with a language like Japanese. Our national approach to language study is "two years in college" or "three evenings a week for six months." Told that it might very well take eight hours a day for two or three years *plus* even longer years of residence and practice, we boggle—and begin to look around for interpreters (a futile alternative), or talk about its not really being so necessary to know Japanese, or utter some poppycock about most of the people in Japan speaking English, anyway.

5) Anthony Burgess once said that the British are suspicious of linguistic ability, associating it with spies, impresarios, waiters, and Jewish refugees, and it is regrettable that we

Americans are not entirely free of this taint, either. Only too often we tend to view with distaste and uneasiness any among us who become too intimate with a foreign culture and language, especially one outside the more acceptable French, Spanish, German, and Italian bloc. We suggest contemptuously that such Americans have "gone native." Art Buchwald, in his column from Paris, once quoted Air Force Major General W. T. Hefley as saying that he saw no advantage in employing American civilians who are familiar with a foreign country and its language. "If an American knows the local language," the general continued, "he may be injecting wrong ideas into his dealing with the natives."

The concerned observer of this comprehension gap between Japan (as well as other Asiatic countries) and the United States may well ask where the harm lies. Granting that we have almost no Americans who are genuinely expert in Japanese affairs, where and how does this hurt us?

For one thing, because almost none of our diplomats, businessmen, and foreign correspondents are qualified as Japan Specialists, we must rely on Japanese interpretation and translation for explanations of all that concerns both countries. Even assuming that the Japanese are honest in their attempts at explanation, we are still communicating on their terms and from their viewpoint. Although this is not always necessarily bad, it bears an analogy to a baseball team that must play all its games in its opponents' ball park. Disadvantages, friction, and misunderstandings inevitably arise without our own team of experts to explain and judge, to analyze and advise—from *our* point of view.

Let no one think that no blunders, no crises, no tragic misunderstandings have marred the course of our relations with Japan since 1945. There have been only too many, beginning with some notable examples made under the auspices of the Occupation Forces and later encompassing government-level conflicts of interest, opinion, and policy that could have been solved or at least vastly alleviated by the placement of

Japan Specialists in effective positions. In the private business sector, the tragic mistakes are even more numerous. I know of more than twenty American companies that have failed in Japan simply because they did not seek the services and advice of Japan Specialists, evidently preferring to rely on men from their home offices who may have had, for example, a good record for selling soap in Hoboken but who knew next to nothing about selling soap—or even setting up a branch office—in Japan. Since such companies do not advertise their failures, I cannot help assuming that their actual number is much, much larger.

At the level of the individual American living in Japan, language frustration poses a very real danger. No American living in Japan who does not speak good Japanese can escape this danger entirely, except perhaps by spending all his time in those small islands of American culture there, such as the American Club and the Press Club. Elsewhere, he is continually beset by the thought that something is going on that he should know about but can't quite get to the bottom of. He strongly suspects that his secretary's explanation of the reason why the taxation office wants a new report on their office expenses for last year is not quite the whole story and that the maid's version of what the neighbor next door said about his wife is not entirely logical, but there seems to be nothing he can reasonably do to get a fuller explanation. And he is sure that those two Japanese toughs said something insulting to him and his Japanese secretary when they walked out of their office building together last evening, but she pretended not to understand whatever it was they said, so he hesitated to make an issue of it. These are not isolated incidents occurring perhaps once a month. They happen every day. The more contact one has with the Japanese, the more frequently these disturbing questions arise. Even in his attempts to understand major events in Japan, the local American must rely largely on the four principal English-language dailies, which, it has been charged, avoid shocking their foreign readers with outspoken and factual presentation of the news. Past Ambassador to Japan Edwin O. Reischauer often warned his American friends that they were wrong if they thought they knew Japan because they read the English dailies published there. (According to the June, 1967, number of *The Atlantic,* Mr. Reischauer has also said, "I carefully read the best American papers and magazines, but, if I did not have an airmail edition of a Japanese language paper and other current materials sent to me from Tokyo, I would feel in the dark as to what is happening there. . . . I sometimes feel that, in our newspapers, Japan is the least adequately reported country in the whole world. . . . Its importance to us as our second largest trading partner in the world and our chief ally in Asia is obvious, but our press gives it far less space than to any of our other major allies. . . . We are served in our papers only the sketchiest outline of political developments in Japan, with little depth on important undercurrents, and a rather tired round of the same old color stories—Zengakuren, Sokagakkai, and neon lights on the Ginza—but little of the real news of developing Japanese attitudes and actions that could well affect our future in Asia.")

Mr. Reischauer's point about the "rather tired round of the same old color stories" is well taken. Were we to add several more (Kabuki, geisha, Hiroshima revisited, flower arrangement, judo, cherry blossoms, the absence of street names, kamikaze cabdrivers, karate, and Mount Fuji), we would have boxed the compass, for these are the topics about which most of our nonacademic writers on Japan concern themselves. Books that undertake to explain this alien culture to us are so few that one of the best (which is nonetheless imperfect) was written by a woman who had never been to Japan (*The Chrysanthemum and The Sword*, by Ruth Benedict), while another (*Things Japanese,* by Basil Hall Chamberlain) was written before the turn of the century and is still in frequent use, thanks, no doubt, to its lack of competition.

Again quoting the June, 1967, *Atlantic:* "James William

Morley, director of Columbia University's East Asian Institute, lamented recently after a year spent in Japan, 'I can only say that it is shocking to return from that center of dynamism, which seems destined by every measure of educational, intellectual, aesthetic, economic, and political attainment and by every indicator of potential power to be not only *the* great power of Asia but, in the course of the next twenty years, to become one of the three greatest powers in the world, and find the American people abysmally uninformed and unprepared for the future this portends.' " The magazine's writer also supports Mr. Morley by saying ". . . as far as most Americans are concerned, their major Pacific ally [Japan] is all but unknown."

In making unbiased, dispassionate appraisals of the Japanese and their culture, we are further hampered by two other factors, which I identify as The Rush to Judgment and The Compulsion Toward the Interview Technique. Under the influence of the former, we are too reckless in our haste to form sweeping conclusions about Japan. Although we have been in Japan only a few months or even a year or so, we like to leave with a suitcase filled with conclusive, revelatory explanations for every facet of this country that has baffled the West. Yet, judging from my own experience, I doubt that such conclusions are possible for anyone without at least ten years of residence *among* the Japanese (not just in Japan) *plus* access to that all-important tool: the Japanese language in both its spoken and written forms.

The latter—The Compulsion Toward the Interview Technique—affects not only journalists, writers, and researchers but also diplomats, businessmen, and academics. Under its baneful spell, the foreigner seeks the answers to what he wants to know about Japan by the direct and the elsewhere-logical avenue of interrogating Japanese individuals with searching probes. ("How do you feel about America?" "Do you approve of democracy?" "What is your opinion about student unrest?") To such confrontations, the Japanese will all too often respond with evasion, indirection, vagueness, silence, ambiguity, prevarication, or rebuff.

What the seeker after the heart and soul of Japan must do instead is to gird himself with the proper tools (language and formal Japan studies), sharpen his perceptions keenly, immerse himself in the daily life of the average Japanese, and then wait for true understanding of the country and its people to come to him. It may be slow in coming, it may be hard to recognize at first and, contrary to the fond expectations of the Japanese themselves, it may not be wholly or even mostly favorable in its conclusions about them, but eventually such comprehensions will begin to seep through and at last fill the receptable to a sufficient depth.

10

Their Religions

The Western visitor to Japan who asks a Japanese acquaintance his religion (a question not often asked among the Japanese) would be puzzled if the Japanese should answer that he is at once both a Shintoist and a Buddhist. Perplexed, the visitor might then refer himself to a reliable book of statistics and learn that out of a 100,000,000 population, the number of Japanese who say they are Shintoists is 77,000,000 and the number who say that they are Buddhists is 65,000,000.

As this same visitor travels around Japan, he will be impressed by the outward evidences of religion, e.g., 180,000 buildings of worship in an area the size, as I've noted, of the state of California, which has about 25,000. In addition, he will see myriad roadside gods, *torii,* altars, stone lanterns, and other odds and ends of statuary with religious significance, not counting the millions of altars in homes. Yet, if he pursues his inquiry, he will be accurately informed that the National Character Study Committee (organized by the National Institute of Statistical Mathematics) reported as a conclusion of its extensive 1963 survey that 69 percent of the Japanese people do not consider themselves "religious" and that for young people this percentage should be raised to 90.

Many years before this survey was made, however, Westerners had already agreed with this assessment and had characterized the Japanese as "irreligious," "indifferent to religion," "undevotional by temperament," and even outright "agnostic," although it should be borne in mind that these descriptions were offered from the standpoint of the Western world of Christianity. When we see a Japanese bow before a temple or shrine with a smile on his face, we often rush to the judgment that here is an irreverent mocker ready to poke fun at the institutions of his shallow religion. When thunder, flame, and minatory predictions do not emanate from the pulpit or its equivalent, we may question whether this is really a religion or merely a set of easy-to-live-with accommodations casually but cunningly contrived by the Powers of Darkness. We suspect that a religion that does not stir, harass, prod, and exhort its adherents is one that will sit too lightly on their backs and will be too readily set aside when convenience or evil dictates.

This suspicion deepens when we learn that the Japanese have no equivalents of our day of worship or our Sunday church services, that their prayers pay more heed to form than to content, that they have no concept of a universal Messiah, that they do not grapple with evil, that they are careless of the notion of a life after death, and that their religious holidays and observances are, by and large, continued and valued more as community gatherings and social events. In sum, we find that the Japanese have tended to mold their religions to fit their way of life rather than the reverse.

But however heartily Christians may disapprove of—or at least view with darkling thoughts—Buddhism and Shintoism, the Japanese do not return us this courtesy, for their approach to all religions has been fundamentally tolerant and eclectic. Their persuasions—except Nichiren Shoshu and imported Christianity—are not mutually exclusive. Sometimes called a "museum of religions," Japan has generally, with only a few lapses, held its doors open to all religions that care to test their demotic appeal in the arena of their archipelago. Article 20 of their new (1946) Constitution decrees that "Freedom of religion is guaranteed to all," and Japanese magistrates have upheld this provision with fairness and scrupulosity. Nor would it be just to assume that freedom of religion was a new concept force-fed to the Japanese by our forces of Occupation, since they were demonstrating a remarkable degree of religious tolerance four hundred years ago when they permitted St. Francis Xavier and the Catholic missionaries who followed him to proselytize freely within their boundaries and, again, nine hundred years before that when they embraced another alien religion, Buddhism, with pronounced fervor.

Not only do the Japanese permit all religions free entry into their land but most of them also allow at least two religions to enter their homes and private lives. The average Japanese will be taken to a Shinto shrine to be blessed shortly after he is born and in later years he will probably be married by a Shinto priest. When he enters schools, his parents may accompany him to a Shinto shrine dedicated to the memory of a renowned scholar to pray for good grades. Should he become sickly, he may well visit either a Buddhist temple or a Shinto shrine that is known for its divine powers of healing. When he dies, a Buddhist priest will probably officiate at his funeral services and cremation, after which his ashes will find their final lodging in a Buddhist cemetery.

This religious parallelism is seen most clearly in the many homes that maintain both *butsudan* (Buddhist altars) and *kamidana* (Shinto god shelves), which may be serviced daily or only on days of particular religious meaning with offerings of food, flowers, and rice wine and with incense and candles. Odd though it may seem to Westerners, acceptance of the rituals of two religions indicates neither confusion nor inner conflict in the average Japanese. He can live with both, while they coexist in peace and harmony and complement one another in strengthening and sanctifying the family, the community, and the nation itself.

The precedent for this pluralistic concept of religion dates back to A.D. 552, when Buddhism—in the form of sutras and images of Buddha sent as gifts by the King of Paikche in what is now Korea—first came to Japan, which had known only Shinto until then. Prince Shotoku (whose portrait now appears on one-, five-, and ten-thousand yen notes) was able to convince his mother, the Empress Regnant Suiko, that Shinto and Buddhism would not clash with each other because Shinto was the religion of things past and Buddhism that of the future. This oversimplification does not quite hold water, but it was evidently sufficient to persuade the Empress, with whose blessing Buddhism was empowered to sweep through the aristocracy and subsequently to be exalted to the position of state religion. (It did not, however, actually become popular among the masses until the thirteenth century.) Buddhist priests further enhanced this syncretism by declaring ex cathedra that the gods of the Shinto pantheon were actually manifestations of the Buddhas (meaning persons who have achieved nirvana, or enlightenment) already enshrined in Buddhist temples in Korea, China, and India.

It was India in which Buddhism originated but which is today held in spiritual thrall by other religions entirely. Gautama Siddhartha, an Indian ascetic, was born there in 466 B.C., the son of the ruler of a small agricultural republic called Sakya at the base of the Himalayas. At the age of twenty-nine he renounced earthly pleasures and set out to find universal truth, thereby becoming a Boddhisattva (one who is seeking truth). After attaining Buddhahood, he traveled about India for forty years teaching that man's sufferings are caused by his desires and can be eliminated only by detachment. He told his disciples that the soul goes through a cycle of rebirths, the rewards of the next life being determined by the good works of the present one. Despite the implied possibility of pleasant existences, this cycle is basically one of distress. To achieve enlightenment is to end the cycle, and then all sufferings cease. His dying words were "All things are transitory." Nothing supernatural is attributed to his life.

The sutras—Buddhist scriptures that are usually chanted —were written in the succeeding centuries as the religion began to undergo many changes, the principal one of which was its division into Mahayana and Hinayana Buddhism.

Mahayana, or Great Vehicle, Buddhism was the one that reached Japan at the date mentioned earlier, A.D. 552, and was adopted by the Soga clan as a tool in their rivalry against the Mononobe family.

Buddhism's subsequent fourteen hundred years of activity in Japan seem to reflect the very cycle of varying existences that Siddhartha taught. There were times when it was in absolute ascendancy and times when its future was indeed bleak. At times it was suffused with the gentle glow of art, harmony, good works, and peace, while at other times its bellicose monks from their temples atop Mount Hiei descended like a pack of wolves in full cry on Kyoto and swept through the streets of the Imperial capital to emphasize their rigorous demands upon the Court. But above all else the role of Buddhism during those long centuries should be remembered as that of the teacher under whose sometimes kindly, sometimes harsh tutelage Japan grew up. During much of that time all education and care of the sick were in Buddhist hands, and its practitioners introduced art and medicine and deeply influenced most spheres of social, political, and intellectual activity.

Although there has been a plethora of subsects and other splinterings in Buddhism, the present principal sects are Tendai, Shingon, Jodo, Shin, Zen, and Nichiren. The lay organization of Nichiren—the Soka Gakkai—is discussed under New Religions later in this chapter. Zen—the word itself means silent meditation—is apparently the most interesting to Westerners.

Zen Buddhism was established in Japan primarily through the efforts of two monks, Eisai (1141–1215) and Dogen (1200–1253), who brought it back with them from China. Its emphasis on self-discipline, austerity, and meditation appealed to both the samurai and the educated classes. Instead of scriptures or sermons, it depends on intuitive thought (as contrasted with intellectual speculation) which can lead to an aesthetic, instantaneously achieved flood of apperception of the reality of the universe. This may be years in coming, but when, early or late, it is transmitted through a kind of spiritual telepathy, the believer is overwhelmed by this sudden revelation and can then enter into a condition of mystical self-intoxication which allows him to transcend consciousness of his Self and become one with the Universe. In this state, the mind of the believer becomes a holy void and he can ignore the vicissitudes and calamities of life, even as the Indian priest who brought Zen from India to China in A.D. 520 sat and stared in silence at a blank wall for nine years.

The essence of Zen teaching is: "Look within thee; thou thyself art Buddha."

Before considering the influence that this and other religions have had over the thought and attitudes of the Japanese, both past and present, it would be well to emphasize that such influences are seldom delineated and set apart from those of other religions. Instead, the lines of demarcation have become blurred over the years, for Japanese religious influences are like streams in a broad, flat, soft-soil plain, now and again joining forces to erode a wider bed, then later separating to seek out other individualistic paths to pursue. Farther on, one stream may weaken and be absorbed by another, only to gain vigor from this confluence and strike out on its own again later.

Prince Shotoku, who has been called the Father of Japanese Civilization, is supposed to have remarked that Shinto, Buddhism, and Confucianism form the tree that is Japan. Shinto is the root (the character of the people and their national traditions), Confucianism the trunk and branches (code of ethics, educational systems, and legal institutions), and Buddhism the fruit and flowers (the flowers of spiritual life and the fruit of religious sentiment). Although there was a sharp break between Buddhism and the other religions beginning in the fifteenth century, these three systems have over the centuries become closely and subtly interwoven in the minds and hearts of the Japanese to the extent that it is safe to say that no Japanese is entirely unaffected by the influence of any one of the three, consciously or unconsciously.

As noted above, Buddhism has influenced most spheres of social, political, religious, and intellectual activity in Japan. By extending Prince Shotoku's analogy about the tree of Japanese life, one could say that what was the fruit and flower (Buddhism) of the tree in Shotoku's time produced seeds that in time became the roots, trunk, and branches of other trees throughout the forests of Japan.

Buddhism was the means by which much Chinese and Korean culture was brought to Japan. Its first truly significant influence on the Japanese was that it taught them to think more deeply on the problems and meaning of human existence. It contributed to the language itself and to the spread of its use, through which its priests then taught the people the elements of philosophy, logic, and the natural sciences as they were then understood on the continent. Although the Japanese concept of political institutions had its source in Confucianism, it was the Buddhists who delivered these concepts to the Japanese and interpreted and expatiated on them. In the field of the arts Buddhism extended itself far and deep. Not only did it influence all the arts but it even created some of them. Japanese sculpture is almost entirely a Buddhistic product, while architecture and the neat simplicity of the interior of present-day Japanese homes lag not far behind. The most famous names from Japan's finest era of painting belong to Buddhist priests. Its influence is also strong in music, which is little appreciated by the Western ear, and although poetic forms may owe more to Shinto, the point of view is more often Buddhistic. It contributed to Bushido (see below) the ideas of negation of self and asceticism, thus raising the proper samurai above the level of the pleasure-bent robber baron of the Middle Ages in Europe and assisting many of them to become learned and capable administrators of the Tokugawa and early Meiji periods.

But it is in the fields of religion and philosophy that Buddhism brought its most significant gifts to the people of Japan. Not only did it import its own beliefs but Buddhism also, in accordance with its code of tolerance, gave other religions a helping hand along the way. Its priests helped to propagate Confucianism for the desired orderly society that it would bring and let Shinto live at a time when, in Buddhism's ascendancy, the imported code might well have been able to crush the native one. It has provided its Japanese believers with the comfort and assurance of eternal salvation and has instilled a sense of close relationship between the living and the dead. And it enlarged and raised the conception of man's destiny and the ways by which it can be achieved.

Before the advent of Buddhism in the sixth century, the only Japanese religion was a poorly defined body of native rituals and beliefs that were without even a name. (Later it was called Shinto, or the Way of the Gods, to distinguish it from Buddhism.) The Japanese believed that there existed a spiritual essence in all animate and inanimate objects as well as in the forces of nature and even such phenomena as the echo. For one reason or another, they respected, even revered a great many of these spiritual essences, including some believed to exist in objects and forces neither pleasant nor beneficial. The more awe-inspiring, extraordinary, mysterious, superior, or even malignant the vessel, the more likely it was that the Japanese regarded its essence—its *kami*—with respect.

Some understanding of the word *kami* is necessary in any attempt to grasp Shinto. Originally it meant "above" and by extension, "superior." Because the Japanese bowed low before the objects whose spiritual essences they revered, these essences came to be called *kami*. Later, when Chinese writing was brought to Japan, one *kanji,* or character (上), was assigned to the *kami* that meant *above,* while another (神) was given to the one that meant *spiritual essence.* Centuries afterwards, as Western learning began to flow into Japan, various English translations were made of the *kami* that originally meant spiritual essence, among them being mind, spirit, God or god, soul, deity, and superior being. When Christian missionaries sought a Japanese word to convey our concept of one omniscient Creator—for which there was no equivalent in any of the erstwhile Japanese religions—they had no choice but to use *kami* (to which they added the respectful suffix *sama*). Our Christian God thereby became *Kami* or *Kami-sama,* but then this translation proved to be a two-way street. Upon learning that the Christian God was called *Kami,* other foreign students of things Japanese too readily assumed, when they heard a Japanese use the word *kami* in speaking about his own religions, that he meant God as we use the word. Not soul or spirit or spiritual essence or even god—but God. And if a Japanese happened to mention that he regarded his Emperor as a *kami* (contrary to all other Japanese, the Emperor alone had this status while living), the Westerner interpreted this to mean that the Emperor stood in relation to the Japanese as God Almighty stands to us.

To be sure, the Emperor of Japan was more, much more, than what is implied by the two words "superior being." He and the Emperors who preceded him stand very high in the Shinto pantheon, lower only perhaps than the mythological group of deities that created Japan, but even so he could not be equated with the one supreme Christian God.

In addition to the long line of Emperors, the spirits of winds, storms, rivers, mountains, and even stones were regarded as *kami,* as were deceased national heroes, famous scholars and officials, real and imagined ancestors, clan chieftains, and others. Toward most of these *kami,* the Japanese felt love and gratitude and often a desire to placate or console. They installed them in countless locations throughout the country and venerated them with offerings, prayers, and obeisances. They asked the intercession of appropriate *kami* for success in war, bountiful crops, and fertile wives. Prior to these acts of reverence, they were especially careful to cleanse themselves physically and to seek ceremonial purification after contact with such "defilements" as wounds, illness, sexual intercourse, menstruation and death.

Each clan had a *kami* (called *ujigami*) which it came to regard as its own tutelary deity. This *kami* may or may not have been an actual clan ancestor. If Clan A defeated Clan B in war, Clan A's tutelary deity assumed a position higher than that of Clan B in the rudimentary hierarchy of *kami* then forming. One particular *kami* of the sun (later called Amaterasu Omikami, or the Sun Goddess) was the tutelary deity of a clan from whom the present Emperor is descended, and as the power of this clan rose, so rose the ranking of the Sun Goddess, who became at length the central deity in Shinto.

After the coming of Buddhism with all its gorgeous ritual, exalted moral code, impressive temple architecture, profound metaphysics, adventitious gift of a written language, body of sutras, history even then a thousand years old, and concomitant offering of arts and general knowledge, Shinto, as might be expected, went into a sharp decline. That the Buddhist priests did not stamp it out entirely is plain indication of the benevolent nature of their religion. Instead, they let it live and even recognized, as noted above, many of its *kami* as manifestations of their own Buddhas.

This stage of low posture for Shinto continued until about 1700, when a reaction set in and such scholars as Hirata, Mabuchi, and Motoori illumined the way for a national revival of interest in and respect for all that was old and all that was indigenous. Shinto was rejuvenated, while Confucianism and Buddhism were scorned. After the Meiji Restoration in 1868, Shinto's fortunes rose even more swiftly, for the new national government in Tokyo decided to utilize it as a tool in the accomplishment of one of their most important tasks: that of unifying the nation and instilling patriotism in the people.

During the Tokugawa Era, which ended in 1868, Japan had been a loose federation of small and large fiefs, the chiefs

of some of which were closely allied to the Tokugawa shogunal family, the de facto rulers, by blood or marriage, while
the chiefs of others were cool or even hostile to the Tokugawa
and were held in check by a system of hostages, spies, heavy
taxation, and, of course, military prowess. In theory, all Japanese paid homage to the Shogun in Edo and, beyond him, to
the dim figure of the Emperor, surrounded by his often effete
and sometimes poor court, in Kyoto, but in actual practice
whatever loyalty the average Japanese could muster focused
on the feudal hierarchy in his own fief.

With the restoration of the Emperor Meiji, the fiefs were
abolished and the daimyo, or feudal lords, dethroned. The
dedicated leaders of the new government that had wrested
control of the country from the Tokugawa dynasty realized
that, in order to compete with the Western powers which, led
by the United States, had shouldered open Japan's long-closed
portals, they would have to inculcate in the people a spirit of
national unity and purpose and of patriotic devotion as well
as an eagerness to strive and even to sacrifice self for country.
Although they had an Emperor at whom to direct this national
devotion, his throne and glory were tarnished from long
neglect. They were in need of an implement with which to
restore, polish, and enhance his nimbus, and the implement
they selected was their ethnic religion: the Way of the Gods.

One of their first acts was to divide Shinto into the sub-
divisions of State Shinto and Sectarian Shinto, with the latter
retaining most of the religious aspects of the preceding form
and the former becoming a suprasectarian arm of government
whose true purpose would have been more adequately revealed
had it been named, say, the National Bureau for the Implan-
tation and Promotion of Unquestioning Patriotism. In 1884,
the government declared that State Shinto was not a religion
at all but a cult, thus removing it from competition with
proper religions, arranged direct and ample financing for its
priests and facilities, and, as if it still had not made its point
clear, forbade the priests from preaching any religious dogma.

It was as if the U.S. Congress had sponsored and financed a "Love America Society," in which all Americans automatically became members and whose leaders were charged with, among other things, the supervision of frequent recitations of the Pledge of Allegiance by all citizens and of properly respectful flag-raising ceremonies, management of Arlington National Cemetery, maintenance of historic battlefields, encouragement of military service and ardor, group singing of "The Star Spangled Banner" in theaters and other places of public assembly, and formal teaching of a glorified version of our national history in which many of our presidents and generals were raised to godhead status.

In December of 1945, however, our Occupation Forces caused the government of Japan to withdraw all official support from State Shinto, whose priests and properties thereupon coalesced with Sectarian Shinto. Correctly identifying State Shinto with the Establishment that lost the Pacific War, the Japanese people turned cool overnight toward their former national religion, and the priests and shrines that had subsisted on governmental financing found themselves in grievous monetary trouble. To eke out the scanty contributions from diminishing adherents, they converted part of their precincts into parking lots, kindergartens, and wedding halls. One—the Karasawasan Shrine in Tochigi Prefecture—began raising grapes, peaches, mushrooms, and hogs for the tourist trade and then expanded its income potential with a hotel and a golf course.

Nowadays, however, Shinto is regaining strength and has 200,000 priests in 99,000 shrines with, as noted before, 77,000,000 adherents. Although it never had anything comparable to our Bible, its priests are now being trained to transmit to their parishioners a growing body of Shinto doctrine together with much of the traditional ethics that are no longer taught in schools. It has no images but uses instead symbols (for example, a stick with strips of paper attached to it) for its *kami*. It has no regular services, but ardent Shintoists may worship before the *kamidana* in their homes every day while the less devout may visit a shrine occasionally, especially on religious holidays and festivals. These acts of devotion at a shrine consist of rinsing the hands and mouth at the ablution basin, clapping the hands twice before the sanctuary to get the attention of the *kami*, bowing, praying silently, and leaving an offering. A priest may participate in more elaborate ceremonies, while the worshipper at home may only kneel, bow, and pray. The prayers are stereotyped expressions of appreciation and awareness of the bond between the living and the dead and between the individual and his community and nation. The worshipper does not specify his sins and ask forgiveness nor does he request certain blessings in return for which he will mend his ways. The central belief of Shinto is that man (that is, Japanese man) is innately good and that he should follow his genuine natural impulses.

Shinto shrines can be identified by the *torii* set before them. These are gateways of two upright wooden or concrete columns topped by two more cross-pieces, the higher of which curves gently upward. There are usually three of them, and they progressively purify the worshipper as he passes through each. *Torii* is written with two characters meaning "where the birds are," but this does not refer to an occasional bird's preference for the cross-pieces as a roosting site but to an ancient custom of hanging from them dead birds as offerings to the *kami*.

Prince Shotoku's analogy of Shinto with the roots of the Japanese tree is well taken, because Shinto extends deeply and widely into the soul of Japan, like the many roots of a banyan tree. More than a religion, Shinto has been called a "whole set of emotions and attitudes that influenced art, work, play, tastes, sex, colors, shapes, language, and everyday lore." Shinto is so all-pervasive that it functions like a second nature and, as such, may often pass unnoticed by even the Japanese themselves, to say nothing of foreigners.

Through its teachings about the origin of Japan and the

unbroken continuity of the Imperial line, it has specifically wrought a strong sense of national unity and social solidarity in the Japanese. In rural areas, it still acts as the most cohesive force in that the shrine is the center of most festivals and other community observances. With its emphasis on purification and the role of water therein, it has fostered and sustained the Japanese love of cleanliness. By teaching that there is a *kami,* or spiritual presence, in every tree, rock, hill, and stream, it is responsible for the pervading desire to appreciate and commune with nature, not to conquer it. With its emphasis on intuition and the subconscious knowledge of reality, it has saved the culture of Japan from becoming too entangled in the intricacies, unrealities, and static formalism of imported dogmas. Its emphasis on individual self-development, creative action, the reality of life, and the universality of the divine spirit has strongly influenced the development of Buddhism in Japan. The general association of beauty with practicality in the Japanese is a Shinto contribution, saving the Japanese from the often debilitating effects of addiction to art for art's sake. Shinto emphasis on vitality and creative effort is to be seen in much of the country's literature, while its compression of ideas and its avoidance of elaborate self-expressiveness are clearly reflected in the tanka and the haiku, those two brief poetic forms whose popularity is such that the Japanese may well be described as history's most poetic race. And Shinto interest in novelty, self-creativeness, and self-reliance is the force that has always enabled the Japanese to consider at least and perhaps to adopt imported religions, principles, systems, and technologies and not only to survive but even to succeed in this twentieth century.

Confucianism can be described as a semireligious system of ethics, a code of moral truths aimed at the establishment and maintenance of social and political order. Confucius based his teachings on the harmonious functioning of five relationships: those between father and son, ruler and subject, husband and wife, older and younger brothers, and friend and friend.

Although it was brought to Japan early in the Christian era, Confucianism lay largely dormant until the early part of the seventeenth century when Ieyasu, the first Tokugawa Shogun, recognized the Confucian classics as a source of the political and social stability he was seeking to establish and had them printed in Japan for the first time.

Whereas the father-son relationship had been given primacy in China (and had been the strength of the Chinese familial system), Tokugawa preferred that the Japanese give primary obedience to their rulers (to the clan chiefs and through them to the House of Tokugawa); but otherwise the Confucian teachings fitted in perfectly with how he thought feudal Japan should be governed. For the next two hundred and fifty years the entire intellect of the country was molded by the ideas of Confucius, himself a minor government official who had confined his teaching to the practical details of morals and government while avoiding extensive contemplation of the hereafter.

Although Confucianism can hardly be said to exist in Japan as a religion any longer (there is but one Confucian temple in all of Tokyo), its impress on the culture is unmistakable. Social harmony, political organization, moral teaching, and educational and legal institutions are among its contributions.

Confucianism further had a most meaningful influence on Bushido, or the Way of the Warrior. Almost a religion to the samurai, this code of theirs was such that their first thoughts each day were supposed to be focused on death, for the courage with which each died was the ultimate proof of his worth as a warrior, and he should, therefore, be prepared to meet death whenever it came his way. Inazo Nitobe wrote, "What Japan was she owed to the samurai. They were not only the flower of the nation but its roots as well. All the gracious gifts of Heaven flowed through them." While granting that Nitobe may have waxed over-enthusiastic on his favorite subject, it is nonetheless true that the samurai, influenced by their code and by Confucianism, contributed largely to government and society during Tokugawa days and during the early Meiji Era, when they had been shorn of their topknots and deprived of their two swords.

It was Sogo Yamaga who systematized Bushido by applying the principles of Confucius to military science and the life of the warrior. To loyalty and courage Yamaga added such Confucian virtues as serenity, magnanimity, discernment, firmness, and sincerity, for it was his aim to see the samurai expand beyond their role as swordsmen and bodyguards and become men of learning, capable of taking leading roles in civic administrations.

In 1549, three Jesuit missionaries landed in Kagoshima at the southern tip of Japan. To these Catholic priests, one of whom was St. Francis Xavier, must go the credit for bringing Christianity to Japan.

Between that year and 1635, these and other missionaries who followed did what was, on the surface at least, a truly remarkable job of converting Japanese to Christianity. In 1582, there were eighty missionaries and 150,000 converts in Japan, but by 1635, the year of the ultimate repression, the number of converts had grown to somewhere between 200,000 and 300,000 and included many daimyo, generals, and persons of cultural and material attainments.

Several factors, however, must be considered in connection with these reported conversions. First, certain similarities (candles, images, rosaries, altar flowers, incense, processions, and shaven heads of priests) between Catholicism and Buddhism led many Japanese to believe that the newly imported religion was still another of the numerous sects of Buddhism and, as such, had the approval of one thousand years of custom and familiarity. Second, the Japanese were quick to note that merchants with exotic commodities and firearms often accompanied the priests, so the many desiring to trade assumed that a warm welcome given the religious half of the team would result in reciprocity from the commercial half. Third, the priests devoted their staunchest efforts at proselytization to the feudal lords, who, if won over, sometimes ordered their subjects to become Christians en masse (and who were also known, when disappointed with the resultant benefits, to abruptly command their people to revert to Buddhism with equal ease). Last, the Christian timing was apt, for the powerful Nobunaga Oda (1543–1582) was trying to unify the country and welcomed the Christians as a weapon for use against the unruly Buddhist monasteries in and around Kyoto.

Although Nobunaga's successor Hideyoshi Toyotomi was at first tolerant of the Christians and their activities, his benignity turned to dark distrust when he was told by Protestant traders from England and Holland that the Catholic missionaries were harbingers of Spanish soldiery, who would, as in the case of Mexico and the Philippines, come to conquer while the priests converted. In 1587, Hideyoshi issued an edict banning Christianity but did not begin to enforce it until ten years later, when he had nine Catholic missionaries and seventeen Japanese converts crucified. (The Japanese courage and equanimity in the face of this difficult death is said to have exceeded that of their foreign mentors—the first time that Catholicism had encountered such fortitude in non-Europeans.)

Hideyoshi died before he could carry out his intent to suppress Christianity, and his successor Ieyasu Tokugawa was at first too beguiled by the potentialities of trade with Europe to take up the cudgels himself. At length, however, he too became suspicious and then antagonistic and so initiated a series of repressive measures that culminated in the massacre of more than 30,000 Christian converts in Shimabara in early 1638. (Some authorities believe that the Shimabara Rebellion drew as much momentum from economic and political unrest as from religious differences, that it just happened to take place in a district in which many Christians lived.) Be that as it may, the rebellion brought on the expulsion of the missionaries, an absolute interdiction against all Christian converts and activity, and the closure of Japan's gates (except for a handful of non-Catholic European traders on the island of Dejima) to the world for more than two hundred years.

Although the motives of many of the Japanese who embraced Christianity during the years between 1549 and 1638 may be questioned, there can be little doubt that at least some of them had faith of the highest and firmest order, for within a month after the construction of a Roman Catholic church in Nagasaki in 1865, four thousand Japanese Christians from the nearby village of Urakami came to the church to rejoice and to explain to the priest that they and their forebears had secretly kept the Christian faith alive for 225 years. Although Japan was then in the process of opening its doors to the West, the laws against Christianity were still in force, and the Tokugawa Shogunate arrested all four thousand and banished them to other feudatories. Fortunately, the Tokugawa regime collapsed before more serious harm could befall this stouthearted assemblage. Ironically, the same Catholic church, which the four thousand faithful from Urakami later joined, met complete destruction at our hands when we dropped the second atomic bomb on Nagasaki in August of 1945.

With the fall of the Tokugawa government and the restoration of the Emperor Meiji, there began a cycle of fair and foul weather for Christianity in Japan. In 1872 the Meiji government lifted its ban on Christianity and allowed free missionary activity, but it was not until the 1880's that Japan began to fully realize how much it would have to learn from the West. In the massive importation that soon followed, not only was Christianity included but it became, in fact, so popular that one prominent magistrate was prompted to predict that it might even be named the official state religion.

During the 1890's, however, reaction set in and a rising tide of nationalism dampened the prospects of Christianity considerably. Then the sight of Christian nations slaughtering each other in the bloody baptism of the First World War aroused serious doubts in the minds of the Japanese about the efficacy of Christianity and the sincerity of those who embraced it, but the humanitarianism of Wilson's Fourteen Points and the fast, unstinting aid we sent to Japan after the Great Kanto Earthquake of 1923 helped restore some of its prestige. Unfortunately, the passage of the Oriental Exclusion Act by the U.S. Congress in 1924 nullified these benefits and Christianity again went into a decline, which was hastened and lengthened by the rising antiforeignism of the 1930's.

As might be expected, the Allied victory in 1945 reawakened an interest in Christianity and led to an abolition of all restraints on religion. Even so, the number of native Christians in Japan today is only about 800,000, well under one percent of the population. Approximately 40 percent of these Christians are of the Roman Catholic persuasion and 41 percent Eastern Orthodox. The remainder are Protestant, if we include in their ranks the 75,000 members of the "Churchless Christian Movement" begun by Kanzo Uchimura.

That Christianity has not fared better in Japan must be attributed to the exclusive nature of the religion, which isolates its converts from the community around them, and the traditional preference of the Japanese for a less forbidding religion with a more benevolent confidence in the innate goodness of man.

It is estimated that one in every five Japanese is an adherent to one of the 171 so-called New Religions, one-third of which can be loosely classified as Shintoist, one-third as Buddhist, and the remainder as a jumble of miscellany. Once included among this miscellaneous classification but now sadly defunct were *Denshinkyo,* whose believers worshipped electricity and Thomas Alva Edison, and *Bosei-kyo,* whose followers regarded sexual acts as primary healing agents.

Although they may have had much older roots, most of these New Religions rose to prominence after the end of World

War Two because their believers were disenchanted with the
theretofore established religion (Shinto), and because Occu-
pation-inspired reforms freed all genuine religions from the
trammel net of the 1939 Religious Bodies Law.

Obviously, when one is speaking of that number of separate
religious entities, there must be considerable variance in size,
organization, belief, ritual, and congregational makeup; nonetheless some generalizations can be made that have application
to most of them. They have, for example, tended to concen-
trate their initial efforts at proselytization on farmers and
workers, only later advancing on the middle classes. The organization, direction, and control of their priests are less formal than in the older religions. They draw their theology from
several, sometimes many sources. Their doctrine and philosophy are weak. Their appeal is based on hope for a better life
and on ritualistic or magical curative powers. They have
strong leaders. (In sixty or so of the 171 New Religions, the
leaders have laid claim to divine inspiration or revelation.)
With the notable exception of the Soka Gakkai, they are
tolerant of other religious creeds. They are easy to understand
and easy to join. They have their own Meccas in Japan. They
preach that their promised rewards can be enjoyed in this life.
They offer highly emotional ritual performances. They appeal
to unsophisticated persons who may have suffered grievous
bereavement or injury in war or who have lost their convictions about the purposes of life. And they implant in their
followers a feeling of personal dignity and importance.

Although the New Religions have often been contemptuously ignored or belittled as appealing only to the ignorant
and superstitious, some authorities regard their rapid growth
and incontrovertible vitality as one of the three most significant
developments in the history of Japanese religions (the other
two being the adoption of Buddhism beginning in the sixth
century and the rise of the demotic Buddhist sects in the thirteenth).

Chief among the New Religions, in descending order based

on the number of their devotees, are the Soka Gakkai, Reiyukai, Tenrikyo, Rissho Koseika, and Seicho no Ie. The first—the Soka Gakkai—is the one that has attracted the most foreign attention.

Contrary to the implication in its name, the Soka Gakkai (Value-Creating Learned Society) appeals more to persons of lesser learning than to the intelligentsia. It is a phenomenon that has amazed Westerner and Japanese alike. In Japan, it boasts a membership of sixteen million, while in the United States (where it goes by the name of Nichiren Shoshu, or the Orthodox Sect of Nichiren) its believers number 170,000, with most of the more recent converts being Caucasian. Its political arm in Japan is the Komeito (literally, "openly illuminated party" but usually given in English as the Clean Government Party), which is now Japan's third-strongest political organization and which predicts that by 1977 it will hold 140 of the 486 seats in the House of Representatives, thus making it the second-strongest. (To date, the Soka Gakkai has demonstrated a remarkable capacity for meeting or surpassing its announced goals.) It is the fastest growing major religion in the world.

Nichiren (1222–1282) was one of the most colorful and turbulent figures in Japanese history. A monk of the Tendai denomination, he became dissatisfied with his and other Buddhist sects and founded the first distinctively Japanese branch of that religion. Preaching that the Lotus Sutra was the perfect revelation of truth and the only written words his followers need know, he stormed through Japan vilifying all other religious beliefs. He sought to appeal to the common man by identifying religion with natural life. His powers of mystical prognostication won fame when the Mongol invasion that he had predicted became a reality. His impassioned preaching and dire warnings stirred much religious fervor and unrest, for which he was exiled and even sentenced to death. (He was spared, almost miraculously.) When he was past fifty, he had a loose tooth removed and handed it to Nikko, his leading disciple, instructing him to use it in spreading the true gospel as Nichiren conceived it. To this molar was attached a bit of flesh, which has reportedly grown until it now covers nearly all of the tooth. Nichiren is said to have predicted that when the tooth is entirely covered, the religion he fostered will have reached its zenith.

After his death, Nichiren's faith splintered into thirty-one groups. One of these—Nichiren Shoshu—is the spiritual parent of the Soka Gakkai, which was established in the early Thirties by a schoolteacher named Tsunesaburo Makiguchi, who had little success in popularizing his beliefs and died behind bars. His successor Josei Toda, however, found the religious freedom of the postwar era more receptive to propagation and growth and by 1951 he had assembled under his guidance five thousand devotees. When Toda died in 1958, the mourners in his funeral procession numbered more than three hundred thousand. Daisaku Ikeda, the present head of the sect, succeeded him.

Much of the Soka Gakkai's appeal derives from excellent staging and its emphasis on quick rewards. ("If you sincerely wish for something hard enough while chanting over and over *'Namu Myoho Renge-Kyo,'* you will surely receive it.") Its success at myriad conversions can be mostly attributed to *shakubuku,* the word the society uses to encompass its efforts to convert nonbelievers. Literally, *shakubuku* means "to shatter and subdue," referring to evil spirits and not the intended convert, although visual evidence may sometimes suggest the contrary.

Since each Soka Gakkai member has a quota of converts that he must bring in or face serious disapproval, *shakubuku* can be a formidable—even frightening—affair. The Japanese wife of an American friend of mine in Tokyo is a member of the Soka Gakkai and she has furnished me several close looks at the methodology. When individual attempts on the part of a member have failed to bring a target to his senses, he summons aid. If the ardent efforts then of a group of six or eight bright-eyed fellow members are still unsuccessful, they may resort to such means as standing in front of the target's residence in the evening and chanting prayers for his soul for hours on end. And should the convert-to-be still be uncowed, his neighbors may even join in the exhortation, if only to achieve peace in the neighborhood.

Of late, however, Daisaku Ikeda has applied the soft pedal to some such methods, now that the Soka Gakkai is growing out of its fitful adolescence and nearing a form of maturity.

In part, the Society's success in politics (it leans to the right but exploits the weaknesses of both the right and left) can be explained by its use of tactics similar to the ones used in *shakubuku* and partly by the fact that its political arm, the Komeito, became active when the "black mist" of corruption was raising its heinous head somewhat higher than usual in Japanese politics. Also, by the statement of a Komeito political worker who said, "In winning the election campaign, we simply disregard the election laws. Since our efforts serve the Soka Gakkai, what we did cannot be wrong." The police did not, however, always take this view and so arrested many members. The Komeito candidates nevertheless won and were seated in the Diet.

When it comes to denouncing other religions, the Soka Gakkai believers are not at all hesitant or retiring. Nichiren himself declared about three other Buddhist sects, "Zen is a religion of devils, Shingon means national ruin, and the Risshu congregation is a pack of traitors." About Christianity, modern-day Soka Gakkai says, "Jesus died on the Cross. This fact is proof that he was defeated by his opposition. . . . But when he was about to be beheaded, our Saint Nichiren shouted to his executioner, 'Time is passing. Be quick about it! Cut off my head!' No sooner had he said this than the gods of the universe came to his aid. Meteors shot across the sky. Thus did Saint Nichiren beat his enemies. Comparing this vitality with that of Jesus, we see that Christianity has no power." About Shinto it comments, "Shinto is a heretical religion that we must destroy." And it calls Tenri-kyo an "absurd and good-for-nothing religion."

In its struggle to grow, the Soka Gakkai once locked horns with Tanro, the giant coal miners' union, which had viewed the role of religion in the life of its miners with cool indifference. In 1953, the Society had only a hundred or so members among the miners on the northern island of Hokkaido but by 1958 this number had increased to more than one hundred thousand. Seeing the dangerous, insecure life of the miners as fertile ground for sowing their seeds, the Soka Gakkai had promised the miners an end to mine accidents, effortless wage increases, good health, and spiritual happiness. When the situation reached the stage of crisis, the union Tanro began to intensify its resistance to this attempt to usurp its traditional role and authority. Its main counter-measures consisted of pointing out the more glaring fallacies in the Soka Gakkai teachings, publicizing the names of miner-converts who were still mysteriously ailing or poor, and suggesting that the more vociferous of the new adherents among the miners volunteer for special hazardous mining tasks, inasmuch as they were presumably protected from all accidents by the Soka Gakkai's escutcheon and promises.

The fact that not many miners volunteered proved to be rather effective in checking the Soka Gakkai's subsequent growth in that segment of Hokkaido's population.

11

Their Extremes

The extremes of which the Japanese are capable in their behavior patterns include mob violence, violence to others in the form of crime, and violence to themselves in the form of self-destruction. One popular theory among foreign writers holds that the origin of such violence owes much to the turbulence of nature in Japan, to the typhoons, earthquakes, and tidal waves that from time to time wreak havoc in this chain of islands. If this theory is valid, however, it would seem that by extension the residents of Florida should be more violent than other Americans because of the hurricanes that sweep across their state—a dubious premise at best.

During my years of residence in Japan, for example, I have experienced numerous earthquakes and typhoons of respectable magnitude but in none of them did I see more serious damage than occasional broken window glass and fallen roof tiles. Nor do I feel that I was unusually lucky. Comparatively speaking, few Japanese have actually suffered physical injury or significant property loss at the hands of nature unleashed. When foreigners read of a terrible typhoon or earthquake in Japan, there is perhaps a tendency to think of this as affecting a large portion of the population. They may not pause to consider that even if ten thousand Japanese are driven from their homes by flood waters, this number is still only one hundredth of one percent of the total population. I spent May Day of 1952—the occasion of the most vicious, unruly mob violence in postwar Japan—carrying on business as usual in my Tokyo office, making calls, receiving visitors, and going out for lunch at Suehiro's on the east side of the Ginza. I did not even know that anything unusual had occurred in the city until I bought a newspaper at Tokyo Station on my way home that evening.

Later that same night, I received a telephone call from my mother in the United States wanting to know if I had escaped injury. It was not easy to convince her that I had not even been aware of the rioting that had taken place that day in the same city with me.

Be that as it may, it would be difficult to prove that the Japanese are any more prone to violence * than the other "civilized" races of the world. Certainly, until the present century, they had engaged in fewer external wars than the average, and today their incidence of crime is the lowest among the major nations.

But what is notable about the violence of the Japanese, such as it may be, is that it stands out in strong contrast to their apparent tractability and submissive humility and that its causes are often quite different from what Americans might expect. It is these causes that we should understand if we are to deal successfully with the Japanese in the future.

A major difference between Japanese and American social attitudes—and one that partly explains the excessive behavior of, for example, their dissenting students—is seen in what could be called the Japanese curve of freedom and restriction. To plot our American curve, we would have to begin low with the restrictions that are placed on us as children and then rise

---

* In June, 1969, the National Commission on the Causes and Prevention of Violence ranked Japan sixty-eighth in the world in total magnitude of strife with a score of 5.9. The country most prone to strife and violence was Congo-Kinshasa with a score of 48.7. Several countries vied for the honor of being least prone with scores of 0, among them Sweden, Norway, Hong Kong, and Taiwan. In forty-first place was the United States, with a score of 10.2, but recent events have pushed us into the more violent ranking of twenty-fourth.

to a peak of freedom during our adult years, when we are, so to speak, on our own. In old age, our curve may begin to descend again, as some of us become dependent on our children or on state welfare for support. But in Japan, this curve would be plotted in precisely the opposite way. The Japanese feel that childhood and old age are their years of greatest freedom, while their adult years are those most restricted by the pressures and demands of their society.

Childhood in Japan, especially for boys, as I earlier suggested, is a time of great freedom and happiness. Boys are usually the "little masters" and, too often, tyrants of the house. They can punch their mothers and pinch their sisters at the risk of only the mildest of reprimands. Resort to physical punishment by their parents is rare. They are permitted to indulge in that kind of childish boastfulness that can be seen in most cultures: "My father is stronger than your father," "I can run faster than anyone else," and so forth.

About the age of ten, however, both at home and in school, the silken straitjacket of discipline, conformity, and compliance begins to tighten around them. Imperceptibly at first. And gently. Very gently. But bit by bit they are pushed into the mold which will prepare them for foreordained roles in their country's society. It is inevitable that they will rebel. When they do, their tantrums are tolerated. They are allowed a period of permissiveness in which to refresh their male egos, but then the light but inescapable pressure toward conformity, responsibility, and docile acceptance begins again and will continue through their most formative years.

Here originates a dualism that is deeply imbedded in the Japanese character. As the boy grows to young manhood, he harks back to the untrammeled freedom, parent-approved aggressions, and self-assertive individualism of the days when he was cock of the walk. His nostalgia for those better days is accentuated by the sure knowledge of the increasing demands to conform that await him. Although varying in degree with the individual, this dichotomy in his nature will remain with him throughout life and will often account for the otherwise mystifying contradictions in his actions and attitudes.

In college, this young man with the dual nature finds himself on the very threshold of adult status, that period which he now realizes will be the most trying of the three stages of his life. He has succeeded, if at all, in entering college after what are surely the most rigorous entrance examinations in the world. Although the pressure to repress his individuality in the interests of a conformist society has been bearing down on him more heavily for several years now, he still enjoys a few free areas of activity, which he knows will soon be denied him altogether. Among his teachers will be many irresponsible intellectuals and leftist sympathizers who, consciously or not, work on behalf of anarchy in their lectures. After graduation, he knows that he must enter a society, a business world that still functions largely on feudalistic principles. Despite the talk of democracy and individual freedom that he hears about him, he realizes that he will not see much of either. He understands that he must accept the future but he resents the necessity. Knowing that the generation before him was responsible for the most massive group failure in his country's history, he is understandably leery of their proffered guidance.

It is in this frame of mind that Japanese students demonstrate, protest, riot, and confront. It is their one last fling before the demands of adult society clamp them firmly into the roles for which they are being molded. It is their last despairing plea for the larger social justice of a future world—before knuckling under to the rigid requirements of the one they are about to enter.

After witnessing the violence of Japan's protesting students, some Western observers are tempted to predict chaos or an extremist regime in Japan in due course, but, although these demonstrations are serious enough, it is unwise to think that they per se will serve to bring about any far-reaching changes in Japan's form of government within the next few decades.

Concerned Japanese have conducted occasional studies to

determine what happens to these rebellious students after graduation. According to the findings of the four studies I have read, the pattern is nearly inflexible: The graduates find jobs in business or in government. During the first few months, some vestiges of their previous rebelliousness may still be apparent, but by the end of the first year, they are, by and large, the same amenable cogs in Japan's social works that their older coworkers and neighbors are. When queried, most of them say that they can hardly recognize themselves as they were a scant year or so before.

Even so, such violent resentment during student days must leave a mark of some kind on their characters, if only to widen, even slightly, the dualism mentioned earlier. It would be a mistake, however, to assume, except in a few extreme cases, that the experience of campus disorder will inspire these young men of today to lead the Japan of tomorrow down the road toward political extremism.

As suggested above, the society which these students, as well as all other Japanese, enter is one that requires extreme circumspection, repression of individuality, and conformity of its members, among whom will be men and women who sometimes find themselves pushed beyond the limits of their endurance and patience. When this happens, violence often results.

Although normally persevering and patient, the Japanese have a disconcertingly short fuse when they feel that they have been *baka ni sareta* (ridiculed), either as individuals or as a group. In bringing conformist pressures to bear on children, laughter and ostracism are a parent's most forcible threats, *"Hito ni warawaremasu yo* (People will laugh at you)" and *"Mo shirimasen yo* (We won't have anything more to do with you)" being warnings heard almost daily in homes. The Japanese are acutely sensitive to any possibility that they will be laughed at for behavior, clothing, or speech that is out of the ordinary or not group-approved.

In later years, the Japanese develops a sense of duty (*giri*) to his name and reputation, any slurs against which are keenly felt and resented as attempts to humble and mock him. Take, for instance, the case of a young man who has studied English in middle school, high school, and college. Upon graduation, he becomes a teacher of English in a rural middle school, but his English ability is spotty. Since he has never lived in—or even visited—an English-speaking country, his spoken English and its pronunciation will be poor, although his comprehension of difficult passages from English literature may be excellent. Nevertheless, he must never confess any such weakness. If he strives to improve at all, he must do so in the privacy of his room or completely away from his environment. Even if he meets a native speaker of English whose fluency and pronunciation are infinitely superior to his, he will almost never request assistance or advice. As a properly designated teacher of English, he cannot admit to any ignorance of that tongue. To do so would cause loss of face. It would mean that he had failed to try to protect his name and reputation.

To the same extent that he strives to shield his good name from slurs the Japanese will resent imputations against it. When these become too frequent or too abrasive, he may feel that his "face has been broken," that he has been ridiculed.

What applies to the individual also applies to the nation. The Japanese are extremely sensitive to what other nations think of them. When events of international interest occur in Japan, it is quite common for news commentators to relate what has happened and then hasten to describe foreign reactions, as reported by their correspondents in Washington, Paris, London, Moscow, Berlin, Rome, and other world capitals. Accordingly, when they feel that they are being "made light of," violence, in the form of war, can be the ultimate result.

Part of our own troubles with the Japanese during this century can be traced to occasions in which they felt that they, as a nation, had been held in contempt. The Five-Power Naval Treaty, for example. Or England's abrogation, at United

States insistence, of her 1902 treaty with Japan. Or the California Exclusion Act.

Few Americans today understand the intensity of the resentment harbored by the Japanese when we closed our doors to all but token immigration from their country. They interpreted this as a blatant announcement to the world that we regarded them as an inferior race not fit to live on American soil. Although subsequent Japanese expansionism on the continent of Asia (and, later, of course, the Pearl Harbor attack) was a more immediate and, to us, meaningful cause of the Pacific War, some authorities question that Japan would have chosen this road to eventual collision with the United States if the humiliation seared into their national consciousness by the Exclusion Act and the Five-Power Naval Treaty had not provided fertile soil for the growth of bellicose resentment.

Despite this sensitivity, the Japanese are capable of accepting and living with stark defeat, as they amply demonstrated during the first years following the Pacific War, as long as their noses are not rubbed in it. Our decisions to leave their Emperor on his throne and to manage the country through Japan's duly established governmental machinery were wise ones in this respect, because, in so doing, we took advantage of a control apparatus that had long been accepted by the people and whose alembic could considerably lessen the sting of humiliation that might otherwise have been felt in more directly expressed requirements on them.

Another attitude influencing violence in modern Japan is to be found in the pages of her history: namely, that violence animated by loyalty to a clan chieftain or feudal lord was worthy of exaltation, even though doomed to failure. The revenge motive was strong; murderous efforts to wipe away slight or fancied stains on the feudal lord's escutcheon were common. Indeed, vendettas almost achieved the status of a national passion, like bullfighting with the Spaniards, and Japan's most famous adventure is the story of the forty-seven samurai who endured many months of hardship and shame in order that they might at last avenge their lord, who had been commanded to commit hara-kiri following a fight with the Shogun's Master of Court Rituals over a question of appropriate dress during Shogunal audiences.

This willingness to kill and then to die for hopeless causes has filtered down through the years to us today in the forms of the "assassination mentality of the Japanese" and the minority-inspired violence in their politics.

What with our own disgraceful record in recent years, we Americans are hardly qualified to speak disdainfully of foreign assassins, but it is nonetheless true that assassination did become a formidable political weapon in Japan during the decade preceding World War Two and that it is still far from being a dormant phenomenon. Witness the classic assassination in 1960 of Inejiro Asanuma, chairman of the Japan Socialist Party, by a knife-wielding youth only seventeen years old. I call this case "classic" because the boy stabbed Asanuma with exceeding skill and dexterity in surroundings where his instant capture was foreordained, and because he quietly hanged himself in his cell soon thereafter with courage and determination. Here was no Oswald hungering for public notice, no Ray seeking material reward, no Sirhan of uncertain mental clarity. Instead, it was a seventeen-year-old boy who struck down his imagined bête noire with all the skill of a master swordsman and who then took his own life without the slightest attempt at histrionics.

In Japan, the "tyranny of the majority" can easily give rise to the violence of the minority when that minority believes that decent consideration is not being accorded its situation. Although the effort is as often as not predestined to failure, the minority often flings itself in wild fury against the battlements of the "oppressive" majority, as if trying to purchase public sympathy for their cause with their life blood.

It is being aptly said these days that the Japanese support the cause of peace—even with violence. Many students, labor unionists, and leftists, abetted by a deplorable number of teachers and other intellectuals, storm through the streets of Japan's cities in their continuing struggle against any effort on the part of their government—or the United States—to involve their country more closely with the task of defending the Free World's perimeter along the Asian continent. While it is obvious that much of this protest is designed mostly to embarrass and hamper the party in power, it is equally undeniable that there is an extremely strong sentiment against war—of any kind or for any reason—among the Japanese, and according to a poll conducted in 1970 by a leading news service, nine out of ten of them are in favor of retaining the antiwar clause (Article 9) of their Constitution.

The Pacific War and its aftermath are still vividly alive in the memories of a great many Japanese, while even those who are too young to recall those days have been kept at least partly aware of their country's failure and suffering by the survivors of Hiroshima and Nagasaki and the continuing demonstrations against nuclear weapons, by the one-armed or one-legged (or both) veterans in white who begged for charity on the trains and street corners for many postwar years, and by the physical presence of a conquering (even though benevolent) foreign army.

I have often been asked by American visitors to Japan if I thought that the Japanese truly regret their attack on Pearl Harbor, and I have had to answer this question in the negative. To be sure, many Japanese regret the Pacific War itself—because they lost it and because this loss brought about extensive suffering to them. And there are some who regret the Army-fomented lust for expansionism that pushed Japan into fatal collision with the United States in 1941. But I know of very few apparently sincere expressions of regret about the nature of the attack on Pearl Harbor, and even these few for the most part emanated from Westernized Japanese who had reason to believe that their remarks might eventually reach American ears.

With war as with other forms of international competition,

the Japanese play the game to win. The Western world's concept of sportsmanship (it's *how* you play the game that counts) holds little meaning for the Japanese, especially when applied to war. (Although their warrior class had a respected code of chivalry in feudal days, it differed largely from European notions of gallantry and honor.) Since the surprise attack was—in our own era—an internationally accepted mode of waging war after hostilities had begun, the Japanese could see little reason why it should not also be acceptable as a means of initiating conflict, with obvious advantages to the attacker.

A possible explanation for this attitude toward unannounced attacks is that, until a hundred years ago, Japan had had almost no experience in international warfare, where prior declarations of hostile intent should have been encountered, but had learned what she knew of waging war from the conflicts between clans and factions within her own boundaries; in these, a formal declaration of war, signed and delivered, was certainly not the common thing. For instance, Ieyasu Tokugawa captured Osaka Castle (and thereby won for himself and his 250-year dynasty control over all of Japan) by what historians have called a "most repellent deceit." Further, treachery played an important role in wresting this same control from the last of the Tokugawa line, when a force of samurai from Tsu turned their coats the night before the last major battle (near Osaka in 1868) between the Shogunal and the Imperial armies. Again, at the beginning of the Sino-Japanese War in 1894, the Japanese navy struck the first blow and sank a Chinese warship before war was declared. And yet again, in February of 1904, a Japanese destroyer squadron attacked Russian naval vessels anchored in Port Arthur without warning, moving Czar Nicholas II to lament in his diary, "This, without a declaration of war! May God come to our aid." (It is interesting to note how attitudes can change with shifting alliances: In reporting the Japanese attack on Port Arthur, the *Times* of London praised the Japanese for what they had done: "The Japanese Navy has opened the war by an act of daring which is destined to take a place of honor in naval annals. . . ." But when the Japanese attacked Hong Kong (and Pearl Harbor) on December 7, 1941, the British chose entirely different words to describe this similar Japanese "act of daring.")

While the Japanese may not feel that they were wrong in launching an unannounced attack on Pearl Harbor in 1941, they are perceptive enough to realize that this attack has been widely condemned in the Western world, so they and their apologists have taken up the theory that Franklin D. Roosevelt and several of his top advisers had determined to force Japan into initiating hostilities against the United States because they believed that they could not otherwise rally the full support of the American people for such a war. These apologists point to Cordell Hull's note to Japan of November 26, 1941, as an ultimatum that no independent nation could in good conscience accept. (Admittedly, this note was extremely raw in tone and made demands on Japan that no reasonable government official could have then expected her to accept, but Japan's apologists conveniently ignore the fact that the Pearl Harbor attack was being actively and concretely planned at least two months before the date of the Hull note.) Unfortunately, however, there is other evidence—and from United States sources at that—to show that Roosevelt and two of his top assistants had at least commented on the desirability of having Japan begin the conflict, which makes it easier to construe the Hull note as an ultimatum that deliberately left Japan little alternative.

Another Japanese view of the Pearl Harbor attack was one that I encountered for the first time in the December 17, 1966, issue of the weekly magazine *Shukan Shincho* but have seen and heard elsewhere several times since then. According to this view, the United States really shouldn't be put out with Japan about the attack. After all, did it not set in motion a chain of events that converted a depression-stricken, semi-isolationist United States into the richest and most powerful nation on the globe? The clear implication was that we should be, if anything, rather appreciative of the favor.

To Americans who are puzzled and distressed by the soaring rate of crime in the United States (it has increased eleven times as fast as the population since 1960, while police solutions of serious crimes have fallen off by one-third), even a cursory look at the condition of law and order in Japan should be both refreshing and inspiring.

First of all, crime is generally on the *decrease* there: In 1935, for example, the number of arrests made by the Japan police totaled one and a half million from among a population of sixty-eight million. Thirty years later, the total barely exceeded one million—a reduction of one-third, although the population had grown by half again to one hundred million.

Some figures are even more dramatic: In 1965, the number of arrests for fraud and embezzlement was only one-sixth of what it was in 1935, while during the same period counterfeiting dropped by two-thirds and abuses of official power by one-half. In 1970, New York City police had to contend with 74,102 holdups and muggings, while the police in Tokyo, a larger city, were faced with only 472.

According to Interpol statistics, Japan has the lowest crime rate in the world (3.6 per 100,000 people, compared to 667 in the United States and 540 in England). During the five-year period between 1960 and 1965, crime increased by 55 percent in Great Britain and by 40 percent in the United States, but it *decreased* by 2 percent in Japan.

Within this framework of overall decrease, however, juvenile crimes are increasing. In 1965, juveniles accounted for more than half of the arrests on suspicion of violence, theft, robbery, and intimidation. Interestingly enough, only 4 percent of the juvenile offenders came from really poor families, while 43 percent were the products of middle-class homes. (A considerable percentage was recorded without accurate indication of family income level, but the police believe that these, too, were mostly from the middle bracket.)

On December 6, 1968, the manager of the Kokubunji branch (on the western outskirts of Tokyo) of the Nihon Shintaku Bank received an extortion note. He was ordered to leave three million yen ($10,000) in a certain place at a specified time. Otherwise, the note warned, his home in Tokyo would be blown up.

The branch manager did not comply, but he informed the employees at his bank of the threat.

Four days later, in the morning, four employees left the same bank in a Cedric car and started out for the Toshiba factory in Fuchu, a few miles south. They were carrying something of considerable bulk and value: three hundred million yen.

Japanese companies customarily give bonuses to their employees twice a year: at the end of June and at the end of December. But many, like Toshiba, were passing out the year-end bonuses fairly early in December this year, to give their employees more time for their New Year's shopping. Usually the bonuses equaled about one month's wages but sometimes ranged as high as two or three months'. It was the bonus money for Toshiba's Fuchu factory workers that the four bank clerks were delivering that morning. And it was all in cash; Japanese companies don't pay salaries or bonuses by check.

At nine o'clock, as the Cedric was driving down the road that goes past Fuchu Prison, a uniformed patrolman on the familiar white motorcycle of the police forces waved the bank car over to the side of the road. The patrolman, whose face was largely concealed by his helmet and scarf, hurried over to the halted vehicle.

"We've just had a call from the police station in Sugamo," he said tersely. "The home of your branch manager has been blown up."

Sugamo was the district of Tokyo in which the branch manager resided.

"And we've learned," the patrolman went on, "that there's a charge of dynamite planted somewhere in this car. It's set to go off any minute now." He began at once to inspect the car.

In less time than it takes to tell it, the four bank clerks were out of the Cedric and running for the ditch, completely forgetting the money entrusted to their care. As they threw themselves into the presumed safety of that declivity, the patrolman climbed in behind the wheel of their car and drove off with the three hundred million yen.

Perhaps it is needless to say that the man who had made off with the largest cash haul in Japan's history was not a genuine policeman. At the date of this writing, they still have not found out just who he was.

Despite the above implication, the efficiency of the Japanese police represents a primary reason for the low rate of crime in that country. On the whole, they are capable, dedicated men and women. And there are fewer of them. Japan has one policeman for every 729 inhabitants, while the United States has one for every 502 and France has one for every 347.

Furthermore, they are often emasculated by inadequate and outdated laws. For example, Japan has no law that specifically provides for punishment of criminals convicted of kidnapping for ransom, which is a crime only recently imported. It has no law against espionage. It has no law against incest. It has no treaty of extradition with any country but the United States. It has no law against statutory rape. (Forcible violation of a girl under thirteen years of age is, however, a crime.) Unless he has a warrant of arrest or sees the man actually engaged in an offense, the policeman is not authorized to search a suspicious person for weapons. If he uses force in apprehending any member of a mob, the policeman risks prosecution for attempted murder, false arrest, or afflicting bodily injury. (Labor, student, and leftist organizations are alert for such opportunities to harass the gendarmes.) Only in a state of national emergency, which has not been proclaimed since the end of World War Two, can the police use force to subdue unruly demonstrators, which explains in part the mob violence and wild abandonment of recent years.

(A careful study of known student-participants in the Security Treaty riots of 1960 showed that almost no athletes were represented, giving rise to the intriguing theory that rioting is merely another sport, a chance to burn up excess youthful energy.)

Hampered though they are by comparatively small numbers and by certain legal restrictions, the Japanese police turn in a very creditable performance. Where the arrest-rate for all crimes is 25 percent in the United States, it is 35 percent in Great Britain—and 51 percent in Japan. For robbery, it is 38 percent in the United States and 83 percent in Japan. And for murder it is 98 percent in Japan as against 91 percent in the United States.

The credit does not, of course, go entirely to the police. Several other factors are involved, among them Japan's geographical isolation, limited space, traditional respect for authority, family pride and honor, common language, labor shortage, and lack of a land border that criminals can easily cross to escape.

Also, the public shows an amazing degree of cooperation with the police, which is surprising in consideration of the harsh repression of the Twenties and Thirties and the traces of police arrogance that, unfortunately, still remain. (A hangover from Japan's feudal era, which was characterized by the Japanese expression *"Kanson Mimpi,"* meaning "Respect officialdom; despise the common man.") A recent survey of three thousand citizens showed that 60 percent of them looked upon the policeman as "a kind and warm-hearted friend in times of need," while 23 percent replied that they had no complaint at all against the police.

One of the postwar innovations (inspired by the United

States) designed to bolster police strength and efficiency was the substitution of .45-caliber Smith & Wesson revolvers for the deliberately dulled swords policemen carried until 1945. Police view this "improvement," however, with mixed feelings; in a gun-short country where none but the police are ever authorized to carry a concealable firearm, too many petty criminals have become murderers during fights ensuing from their attempts to steal policemen's revolvers.

One of the most bizarre mass murders and bank robberies in Japanese crime annals took place in a small suburban bank in Tokyo on the twenty-sixth of January, 1948. It still arouses large numbers of Japanese to heights of furious emotion and is more of a cause célèbre in that country than the case of Caryl Chessman was in the United States.

At about three-thirty in the afternoon of the above date, a middle-aged man with a scar on his face appeared in the Shiina-machi branch of the Teikoku Bank in Toshima Ward in Tokyo. He was wearing red boots (not as uncommon in Japan as they would be in the United States) and an armband identifying him as a "technical official" from the Toshima Ward Office. He asked to see the branch manager.

The branch manager being out, the visiting "official" was taken to the desk of the manager's assistant, to whom he showed a business card that further identified him as a medical doctor.

"There has been an outbreak of dysentery in this neighborhood," he told the assistant manager, "and a man who now has the sickness tells us that he has come to this bank several times recently. Will you please assemble all your employees? I must ask you to take preventive measures against dysentery."

The doors of the bank had just been closed for the day, so the assistant called the other fifteen employees of the bank together to hear the "ward-office doctor" explain what had to be done.

Very carefully the man in the red boots laid out sixteen doses of medicine, in the form of white powder, and asked that each employee fill his own teacup with water. He cautioned them that the medicine could have a harmful effect on the enamel of their teeth if they did not place the dose on their tongues carefully and swallow it all down with one gulp of water.

At the "doctor's" signal, all sixteen employees picked up their cups and followed his instructions to the letter.

Almost immediately they began to feel tearing internal pains and then staggered off toward the water cooler, where they all collapsed in quick succession. Of the sixteen bank employees, twelve died.

The man in the red boots gathered up 164,000 yen and a few checks, and then fled.

On the twenty-first of August, one Sadamichi Hirasawa, a fifty-seven-year-old artist living in the city of Otaru in northern Japan, was picked up as a suspect. In jail, he first tried to commit suicide and then, on the twenty-seventh of September, he admitted giving a derivative of prussic acid to the sixteen employees of the Teikoku Bank.

Although he later denied having admitted guilt, Hirasawa was sentenced to death, whereupon began an almost comically long series of appeals, stays of execution, reversals, retrials, and signature-gathering campaigns, all of which have left Hirasawa today exactly where he was over twenty years ago: in prison awaiting execution. (At this writing, he is reported to be seriously—perhaps terminally—ill.)

In Japan, most criminal cases are tried before three judges who, sitting together, decide the question of innocence or guilt, and this system seems to work very well. (The new Chief Justice of the United States, Warren Earl Burger, also questions the principle of trial by jury, was quoted in *Time* magazine of June 20, 1969, as saying, "If we could eliminate the jury, we would save a lot of time. You can try a case without a jury in one day that would take you a week or two weeks with a jury.")

Japan did experiment with trial by jury during the years between 1928 and 1943. The accused were given the right to choose between jury trial and trial by judges. The number who chose the former averaged only thirty a year during that fifteen-year period, almost all of the accused evidently preferring *not* to be judged by their peers, so jury trials were abandoned.

The absence of trial by jury is one of the weightiest reasons why many Americans watched uneasily when the U.S. Armed Forces, in October of 1953, gave Japanese courts primary jurisdiction over military men and their dependents for offenses committed off-base in Japan. They were worried that the Japanese, perhaps still smarting from their defeat in the war, might take advantage of their new power to punish American offenders more severely than their offenses warranted.

They need not have been concerned. Japanese courts bent over backwards to show leniency to Americans haled before them. In numerous instances, they were so forgiving that they let go scot-free culprits who deserved at least some manner of punishment, and our military prosecutors had to seek out other charges (to avoid double jeopardy) with which to bring these men to even lesser justice.

By May of 1957, three and a half years later, when the bulk of our forces had left Japan, the Japanese police had apprehended 27,000 U.S. citizens, of which number they indicted only 500 (an arrest-indictment rate much lower than that for their own countrymen). Approximately half of the 27,000 were for traffic violations, of which only eleven were prosecuted.

Of the above 500 indicted, some 30 percent were punished only with fines—and small ones at that. At the end of this time, May of 1957, only thirty-seven American citizens were serving sentences in Japanese prisons, none of which exceeded fifteen years in length. The death sentence was never meted out to an American, although more than a few Americans had killed Japanese under a variety of circumstances.

The U.S. Defense Department confirmed in a Senate hearing that American offenders generally got lighter sentences from Japanese courts than they would have received from our own and went on to testify that the Japanese had built a special jail for the confinement of Americans that was "far and above" the standard for Japanese prisons.

During the Sengoku Era of Japanese history, the commander of one of Lord Mori's castles, Muneharu Shimizu, was ordered to commit hara-kiri: suicide by disembowelment. On the evening of the hara-kiri ceremony, a loyal vassal of Shimizu's—a man named Shirai—sent a message to his master begging that he deign to come to Shirai's room. Although understandably preoccupied with thoughts and preparations for his departure from this world, which was to take place in less than an hour, Shimizu took the time to go to his favorite vassal's quarters in a far corner of the castle. When Shimizu got there, Shirai was sitting with his legs crossed on the tatami matting. Humbly he asked his master to sit down beside him, whereupon he began to tell Shimizu that he should not fear death, that he should approach it with courage and equanimity, and that self-disembowelment was not, after all, such a fearful demise.

Shirai coughed once and swayed slightly. Then he opened his robe.

"You see, sire," he said, revealing the slash across his abdomen, "I committed hara-kiri myself as soon as I was sure that you were coming. I wanted to show you that it is not so difficult. . . ."

Overcome with gratitude, Shimizu rose to his feet beside his faithful vassal and unsheathed his long sword. With tears in his eyes, he raised his blade and with it cut off Shirai's head, thereby performing the act of *kaishaku* and according his old friend high honor. After a few minutes of silent grief, he cleaned his sword and then walked back to meet his own end —with renewed courage.

A similar but little-known incident took place in 1944 in

Cowra, Australia, when the Japanese inmates of a prisoner-of-war camp broke out of captivity and fled into the Australian countryside one night in August. When the Australian guards entered the prisoners' barracks after the break, they found the bodies of eleven Japanese hanging from roof beams. Interrogation of prisoners recaptured later revealed that those eleven men had been the instigators of the escape and that they had hanged themselves in front of all the other prisoners to demonstrate their own willingness to die and to give their comrades courage.

These two instances should suggest that the Japanese institution of suicide is a remarkable, if not unique, phenomenon in mankind's annals of reasons for and methods of self-destruction. Although Westerners perhaps think of hara-kiri first in connection with Japanese suicides, the earliest recorded cases in Japan were accomplished by hanging and self-incendiarization, the usual manner of the latter being for the victim to set fire to his own home with himself inside.

Yoshiteru Murakami, a warrior of Japan's feudal days, managed to combine both self-incendiarization and hara-kiri in his own dramatic demise, when he and his master, Prince Morinaga, were trapped in a house by their enemies. Wanting to distract the foe so that his master could escape, Murakami climbed to the roof with a torch in his hand. With it, he set fire to the thatch, which blazed up brightly while Murakami yelled taunts to the enemy samurai below in the garden.

"Dogs!" Murakami shouted. "I am Prince Morinaga. Watch! I'll show you cowards how a true warrior dies."

In the light of the leaping flames from the thatched roof, Murakami glanced back and saw the dim form of Prince Morinaga disappear over the garden wall at the back side of the house. Reassured, he turned back to the now intently watching foe clustered below him.

Silently he shed his outer robe and withdrew his dagger. Steeling himself, he made a long, deep slash across his abdomen, just below the navel. Despite the excruciating pain and the now-blinding heat, he kept his body straight and his face impassive. As his intestines came tumbling out through the cut, he seized a handful with his left hand and cut them loose with the dagger in his right.

Tossing the dagger aside, he threw the ropy intestines down into the faces of his startled enemies. Then with one final effort he unsheathed his long sword, inserted the point in his mouth, and fell forward on it and into the flaming thatch.

This was one of the first recorded instances of hara-kiri, or seppuku (both mean *stomach-cutting*) in Japanese history and took place long before it had become a formalized ceremony, encumbered with almost as many traditions and rules as the coronation of a monarch.

Sen-no-Rikyu, one of a long line of justly celebrated tea-ceremony masters, was another who cut part of his own intestines free from his body. He had been ordered to commit seppuku by Hideyoshi, the de facto ruler of Japan at the time, for reasons Sen-no-Rikyu thought were unjust. Although he followed Hideyoshi's orders, he made his indignation known by cutting loose a portion of his own intestines, piling them in coils on a tray, and insisting, with his dying breath, that they be delivered to Hideyoshi.

Seppuku became popular among the Japanese as a means of ending one's life partly because the stomach was regarded as the seat of all emotions, the abode of the soul. Their language has many expressions that support this: *"Hara ga tatsu* (The stomach stands up)"* means to get angry. *"Hara-guroi hito* (a man with a black stomach)"* means a sly, cunning man. *"Hara wo kimeru* (to decide the stomach)"* is the equivalent of to make up one's mind. *"Kare no hara ga yomenai* (I cannot read his stomach)"* is similar to saying "I cannot understand what's in his mind."

One little-understood aspect of formalized seppuku is that the stomach-cut alone was usually not fatal. This incision was made from left to right just below the navel but was not deep. The above-quoted cases in which the intestines poured out through the wound were exceptional and took place before seppuku became a ritualized method of punishment. Some men, in fact, barely scratched themselves with the tips of their daggers. It was after this cut had been made that the kneeling man signaled, by nodding his head or raising a finger, for his assistant, who was waiting poised to his left rear, to chop off his head. The role of this assistant also became formalized and required great skill. Some were able to lop off a head and leave it hanging from the trunk of the body by only a shred of skin. To cut the head off entirely was considered poor form, since it was likely to roll around and perhaps even bespatter distinguished witnesses with blood.

Nowadays, however, seppuku—together with Bushido, the Code of the Samurai—has fallen into disuse. There have been several subsequent cases (those of novelist Yukio Mishima and of a Japanese doctor named Tamano in—of all places— Fort Worth, Texas), but the last significant number took place at the end of the Pacific War. (Admiral Onishi—a primary force in the development and use of the Special Attack [Kamikaze] Corps, which was another colorful facet of Japanese suicides—was among those who disemboweled themselves soon after learning of Japan's decision to surrender. Onishi made the stomach-cut before dawn on August 16, 1945, and then, having no assistant, tried to bring on death by cutting his throat. Neither cut, however, was deep enough, so he lingered on in pain until his final breath at six o'clock that evening, in the meantime having refused all offers to either hasten or hinder his departure.)

While nothing has taken the place of seppuku, which was both a ceremony and a punishment ordered by the authorities or a feudal lord, other forms of Japanese suicide are, of course, still with us, rich in variety and significant in number.

One popular fashion of exit-making is called *kisha-ojo:* throwing oneself in front of a train. Sometimes a pair of unhappy lovers will tie themselves together with the girl's sash and then fall onto the tracks. In another common method of double suicide (which the Japanese call *shinju,* meaning to reveal the heart), the star-crossed lovers, again bound to each other, leap from a high cliff into the sea or a river.

Committing suicide to draw attention to oneself or to one's dilemma is by no means limited to Japan, but this reason deserves special emphasis there and helps to explain the often bizarre ways by which the Japanese voluntarily depart this life.

Jumping from the top of department stores to sidewalks below is one such method that should surely be classed as a strong bid for attention, especially when we consider that the majority of such acts take place during rush hours.

At noon of one spring day in 1948, I was looking out from the window of my office in Osaka and happened to see a man jump from the top of a department store across the canal from my building. He landed on top of three young office girls, who had been walking along hand in hand enjoying the sunshine, killing one and injuring the other two. I had first caught sight of him when he climbed over the guard wire and noticed that he had placed a black box on the ledge beside him before taking his final leap.

The deaths and injuries had, of course, drawn quite a crowd, but the people on the street could not see the black box eight stories above them, so I left my office, crossed the canal by a nearby bridge, and went up to discover that the box was a portable record player and that the record to whose strains the young man had dived to his death was *Mood Indigo*.

Throwing oneself into the pit of a volcano is another familiar method of self-disposal, in which perhaps tidiness is a factor, since there really is no problem of disposal of the corpse, it being swallowed up by molten lava. For those so inclined, the active volcanoes of Mihara (on Oshima) and Aso (in Kyushu) are highly regarded.

Other places that have become famous as suicide sites are Nishikigaura, a seaside cliff near Atami from which lovers leap, and Kegon-no-taki, a waterfall near Nikko into whose tumultuous basin singles and couples alike plunge with ultimate abandon.

In a recent year the mistress of the president of a Tokyo company took a bath, killed herself, and took revenge on her patron and his wife all at the same time. The company president had decided to break off the liaison with his mistress and to spend more time with his wife (surely a newsworthy item in itself in Japan), but the extralegal bed-mate demanded more consolation money than he was willing to give. With things at this impasse, he moved his few possessions out of his mistress's apartment. Before he did, however, she was able to lay her hands on the key to his legal domicile long enough to have a duplicate made.

A week or so later, the man took his wife out for dinner one evening (another newsworthy happening), and the ex-mistress, who had been spying on their home for several nights, used her duplicate key to gain entry. Once inside, she drew a hot tub, found a razor, and undressed. After a leisurely bath, she settled herself comfortably in the steamy water and cut both her wrists. I suspect that she may have died gleefully imagining the look on the face of her ex-lover's wife upon finding a strange woman taking a blood-bath in her bathtub—and the repercussions that were to follow.

Whether revenge or remonstrance or what have you, the reasons for which the Japanese do themselves in are often as unusual as are their methods. Failing an examination at school, losing a contest or game, and even a desire to call the attention of a foreign country to Japan's problems are oft-encountered examples. And up until the end of the war in 1945, men were known to kill themselves for very slight and even unintentional acts of discourtesy to the Emperor and the Imperial Family, e.g., momentarily holding the Emperor's photograph upside down or allowing the Imperial train to depart two minutes late.

These and other reasons are often so seemingly unimportant that the foreign observer is led to the possible explanation that the Japanese simply do not hold life, theirs or anyone else's, as dear as we do. Or that they do not regard death as the awful, ultimate tragedy that we believe it to be. I, for one, place some credence in the latter explanation. My own observation of death in Japan has suggested to me that many Japanese continue to feel the immediate—almost physical, even if unseen—presence of loved ones who have died in the not-distant past. These souls or spirits apparently hover in and around the home instead of going away to some Western concept of heaven a million light years off in space. With the passage of time, these spirits supposedly wander hither and yon on increasingly distant journeys, but they seem to do this gradually to accustom the living to their absence—and to return unfailingly at seasons like *O-Bon* and anniversaries of their deaths for visits.

Although Japanese students lead world studentry in suicides, the statistics covering all other segments of the population do not, surprisingly, support the notion that the Japanese people as a whole hold the record for the highest incidence of self-induced deaths. West Berlin stands tall atop this heap, with a rate of 41 per 100,000 people, and Hungary follows with 30 per 100,000. Also ahead of Japan (whose rate is 15) go Austria, the rest of West Germany, Denmark, Sweden, and others. That of the United States is 11, Italy's 5, Ireland's is 2.5, and in Egypt suicide is virtually unheard-of, the figure being 0.1, or one hundredth of what it is in the United States.

The most tragic aspect of suicide in Japan is that it all too often is an activity of youth: students who have failed to pass their college entrance exams for the second or third time, lovers who have been denied parental permission to marry, young widows who are having difficulty raising their children, and men, still under thirty, who die in apology for the sins or debts of their fathers. (In contrast, we find high rates of suicide in the United States among doctors, older divorced men, top executives, artists, and—significantly—psychiatrists.)

But whatever the age or reason, suicide in Japan stands far apart from suicide in the Western world because of prevailing attitudes toward it. Although our Bible (in which seven suicides are listed) does not specifically forbid the taking of one's own life, both church and state have long brought moral and legal force to bear against it. (In the Middle Ages in Europe, everything belonging to a person who committed self-murder was taken away, his body was dragged through the streets and exhibited, and he was buried at a crossroads after a stake had been pounded into his heart.) But in Japan as well as in much of Asia, suicide—for reasons of sacrifice or renunciation or expiation—has usually been regarded as admirable and even worthy of adulation.

Several years ago, while I was engaged in research for a book I was writing in Japan, I happened to visit an ancient temple, the Toshoji, in Kamakura, where the priest acquainted me with a story that I think must be the most wondrous in all suicide annals. It was so fantastic that I could not accept it without further substantiation, so that same week I visited four museums and libraries in Kamakura, until I was at last satisfied that this story was not merely an old priest's imaginative maundering.

The seacoast town of Kamakura was the seat of government in Japan in the 1300's. The Emperor, cloistered in Kyoto, did not rule. The Shogun—the exalted "barbarian-subduing generalissimo"—had set up his *bakufu,* or military-camp government, far to the east in Kamakura to keep his samurai from catching and falling ill with the effete manners of the court, but he, too, at length surrendered his authority to a line of regents: the Hojo family.

One of the Hojos, Takatoki, held the reins of power in Japan on the fifth of July in 1333, when his capital was besieged by General Yoshisada Nitta, an adherent to the Impe-

rial cause. By evening of the day in question, it had become
evident that the Regent Takatoki's army was defeated. A
strange man who is best remembered in Japan today because
of his fondness for the hundreds of dogs he kept in princely
style, Takatoki quickly decided what it was that he then must
do.

First, he had his wife and child disguised as fisherfolk and
smuggled out of his beleaguered capital in a fishing boat bound
for the island of Oshima. Next, he announced his own inten-
tions to his followers, many of whom insisted on being allowed
to accompany him.

At length a long procession left the same temple where I
first heard this story and walked through the evening dark in a
northeasterly direction, toward the low hills that ring much of
Kamakura. Every fifth man or so carried a torch, giving the
line of march the appearance of an elongated, slowly crawling
glowworm. At the outskirts of the capital, the road they were
following began to climb along the slope of the first hill, becoming a narrow, winding path that fell off sharply into a
brush-filled ravine to their left and below. While most of the
men were still strung out along this track, the head of the
procession reached the large cave to which Takatoki had been
leading them.

The cave resembled a room that had been half cut away and
exposed (it is still that way today, more than six hundred
years later), and an overhanging cliff made it appear roomier
than it actually was. Under the ledge of this cliff Takatoki
halted, even as a soft mist began to fall. Some of his followers
gathered around him, while others crowded back into the cave,
but the majority remained standing along the path behind and
below their ruler.

Takatoki spoke briefly to an old retainer beside him, who
passed the message on down the line. The men carrying
torches, which were now beginning to sputter in the gradually
increasing rain, stuck them upright into the soft earth beside
the path. Then they all began to make their preparations,

Takatoki himself removing his outer robe and unsheathing his short sword.

At that instant a commotion was heard from below. Soon a young girl of striking beauty appeared, hastily pushing past the men standing in her way. Crying "Wait! Wait!" she rushed up to Takatoki and threw herself down at his feet.

"Lord," she sobbed, "take me with you. Please!"

For a moment, the austere tension eased off Takatoki's face. The girl was his mistress, whom he was said to love far more than his wife. (He had sent his wife and son to safety so that the Hojo family line would not be broken.) He touched her bowed head lightly, then nodded to a retainer poised behind her, who drew his knife and deftly cut the lovely girl's throat, severing the carotid arteries.

The others returned calmly to the business at hand.

Although Takatoki had been a wastrel much of his life, he now showed no weakness of spirit or purpose whatsoever. Kneeling among his followers, he quickly made the prescribed stomach-cut across his abdomen and then signaled for a retainer to finish the job. The retainer inexpertly cut too deep, and Takatoki's head rolled away, completely severed from the trunk of his body.

His followers took their cue from this liege lord. With no hesitation, half of them knelt and made the gash across their abdomens, while the other half served as assistants and chopped off their heads. Then half of those still alive knelt and sliced themselves open below the waist and were in turn decapitated. At the end, of course, a few remained who had to make their own stomach-cuts deep enough to let their lives spill out through them.

A group of servants who had accompanied the procession stood back in the shadows at a respectful distance watching in dumbfounded silence this bloody event, which was to become known as the "night of the mass hara-kiri at Kamakura." It was they who carried the report of what had happened there to the incredulous General Nitta.

As the closing curtain descended, the servants saw the last of the torches sputter out in the rain and heard the intermittent sounds of several of the heads that were slowly working their way down the slope from the path above, catching now and again on a rock or bush but then rolling on.

What they witnessed during those few brief minutes along that torch-lit path had been the self-sought death of Takatoki's mistress and the suicides by hara-kiri of Takatoki Hojo and no less than eight hundred and seventy-three Hojo warriors and retainers.

12

Their Business Ethics
and Attitudes

Not long ago a leading company of management consultants based in New York City reported that seven out of ten American businessmen assigned to work in Japan are falling short of their sales and profit goals. Another assessment went even further by maintaining that nine out of ten were performing inadequately in comparison with what they had done in comparable positions in the United States.

Although the underlying blame for this regrettable situation must be laid at the door of those executives who assigned men knowing nothing of Japanese affairs to such positions in the first instance, the more immediate causes are language frustration and two business codes that are seemingly light years apart, for most of the thinking and behavior of the average Japanese businessman today arises from concepts that held sway during Japan's feudal era, which ended only one hundred years ago. Since then the Japanese have always shown themselves ready enough to import Western technology but not the philosophy of business that developed side by side with this technology.

That was an era in which, for example, merchants were not permitted to stand in the presence of samurai. If they were so audacious as to try, they stood an excellent chance of being shortened by a head, because the samurai ruthlessly cut down anyone who acted "other than expected." In the social structure of those days, the Emperor and his family stood at the top, followed by the court nobles and lords of the realm, the samurai, the farmers, the artisans, and finally the merchants or tradesmen, in that order. The merchants stood above only the Untouchables, who weren't really considered part of the social order at all.

The merchants, however, accumulated wealth, although the Tokugawa Shogunate forbade them from making a display of it. This prompted them to devise odd ways of getting enjoyment from their possessions, such as wearing garments made of cheap, coarse cloth on the outside but lined with heavy, expensive silk. This "shabby outside, luxurious within" tendency still obtains in certain facets of Japanese life.

The samurai, on the other hand, were contemptuous of money. To ask the price of anything was beneath them. Their attitude was summed up in the proverb, *"Bushi wa kuwanedo taka-yoji"* or, "Although he is hungry, the warrior holds his toothpick high" (that is, as if he had just finished eating). In one sense, these warriors were like the slaves of the Old South: as long as their liege lord retained his domain and power, they did not need to think of money, only loyal service. But when their feudal lord fell from favor or was conquered in war, many of his samurai were forced to become *ronin*—masterless warriors—who wandered over the country trying to sell themselves as fast swords and sometimes falling into lawless habits.

Here it was that the samurai and the merchant at last found a common meeting ground. The samurai needed, though he hated to admit it, the merchant's money, while the merchants wanted to see their grandchildren enter life with samurai blood in their veins. So it was that Japan's early businessmen forced a wedge into the door of expanded social acceptance, but many of the old postures remain even today and the uneasy blending of samurai blood with merchant money spawned a strange dichotomy within merchant-class attitudes themselves.

One day some years ago, when I was working in Tokyo as

a freelance writer, I walked into a bank in Nihombashi and said to the guard-receptionist, *"Sumimasen ga kashi-kinko no kakari wa dochira* (Excuse me, but where are your safety-deposit boxes?)"

Using his directions, I found my way to that section of the bank and was soon involved in the following dialogue—in Japanese, of course—with a clerk:

> Seward: "I want to rent a safety-deposit box. Can you tell me what sizes you have and how much the rentals are?"
>
> Clerk: "May I ask who introduced you to us, sir?"
>
> Seward: "No one in particular. I just happened to hear that you have such boxes for rent."
>
> Clerk: "Yes, sir, we have. Will you give me the name of your company, please?"
>
> Seward: "I'm not with a company. I'm self-employed."
>
> Clerk: "Oh."
>
> Seward: "Well?"
>
> Clerk: "I'm afraid we can't rent you a box unless you have an introduction from one of our regular customers or unless we can check the credentials of your company."
>
> Seward: "If you like, I'll pay a year's rental in advance. Even two years."
>
> Clerk: "It's not that. It's a question of trust."

I could already see that I was heading for another of those encounters that can seriously and sometimes permanently unsettle Americans living in Japan, but I foolishly persisted.

> Seward: "Trust? Whose trust?"
>
> Clerk: "It's a question of *your* trustworthiness, sir."
>
> Seward: "But why? I'm going to leave *my* money and valuables in your bank, so why should you have to trust me? It's *your* trustworthiness that I should be asking about. How do I know I can trust you? Come now, let me see your credentials. Do you have a certificate from the Metropolitan Police Board saying that this bank can be trusted?"
>
> Clerk: "Heh, heh. You foreigners are certainly different, aren't you?!"

Seward: "Be serious, man! All that I'm proposing is that I pay you money in advance to let me leave my money on your premises. Now how could I possibly cheat you? Even if I were a known criminal with a dozen convictions, how on earth could I conceivably take advantage of such a situation to defraud you of any money or anything else?"

Clerk (miffed): "You foreigners just don't understand Japan, do you?"

Seward: "We'll never understand it if you don't try to explain it to us."

Clerk: "I'm afraid I can't help you."

Seward: "Don't you *want* to rent your safety-deposit boxes and make money?"

This question genuinely surprised the clerk. He looked as if he had never considered the matter in that light before, but he said nothing.

Seward: "You certainly don't give a damn what the public thinks of your bank, do you?"

Clerk (angry): "Well, you're the one who came here asking to do business with us, aren't you?"

Exit Seward, aging visibly and without safety-deposit box.

Curtain.

This incident suggests several aspects of business in Japan:

1. The accepted way of doing business (following established methods) is more important than results (sales and profits).

2. Public relations—that is, relations with unknown persons who, even so, are potential customers—are of little moment.

3. The party who makes the opening move in a business transaction places himself in the weaker position.

4. A formal introduction is of paramount importance.

The Japanese feel that anyone who introduces one person to another should take responsibility for actions of each involving the other thereafter. The introducer in effect becomes go-between, policeman, arbiter, jury, and judge. If Party A ever wrongs Party B, then B will go to the man who introduced them and demand that he take corrective action. This is reflected in the fact that in the United States there is one lawyer for every 830 persons, but in Japan there is only one for every 14,000. More than fifteen times—proportionately—as many lawyers in our country as in theirs, *because* the introducer in Japan does much of the work—by extralegal methods, of course—that we would expect a lawyer to do here.

Another conclusion to be drawn from the incident at the bank is that the Japanese feel that the man who makes the opening move or the first approach in any business transaction puts himself by definition in the weaker position.

This serves to explain, at least in part, the traditional lack of business aggressiveness in Japan. To be aggressive, you must usually approach the other party, but there your aggressiveness turns against you and places you in the weaker position. And this means that you do not get as low a price as you would have got otherwise or as early a delivery date or possibly as high-quality merchandise.

Not only is he not aggressive but the average Japanese businessman even tends to the opposite extreme of being self-effacing, reticent, vague, and introverted. In American terminology, he would make the world's worst salesman. (The success of much of Japan's foreign trade today can be attributed to *non*-Japanese distributors and, of course, to merchandise of lower cost and good quality.) The verb *to sell,* in the sense of aggressive efforts at marketing, does not sit well with the Japanese, and to offer a college graduate a job as a salesman at almost any level of income is to insult him.

In the small shops and shop-houses of Japan, sales are usually "soft" to a laughable degree. You should not be surprised if you find no sales person in the shop at all.

But there are some exceptions. The shopkeepers of Osaka are considered more tenacious and hardy in their efforts to make a sale than others. And certain shops throughout the country pay lip service to "hard sell" by having all their employees shout *"Irasshaimase!* (Welcome!)" to the customer when he enters, thus giving him a warm feeling of being wanted, but then they often fail to follow up on that advantage by providing prompt service. Nor do they ever try to sell you anything that you have not specifically asked for. (But I must say that I rather appreciate that.)

In the big department stores of Tokyo and Osaka, which are as large as our largest and through which a very significant portion of all Japan's retail consumer goods flow, the sell is so soft that a customer would probably walk out indignantly if a clerk approached and politely offered to show him that day's excellent buys in suits or socks. Getting any attention at all from one of the clerks, of whom there always seems to be too many, is a problem for most customers but especially for the foreigner, because the clerks who don't speak English (and most don't) become even more shy and elusive in their efforts to avoid a confrontation.

Being conditioned to this kind of reception in Japan's department stores works to the disadvantage of Japanese women when they go to the United States—or at least to that of their husbands. When my Japanese wife was first here she kept coming home from her downtown shopping expeditions with more purchases than she could carry and with a sizable deficit in our budget. At first I thought that this was due to the abundance, variety, and price (often cheaper than in Japan) of the merchandise in our stores, and I was willing to allow her a couple of months to work it out of her system. But when three, then four months had passed, and the dear girl still came staggering home loaded to the ears with boxes, parcels, delivery slips, and expressions of regret over the amounts expended, I decided to make inquiries.

What I eventually had to do was to go with her on several shopping trips and demonstrate the expressions one must use to turn off our over-zealous clerks. Later I made a list of these phrases ("I'm just looking," "Nothing today, thank you," "I think I'm in the wrong store," and so forth) and helped her practice them at home. Her problem had simply been lack of experience in saying No in such situations.

One reason for the vast popularity of Japanese department stores is that, even though their prices may not always be the lowest, the customers trust them. This question of trust is vital in Japan, and one hears it raised often. So often, in fact, that I sometimes suspect that the Japanese don't really trust each other. At least not in the field of retail merchandising. (The undeveloped state of the mail-order business in Japan is another aspect of this distrust; the people do not believe that they would ever receive the goods for which they sent money in advance.) The department stores, however, are universally regarded as trustworthy. They will exchange or take back merchandise; if there is any serious question of customer dissatisfaction, they will refund the purchase money; they will deliver free within the city; and they will not abscond in the night, as smaller business people have been known to do.

As often happens in Japan when the old ways collide with the new, both are forced outwards to extremes, and in some businesses where aggressive salesmanship is a prerequisite, the "sell" can become obnoxiously hard. Door-to-door salesmen, real estate agents, railroad-station touts for inns, drivers of cruising taxis (vis-à-vis Westerners), hostesses in bars that cater to American G.I.'s, fishmongers, and the men who sell neckties and toys on city streets represent this category.

Generally speaking, the Japanese people have always tended to fear direct competition. In competition, except in the case of a tie, someone has to lose and someone has to win. To lose is shameful; to cause another (especially another Japanese with whom one is somehow connected) to lose is discomfiting. The Japanese solution? Avoid competition.

Nowadays, of course, the Japanese must compete in order to live and so they have come to accept competition—but with reservations. What they try now to avoid in business is *excessive* competition, while accepting what they call constructive competition. To outlaw the former while nurturing the latter, the Japanese expect—and welcome—government controls.

In the United States, we think of government's dual role in industry as that of an arbiter in disputes between labor and management and as that of a policeman who seeks to prevent flagrant chicanery. To us, the extent of the Japanese government's control over trade and industry (it supplies through banks an average of 80 percent of businesses' operating capital) would be anathema, but the Japanese are conditioned to accept this because they view trade and industry more as a means for national survival than as an opportunity for individual enrichment.

Japan's government, not surprisingly, welcomes this role (what government ever strives to lessen its own influence?), and to make its work less onerous, while still effective, it seeks an ideal situation in which a comparatively few major conglomerates control the market and production—under officialdom's paternalistic eye.

As suggested above, when some Japanese individuals and companies finally do grasp the message about competition, they plunge right in, sometimes with unusual but not necessarily ineffective results. One Japanese maker of beds is a case in point. This company sponsors two- and three-day conventions which all of its sales personnel must attend to pray, to reflect, and to engage in deep contemplation. They also invigorate themselves by getting up before dawn—in the winter, too—to take cold showers outdoors.

One extraordinary facet of this bed-maker's sales campaign can be observed when a new bed is delivered to a customer. In hopes of persuading others in the same neighborhood of the ineffable glories of owning one of these beds, the maker bedecks the delivery truck with gala trappings and colorful banners that proclaim "Another XXX Bed!" and "A citizen of your town is raising his cultural level!" and "Your friends the Tanakas are now among the fast-growing number of en-lightened owners of XXX Beds!"

In rural districts, where the purchase of such an essentially Western item of furniture as a bed is an epochal event, the manager responsible calls upon not only his own sales force but also those of neighboring districts to assemble two or three dozen employees. With careful timing, these persons reach the customer's house thirty minutes before the arrival of the festive delivery truck, and through various devices, they begin to arouse the interest of the neighbors and attract their attention to whatever activity it appears is about to take place at the Tanakas'. By the time the truck comes, the street leading up to the Tanaka residence is lined with serried ranks of the bed-manufacturer's claque plus twice or thrice their number of bemused passers-by and neighbors. The *sakura,* or cherries, as the Japanese call a claque, begin to applaud and cheer as the truck pulls into sight with brave banners flying. The rest of the audience dutifully follows suit. And then the Tanaka family emerges from their home into the bright wonderful world of owning a genuine XXX Bed.

The actual mechanics of doing business with Japanese companies should be worthy of a full-year course at the graduate level in any college. Without such a background or without the assistance of a seasoned, well-rounded intermediary, the hapless foreigner who knocks at the door of Japanese business is almost certain to face frustration, bafflement, or even defeat within a very short while. Should he succeed without such assistance, then it is likely that he is one of those fortunate few who have a patent-protected product or technology highly desired and hitherto unobtainable in Japan.

This foreigner may be accustomed to flitting about the globe with his well-stuffed briefcase, meeting executives at his own level and finalizing marketing arrangements right and left; but when he comes to Japan, he would be wise to slow down as soon as he gets off the jet at Haneda and remind himself that business negotiations here will seem to progress in slow motion, if at all, in comparison with what he has been used to. Nor is this because the Japanese are lazy or uninterested. Rather, it is due to their strong preference for group action and all that is involved in reaching decisions by the *ringi* (see below) process.

Not many nations have produced fewer political strongmen or dictators than Japan. Ex-premier Shigeru Yoshida had inclinations in that direction, but this was so exceptional that he was given the nickname *"Wan-man"* (meaning One-man). Furthermore, few successful Japanese in any field would be so foolhardy as to attribute their success entirely to their own efforts. Almost invariably, they will credit most of it to the members of their group.

A Japanese proverb has it that the stake that sticks up will get hammered down. In Japanese companies, where lifetime employment is the rule, no one wants to make a decision for which he alone would have to take full responsibility in the event of failure. Such companies, therefore, utilize what is termed the *ringi* process, which means in effect that a proposal is drawn up, usually at the middle-management level, and passed both vertically and horizontally until a sizable group has studied it and concurred in it. Should anyone fail to concur, he will have ample opportunity to present his objections at the numerous staff conferences at which the matter will inevitably be discussed. The man who disagrees will either eventually persuade a sufficient number of others of the validity of his objections, so that the matter will be dropped, or he himself will be persuaded of the worth of the proposal. In any event, if the proposal is approved it will be by an overwhelming majority, if not unanimously, and in the event of later failure no single "stake that sticks up" will get hammered down. It is necessary, therefore, to persuade not only the top man in a company of the value of a proposal but often a considerable number of his subordinates who are concerned in the matter as well.

Obviously this is a time-consuming process, but it appears to work well enough in Japanese business. For one thing, many of the people who will be closely involved later in the new business are being briefed in several or all aspects of it from the very beginning. And for another, it may serve to instill in these employees a strong sense of involvement in the decision whether or not to undertake the business, with the result that they may later devote more effort to it than if the decision to go ahead had been handed down to them from a distant and seemingly cold management committee or board of directors.

Once our foreign businessman has arrived at the conference table of a typical Japanese company, he may quickly want to thrust aside the inconsequentials and amenities and "get down to brass tacks." He has a product which he believes is a good one and which he is willing to sell at what he believes to be a fair price. He lays his cards on the table, and he expects the Japanese to do the same. If the details are agreed upon, they will be put down in black and white, and the resulting contract will become the control center of the proposed business. If the Japanese and American counterparts like each other personally, that's fine, but even if they don't, the business itself is the important thing.

At least that may be the way the foreign businessman looks at it. But the Japanese will tend instead to give personal relationships very high priority. To them, there is little more distressing than open friction, altercations, and angry eyeball-to-eyeball confrontations in business. For this reason, they like to look the foreign businessman over carefully before the final handclasp. Believing that many Americans are more outspoken, abrupt, and perhaps abrasive than they are, they want to feel some assurance that the future years of the business relationship will not be marred by bluntly expressed disappointments, recriminations, harsh accusations, and high-pressure tactics. If it looks as if such will be the course of the relationship, then they would rather not be involved at all, no matter if it promises to be profitable.

Often during the course of such negotiations a crisis will be reached within the Japanese company that will cause further delay in the proceedings. This crisis may be occasioned by internal opposition or by external difficulties with, for example, subcontractors or sources of supply. The Japanese company often will prefer not to go into a complicated explanation of this crisis (hard-to-explain Japanese values may be involved) or even refer to it, which can leave the foreign businessman in a stew of concern and puzzlement. When everything seemed to be going so smoothly, what could have happened? If he has a close personal relationship with some employee of the company, the foreigner may be able to obtain the clarifying details through him. Otherwise, it is best to wait patiently. If his Japanese counterparts have run into outside opposition, they may be "selling their face," meaning that they may be tied up in a series of several seemingly casual visits to the source of this opposition to display their friendliness and respect and to indirectly remind them of the matter at hand.

Even after this crisis has passed, there may be other delays, and sometimes the foreign businessman—thinking to speed things up—may present the Japanese company with his suggestions for the proposed venture, drawn up in the form of a detailed contract. If he does this, he is making a mistake. Eventually a contract will be necessary, but the Japanese are often put off by such a formidable document at this stage in the negotiations. There is nothing at all wrong with putting one's ideas on paper—indeed, it is often to be recommended —but at this point they should be brief, general, and indicative of a certain flexibility.

A time will also come when a compromise may seem to be the order of the day, but here again the Japanese tend to dislike the frank, clear-cut Western style of compromise: "Look, you fellows have been asking for ninety and I've been offering eighty, right? And you say you'll pay the freight. So here's what let's do: I'll have the goods picked up by my trucks and give you eighty-two yen per unit. Have we got a deal?"

To the Japanese, this kind of compromise appears to favor the party who either offered an unrealistically high (or low) price to begin with or who clung more tenaciously to his bargaining position throughout. They would prefer that the final agreement, when reached, be based on sincere attention to genuine actualities on both sides of the conference table.

When the contract is on the point of being signed, the foreign businessman may be dismayed by a Japanese request for much more substantiating data, but this will normally not be occasioned by sudden doubt. Such data may be required when the Japanese company presents the proposal to its government for approval. Furthermore, they like to have such reports on hand to forestall any possible future criticism that the proposed business was not investigated thoroughly enough in the beginning.

When persons are introduced in Japan, one will often hear the introducer mention how many years he has known so-and-so. This reflects Professor Chie Nakane's observation that the relative strength of the human bond (in Japan) tends to increase in proportion to the length and intensity of actual contact. This actual contact becomes what is called a person's "private social capital," meaning the value and utility of old friendships. This can be as important as financial capital in Japan. When a Japanese says that he has known so-and-so for ten years, what he is saying is that during that entire time the man has conducted himself sincerely and in a trustworthy manner, so that he feels confident in introducing him to someone else (and in effect taking responsibility for the man's future actions).

This "private social capital" reflects why expense-account entertainment is so important in Japan. In 1971, Japan's combined corporate "social expenses" reached 3.4 billion dollars, exceeding the entire social-welfare allocation for the year. Seventy percent of this amount went for food and drink at night. (The business luncheon is still not very popular in Japan.) The remainder was spent on gifts for customers and clients during the midsummer and year-end gift-giving seasons. Without this input, the bright lights of the Ginza as well as those of Shimbashi, Akasaka, Roppongi, and other areas would flicker off almost immediately. A drastic revision, for example, in tax-bureau regulations and, consequently, corporate financial practices regarding expense accounting could change night life in Japan catastrophically.

Obviously, a primary reason for all this expense-account spending is that the Japanese genuinely believe that this lubricant is massively beneficial to their business prospects and status. Another reason—lesser, but nonetheless important—is that it is a form of compensation to the employee with those privileges.

The Ten Commandments for Doing Business in Japan

1. Always try to arrange for a formal introduction to any person or company with whom you want to do business. Remember that these introductions should come from someone whose position is at least as high as that of the person you want to meet or from someone who has done a favor for him. Bear in mind also that in taking advantage of such an introduction you are incurring a debt that must eventually be cleared from your books. (See cautions below about direct mention and passing of money.) Because the straightforward, no-nonsense style of negotiation is considered rude, try to get a third party (it can be the man who introduced you) to serve as a go-between. In fact, the go-between should settle the major issues before you meet the other party at all. The tremendous role played by the trading companies in Japan's business world derives partly from their positions as go-betweens and introducing agents.

2. Always strive for a thorough personalization of all

business relationships. In this respect, the Japanese resemble the crusty old Texan of legend who averred that he didn't trust any man with whom he'd never been drunk. Drinking and wenching together promote successful mutual business. The Japanese feel strongly inhibited when sober and unable to overcome their reticence. They need sake to repress these inhibitions, but it is not always the alcohol itself but rather the atmosphere of their "floating world" of bars and restaurants that triggers the release for them. If the president of a Japanese company takes you out in the evening for carousing, you will find that his signature on the bar bill that you both ran up may be more meaningful to your future mutual business than his signature on any contract that you propose he sign. If you are the one who invites him out, take him to an establishment where he can enjoy himself without *enryo,* or constraint. Specifically, this means not to take him to your home (where he will stand on ceremony and feel ill at ease) or Western-style restaurants and nightclubs. This has particular application in the case of older Japanese men. No matter how rowdy the saturnalia grows, take care not to exceed a certain degree of familiarity with this Japanese acquaintance. Do not, for instance, slap him on the back and call him by his first name, unless, of course, he has lived in the Western world for several years and lets you know that he is prepared to accept that degree of familiarity.

3. Never disturb harmony. The Japanese believe that it is better to be harmonious than to be right or to make a profit. If you have something unpleasant or disappointing to relate or to discuss—no matter whose fault it is—endeavor first of all to do it through your go-between. In any case, avoid doing it abruptly or in front of others, especially men who are not privy to the business in question.

4. Never cause a Japanese to lose face by putting him in a position where he must admit failure or say that he does not know something that he should know professionally. (Being discharged is, of course, the ultimate individual failure within the corporate framework, but it almost never happens. Japanese companies are as reluctant to discharge an employee as a father is to disinherit his own child.)

5. Bear constantly in mind the fact that it is the way business is done that is often considered as important as the results. Sometimes even more so.

6. Do not appeal to logic. In Japan, emotional considerations are more important than cold facts.

7. Do not dwell on the subject of money, especially in specific amounts. Leave bargaining over prices to go-betweens or the lower echelons. Never remind your vis-à-vis of how much money you helped him make. Don't talk about how much it cost you both to do the town the previous night, no matter who paid the bill. Leave the handling of cash to others. If you have to turn cash over to a businessman, be sure to wrap it neatly in white paper or enclose it in an envelope.

8. Keep in mind that in Japan time is not money. If a Japanese businessman gives you a specific delivery or payment date of his own accord, it is much more likely to be reliable than one you squeezed out of him. Americans tend to cajole and plead until they have wrung an early promissory date from Japanese businessmen and then they relax, thinking that they have won a victory. It is only later that they learn that they have usually accomplished nothing, other than turning the Japanese against them.

9. Remember that the Japanese prefer to express themselves in language that is vague and ambiguous. If you ask a Japanese how far it is from the Ginza to his home and even if he measured the distance only the day before and knows that it is precisely 5.3 miles, he will still say "a few miles," because to be precise is a form of impertinence. It smacks too openly of an unpalatable display of superior knowledge.

10. Be aware that the Japanese avoid independent or individual action and that their first compulsion in decision-making is to look for precedents. Whereas we admire a man who succeeds on his own without undue reliance on the help or advice of others, the Japanese are not similarly impressed. Long before we coined the phrase, they were already the perfect "Organization Men." They don't like to stand out for any reason, even if it be one of striking superiority. They strive for an organizational ideal of anonymous

consensus. The hoary proverb *"Mazu wa sodan no ue"* expands to mean, "Don't do anything until you have first consulted others." The maintenance of good, ethical relations with other companies (and people) ranks as more important than even production and sales at a profit, although there obviously must be a limit to how far a Japanese can allow himself to be guided by this principle.

Other Important Do's and Don'ts

1. While foreign executives may be largely motivated by profit (and legitimately so, on behalf of their shareholders), remember that a continuing emphasis on the profit motive will not be in accord with the foremost principles of your Japanese counterparts, who may refer more often to steady employment for their own people, corporate growth, national economic welfare, and product superiority.

2. Make only limited reference to contractual obligations between you. The Japanese may not read the fine print in a contract and never quote it. The important thing about such a contract is not so much what it says but rather who signed it and the fact that it exists at all.

3. Don't bring your wife (American or otherwise) to a Japanese-style dinner or to any night-time entertainment except the lavish cocktail parties that are growing in popularity these days. Even if your Japanese host should ask you to bring her, you had better not. He is probably only being polite.

4. Bear in mind that the better quality and lower price of your product usually can't compete against the force of personal obligation on the part of one Japanese businessman toward another.

5. In your first approach to a Japanese company, try to enter at the highest level feasible. You will meet resistance to this because the company officers surround themselves with assistants whose function it is to fend off unknown outsiders. This desire for seclusion, however, does not spring from the idea of being "too busy" or "not wanting to waste time." Rather, it comes from the philosophy that if

the Japanese businessman doesn't meet you face to face, you have not actually entered his network of personal obligation and responsibility, and he is not then expected to do anything at all about you. . . . The problem here is that you may be "locked in" to the level at which you enter. I remember one case in which I made the mistake of approaching a large corporation through a young neighbor of mine who worked for that company as the assistant chief of a certain subsection. He was so far down the ladder that the company president did not recall ever having seen him, as I was regretfully to learn later. In any event, this neighbor kindly offered to make the introduction while we were talking over the fence one evening and I agreed, in a moment of forgetfulness. The next day he introduced me to his immediate superior, the chief of his subsection, and it took me six weeks to work myself up from level to level. And when I at last had my first conference with the president of the company at a long mahogany table surrounded by his staff, my neighbor was still there. Since he made the introduction, his company felt that I should forever be his special project, although my business did not concern his specific commodity area and although the company did not propose to transfer him to my commodity or elevate him in rank. His duties were only to meet me at the entrance of the building, escort me to the president's office, sit beside me during conferences, and go along when I was being entertained at night or when I was entertaining them.

6. Don't praise your own products or services directly. Let a go-between or your reputation and literature do this for you. One American company president whom I know spoiled a proposed enterprise of several million dollars' annual potential by sitting in the Osaka office of his vis-à-vis for an hour and expounding, albeit courteously, on why his own products were far better than anything else on the market.

7. Remember that humility and patience have their uses. The Japanese say proverbially that they expect to call on a company eight times before their visits bear fruit.

8. Always carry and use business cards that give your company affiliation and exact position. I remember one wealthy, influential American who handed out business cards that listed only his name and his telephone number when he was first in Japan. When he realized that he was not getting the same warm reception that he was accustomed to in other countries, he asked me why, and I explained the purposes of the *meishi,* or business card, to him. Until they knew his title and organization affiliation, the Japanese simply did not know how to deal with him. . . . On the other hand, you should be careful about passing out your *meishi* too freely, since they are sometimes used by unscrupulous Japanese to lay claim to high-level foreign connections that they do not really have.

9. Don't expect any significant decision-producing negotiations at the conference table at the first meeting. Remember that the Japanese side will try to outnumber you. If three of you go to the meeting, they may bring ten. They do this for four reasons, and the validity of each varies somewhat with the situation: a) the *ringi,* or group method, explained earlier, b) courtesy to you, since it shows the importance they attach to you and your business, c) the vertical compartmentalization of Japanese business, which means that they actually need more people to provide even preliminary answers than you would have needed, and d) their simple liking to do things as a group.

10. If you meet a Japanese away from Japan, entertain him lavishly. Help him make contacts, get his tickets and reservations, find addresses, and overcome language problems. When you meet him again in Japan, he will repay you manyfold.

11. Be dignified. Maintain an attitude of pleasant reserve, without being cold and stern. Smile and laugh at times, but don't horse around.

12. When you request a Japanese to do something for you, you are, in effect, placing yourself completely in his hands. If, for example, you ask a Tokyo businessman to recommend to you a reliable maker of low-cost pitchforks, do not offhandedly reject his recommendation, even though

you are certain that those particular pitchforks are of miserable quality and exorbitant price. Pretend to give serious consideration to that maker, and when you do finally announce, sadly, that you can't do business with him, offer an acceptable (to the Japanese) explanation as to why.

13. If you must deal with government officials—especially those of the lower echelons—endeavor to have an assistant or go-between do this for you. Otherwise, your feathers are likely to be ruffled by the haughtiness of Japanese officialdom, which still does not truly comprehend its role as servants of the people. The officials, however, will resist your sending someone else to do your business for you, because it pleases them to see foreigners bobbing their heads and touching their forelocks before them, and there will be times when you will have to comply. Still, you should avoid them if you can do so without too much abrasion of feelings.

14. If your Japanese vis-à-vis quotes you a price that you feel is excessive, don't reject it out of hand and especially not with overtones of outraged protest. No matter how unreasonable the price may be, you will insult him if you do not at least pretend to give it serious consideration. After that you can say that you understand his position, etc., and, if only it were possible, you would like to meet his price. Unfortunately, however, a new development in the American market precludes your paying more than half of the price he has just mentioned. Then add suitable words of regret. This applies as well to other business proposals and suggestions in general.

15. Bear in mind that the Japanese are not as devoted to the principle of aggressive advertising as we are. At times they appear to feel that it is beneath their dignity. Even when they do advertise, they will often explain that they were placed in a position where they could not refuse to run an ad, perhaps as a favor to a friend in an advertising agency.

16. In Japan, remember that the word *service* is not always limited in meaning to the repair and reconditioning of manufactured products after a period of use. In fact, the

Japanese often say *afuta-sabisu* (after-service) to express what we mean by service alone. They expand their definition to include a general willingness to favor the customer in many ways, large and small, including entertainment and errand-running. . . . If you get a discounted price in a shop, the clerk may tell you, *"Sabisu desu* (It is a service)."

17. Don't assume that the word *hai* is limited in meaning to simply "yes." Many American businessmen learn this to their sorrow—later. *Hai* can also convey such meanings as "I'm listening" or "I understand" or "Go ahead, I'm following what you say." Remember also that although a Japanese businessman's answer to your request, proposal, or demand may actually begin with *Hai,* followed by a sentence or two of apparent general agreement, you would do well to listen carefully to the rest of what he has to say. In feudal times any inferior who began his answer to a superior with "No" or "I won't" or "It's impossible" stood in active danger of being cut in twain. Accordingly, it became customary to ease one's way into anything short of absolute agreement or instant compliance with such fair words as "Yes, I would be delighted to do as you instruct," etc., until at last approaching that one word *but* most circumspectly and diffidently. Even today this tendency is far from extinct.

In fact, many Japanese simply avoid use of the word *no* entirely, preferring to relay negative reactions by cue words and phrases such as *"Sa, chotto muzukashii desu, ne* (Well, I think it would be rather difficult . . .)" or by letting nonresponsive silence speak for them.

A very large part of this is due to the Japanese desire not to disappoint, not to offend, not to distress. They will often say what they think you would like to hear. It is, therefore, important that you phrase your questions, if possible, in such a way as to give no hint of which answer you would prefer.

Throughout this chapter I have tried to depict Japanese business life as the finely threaded, intricate web of personal relations and obligation that it is: a group-oriented philosophy that regards its industry as a vast family complex in which no effort and no service on behalf of those "in the family" can be too great and in which those outside the family are seldom given any consideration at all.

Be that as it may, it is a system that has worked most successfully for the Japanese in recent years, developing their country into a market that is attractive now and will be increasingly so throughout this decade and the next. It is predicted that by 1985 the average Japanese family will have $20,000 to spend annually, after taxes. Given that level of income and the desire that most Japanese have for imported merchandise, Japan offers to foreign businessmen opportunities of a magnitude that should make the complications involved in entering the market well worth the trouble.

13

Their Democracy

In late 1971, the Emperor of Japan held a press conference for foreign correspondents, the first in history. Although it was not mentioned at the conference, many observers felt that the reason behind this unprecedented event was a recently published book entitled *Japan's Imperial Conspiracy,* in which the Emperor was depicted as having been far more responsible for Japan's entry into World War Two than had generally been believed theretofore in the West.

But the fact that this press conference was held at all is surely a noteworthy comment on the advances made on behalf of democracy in Japan since 1945, because before that date it would have been unthinkable. The activities of the Imperial family were not a subject that the public could make comments on, favorable or otherwise. When ex-Sgt. Shoichi Yokoi recently returned to Japan after an absence of thirty-one years (he had hidden out in the jungles of Guam for twenty-eight of them), he was amazed and distressed to observe the extent to which the public could now interest itself in the affairs of the Emperor: for example, newspaper photos of the Emperor yawning at a banquet in London and the Empress wearing slacks in the snow in Sapporo. Yokoi's voice was literally one from the far-off past when he declaimed that he wanted to go to the entrance to the Imperial Palace, bow in the direction of the Imperial Presence, and respectfully report that he had held out for twenty-eight years in compliance with the Imperial Wish.

When Yokoi fled into the jungles of Guam in 1944, Japan's Emperor was still, by the provisions of the Meiji Constitution, an absolute monarch. If he did not rule as absolutely as, for example, Peter the Great did, it was only because his subjects did not want to trouble him with mundane details and not because there was no basis for such absolutism. Just how much control he did have until 1945 is a point that can be debated, but it is certain that he showed an ample glimpse of it when in August, 1945, he informed his Cabinet, which included some very stubborn generals and admirals, that he desired that his country accept the Potsdam Declaration and thereby surrender to the Allied Powers. No matter what their innermost qualms, the Cabinet members acquiesced without a murmur of dissent.

After the war, his status changed drastically. Although he is now the "symbol of the state and of the unity of the people," he must act *under the direction of the Cabinet* and does *not* have "power related to government." He goes through the ceremony of appointing the Prime Minister, who must be first named by the Diet. He calls the Diet into session, promulgates all laws, dissolves the House of Representatives, appoints and dismisses state ministers, awards honors, proclaims elections, receives in audience foreign VIP's and ambassadors, and performs various other ceremonial functions, but all at the *instructions of the Cabinet*. In short, the Emperor's role today is only to invest the everyday functions of the government with the majesty and dignity of the Imperial Throne.

In a typical year, the Emperor's round of activities might include attending the opening ceremonies of an international sports event such as the 1972 Winter Olympics in Sapporo, meeting foreign royalty upon arrival in Japan, addressing the Diet after the customary New Year's recess and asking its members to extend their best efforts on behalf of the nation, harvesting the first rice in the private Imperial paddy, reporting on the state of the nation to the Imperial ancestors at the Grand Shrine in Ise, awarding honors to a hundred or so worthies, sponsoring a national poetry contest and reading a poem of his own composition there, and pursuing his studies in marine biology during the summer at the Imperial Villa in Hayama.

The government of which he is the symbol is divided—like that of the United States—into three branches: legislative, administrative or executive, and judicial. The executive power belongs to the Cabinet, the judicial to the courts, and the legislative to the Diet. Among the powers invested in the people are those to elect the members of the Diet, to review the appointments of the Supreme Court judges, and to approve amendments to the Constitution.

The Diet is the highest organ of the power of the State and consists of a House of Representatives and a House of Councillors. The former has 467 members, each with an office tenure of four years. The latter has 250 members, each holding office for six years. When the two Houses fail to agree, the will of the House of Representatives prevails, except in proposals to amend the Constitution, in which case the consent of more than two-thirds of both Houses is needed. Each of 117 electoral districts sends from three to five members to the lower House. Of the upper House, 150 members are elected from the forty-six prefectures while 100 are elected by the nation at large.

Universal suffrage is guaranteed and upheld.

The Cabinet is the highest national agency responsible for the administration of the affairs of the country. It has such executive functions as administering the laws, proposing bills and budgets to the Diet, and conducting relations with foreign governments. Within the Cabinet are twelve Ministers who head the governmental departments called Ministries and four so-called State Ministers, who have no portfolio. Since the end of the war, the average life of a Cabinet has been less than one year. It must resign when the Diet fails to give it a vote of confidence and upon convocation of the Diet after a general election. The Prime Minister is empowered to select the members of his own Cabinet, all of whom, however, must be from the Diet.

The Prime Minister himself is responsible to the Diet and must be elected by it from among its own members (except in the event that the House has been dissolved). Since 1955, he has consistently been the leader of the majority party, which now happens to be the Liberal Democrats. He cannot hold a professional position in any armed force.

The courts are all organs of the national government, from the Supreme Court—with its review power—down through the 8 High Courts, the 49 District Courts, the 570 Summary Courts, and the 49 Family Courts. The fifteen judges of the Supreme Court are appointed by the Cabinet and subject to the review of the people. All of the other judges are named by the Supreme Court, appointed by the Cabinet, and are subject to review by the people every ten years. Corresponding to each court are public prosecutors who represent the State in criminal actions.

When asked after the war about the prospects of democratizing Japan, the late Yukio Ozaki—the Grand Old Man of Constitutional Government—said in effect that the U.S. Occupation Forces would have to stay in Japan for one hundred years to have much of a chance of success in such an effort. Because our forces changed from occupation to security status in 1952, we had only seven years in which to do the work that Mr. Ozaki estimated would take at least one hundred.

Where the Japanese actually stand vis-à-vis democracy twenty-seven years after the war's end is a matter for discussion, but it would be safe to begin by saying that they are at least more democratic (or perhaps less *un*democratic) these days than they were, say, in the Thirties. In fact, the present situation might even lull the casual observer into a state of optimistic complacency. This, however, would be both unfortunate and unjustifiable. Granted, their *form* of government is democratic and their nation has achieved three of the *sine qua non*s upon which democracy is founded: national independence, industrialization, and general literacy. Granted, further, a probable majority of the people, if polled, would answer that they believe democracy to be a good thing (although their definitions of democracy would vary), and they would not easily relinquish their recently acquired constitutional rights. Nonetheless, the status of democracy in Japan today is one that gives rise to serious doubts in the minds of competent authorities.

Reflecting their omnipresent adaptability and their genuine admiration for a victor, the Japanese readily embraced the democratic forms held out to them by our Occupation Forces after the war in the Pacific, although admittedly they had little choice in the matter. In the process of assimilation, however, many of them confused democracy with license and dissoluteness. Democracy became equated with permission to pursue entirely selfish goals and was not connected with the fundamental equality of mankind. Nor did democracy's concomitant concept of responsible individualism take deep root in their national consciousness.

Nowadays many Japanese feel that they have given American-style democracy a fair trial—which is hardly true—but that it has brought them more student disorder, labor strife, and political violence than beneficial social reforms. While still not ready to abandon their version of democracy, they are nonetheless beginning to advocate that it be tempered with their traditional concepts of social values and relationships.

These traditional concepts developed within a social hierarchy founded on paternalism, the Confucian canon of decorum, repression of individuality, harmonious relations—at any cost, loyalty as the supreme virtue, and unquestioning acceptance of inequality as the natural order of things—all bound together into a mammoth pyramid of interlocking personal obligations and dependencies. Classes of society were clearly demarcated. Movement between classes was harshly discouraged. Instead, philosophic acceptance of status was inculcated, as was blind obedience to authority. The lower classes were divided into groups which became responsible for the actions of all their members, and this in turn led to extremely close group identification, clannishness, and grinding conformity. (It also resulted in a glaring failure of individual responsibility once removed from group influence.) Ostracism from the group became a most dreaded punishment, and even today the Japanese will subordinate interfamily relations to the interests of neighborhood harmony.

Because no system is perfect in its functioning, there has always been some resistance in Japan to this rigid, conformist society, and rebellion against such restraints has long been a major theme in novels and stage plays. Even so, the rebels—if they survive at all—often seem to eventually become stern dispensers of similar restrictions themselves, even as American college students who endure hazing as freshmen become enthusiastic purveyors of the same callous childishness themselves the next year.

For the Japanese, inequality in both practice and concept has been the rule of their organized social life for almost the entire span of Japan's history. Overwhelming respect and inordinate deference are shown to superior persons on the basis of age, occupation, social status, and rank, while inferiors and strangers are treated arrogantly or utterly ignored.

Within this framework of inequality, each person has his proper place, his station in life assigned by fate. While one is permitted—indeed, expected—to strive to attain the highest level of skill and accomplishment within his particular field of endeavor, he is not encouraged to move into other fields. Nor is he encouraged to display individual initiative, rational judgment, or a spirit of independence. He is taught that it is better to be harmonious than to be right according to his own private convictions. He is not expected to be morally courageous but only amenable to the wills of those above him.

THE JAPANESE

In the United States we pay homage to the man who stands alone against all comers in his continuing struggle for justice or vindication or personal liberty, but such a man would not appeal to the Japanese. They would have preferred that he subordinate his own inner urges to the ambitions of the group.

Perhaps because our forefathers came to this country primarily in search of liberty and because we later fought a terrible civil war over the question of the freedom of one segment of our people, we Americans tend to place a heavy emphasis on the ideal of freedom of choice in religion, occupation, residence, and mate, while we assume, sometimes mistakenly, that all other peoples are filled with this same burning desire for liberty. If you ask a Japanese, without preamble, whether he would prefer to be free or not free, he will almost certainly opt in favor of freedom. But if you could suddenly transport him into that condition of freedom that we Americans regard as ideal, he would quickly lose much of his enthusiasm for it. Conditioned as he is by generations of self-effacing conformity, he actually prefers being a member of a community to independent individual status. This preference is manifested in his tendency to follow a leader, his fear of responsibility, his avoidance of competition, his reluctance to argue his own convictions, his willingness to abide by precedent, and his readiness to submerge his individualism in his group.

I recall some years ago reading a Japanese best-seller entitled *Hadaka Zuihitsu* (*Outspoken Essays*). In the foreword, the author wrote of having seen a flock of geese flying over him one evening, and he went on to wax ecstatic about this splendid concept of goose life. Just think, he wrote, how wonderful it would be if only we humans could conduct ourselves like that flight of geese, all moving in perfect harmony, each in his assigned place, all following the flight leader without question or hesitation.

Astonished, I showed the book to several Japanese friends,

thinking that the writer might be a known eccentric, but they all agreed with his vision of the good life.

Given this Japanese willingness to be led and their acceptance of pervasive social inequality, it should surprise no one to learn that the Japanese also abide by presumptions of racial inequality. Most of them have a deep-rooted belief that the peculiar circumstances of their history have made them a race apart, difficult to appreciate perhaps, but endowed with moral qualities and strength of character that destine them for leadership among nations.

It is strange to reflect that Japan first proposed that the League of Nations adopt the principle of universal racial equality—a proposal which was, unfortunately, defeated. But what Japan was actually advocating then was not so much an elevation of the black and brown races as it was a genuine acceptance by the Caucasian race of the Japanese themselves as equals. Even today the Japanese want to be treated as equals by us while showing almost no willingness to extend the same consideration to the three million *Eta* and the six hundred thousand Koreans within their own boundaries. And there is among them a widespread tendency to regard with disdain and even contempt the other races of Asia. These prejudiced minds among the Japanese conveniently forget, if they ever knew, that, according to the *Shojiroku* (a peerage published about the end of the seventh century) fully one-third of all noble families in Japan proudly laid claim to Korean or Chinese descent.

The whole history of Japanese-Korean relations is a tragic one that is too complicated to explore here, but there are certain striking similarities between the lot of the Koreans in Japan and that of the blacks in the United States. Large numbers of the Koreans, for instance, were brought to Japan against their will as slave labor, while many have taken up crime in Japan only because no other feasible way to sustain life seemed open to them. When the Japan Communist Party undertook to champion their cause, many Koreans became party members, enabling the Japanese, with some justification, to point to their Korean minority as a pack of gangsters, Communists, and malcontents. In contrast to the United States, however, almost nothing is being done in Japan to ease or better the lot of this minority group.

Although the *Eta* (written with two characters meaning "much filth") outnumber the Koreans in Japan five to one, the word *Eta* itself is one that you will almost never hear. It is a taboo word, even as the people themselves are classed as untouchables. In referring to this class of outcasts, the average Japanese uses such expressions as *shin-heimin* (new citizens) and *burakumin* (people of the hamlet), or he may merely raise four fingers in the air in reference to the outcasts' work with four-legged animals (see below).

Several theories about the origin of these outcasts have currency: one is that they were a class of slaves and imperial grave-keepers called *senmin* (literally, low-ranked persons). Another is that they are descendants of Korean captives brought to Japan in the sixteenth century. A third, surely apocryphal, is that they are descended from illegitimate offspring of the twelfth-century General Yoritomo. A fourth is that this class took shape in the seventh and eighth centuries as Buddhist proscriptions against taking animal life spread. And the fifth—and most colorful—refers us back to the time when the Japanese were slowly but surely pushing the Ainu northward out of central Honshu toward their eventual reservations on the island of Hokkaido. Into the wide strip of no-man's-land that long separated these two peoples fled deserters and criminals from both sides who sometimes formed themselves into bands for mutual safety. With the northward advance of the Japanese, these bands were often bypassed in wilderness enclaves. In time, the Japanese came to give these outcasts work that they themselves would not perform: disposal of dead horses and oxen, burial or cremation of the corpses of enemy dead and executed criminals, tanning and working leather, and manufacture of footwear.

Today the plight of the *shin-heimin* (a much more acceptable word than *Eta*) in Japan is far worse, for example, than that of the black in the United States. Weakened by too numerous consanguineous marriages, most of them lead at best a marginal existence in isolated agricultural or cottage-industry communities. Only 10 percent own enough land from which to make a living. Many of the landless are unemployed, while those who have found employment usually work for wages considerably lower than those nonoutcast Japanese would have received for the same job. And automation in large shoe and sandal manufacturing plants is eating away the precarious income of the small-scale footwear-makers among the outcasts.

In addition, they are discriminated against in schools and in marriage. (Engaged couples in Japan religiously have each other's background thoroughly investigated to ascertain that neither is "tainted" with this outcast blood.) Although the Japanese Constitution specifically prohibits such discrimination, little effort is being made to alleviate their suffering. Sending teams of young people, for example, into the outcasts' villages to urge them to vote, to advise them of their rights, to teach sanitation, and to care for their sick is unheard of.

Considered against this background of racial intolerance, suppression of individuality, reluctance to engage in independent thought and action, and lack of enthusiasm for personal liberty and freedom, it is small wonder that their forcibly transplanted democracy is failing to take deep root in the alien soil of the Japanese.

When the National Character Study Committee of the National Institute of Statistical Mathematics surveyed nearly three thousand Japanese from all social classes and age groups in 1963, they found that 49 percent of those polled believed that the desirability of democracy "depended upon the circumstances." Here again we see the typical evasion of an abstract ideal and the preference for judging things in view of prevailing circumstances, for the Japanese in that 49 percent meant that they would approve of democracy when it suited their purposes but would disapprove when it presented some inconvenience or difficulty for them. In short, they might favor democracy today but frown on it tomorrow.

Another factor that militates against the growth of democracy in Japan is the doubt entertained by most Japanese about the desirability of majority rule. While to us it is the very essence of any democratic system, to many Japanese it is anathema, and they may even call it *tasu no boryoku* ("the tyranny of the majority"), a phrase first used by Marquis Hirobumi Ito in referring to Japan's House of Representatives.

The Japanese ask: If the majority is allowed to impose its will on the entire population, what then becomes of the minority's will? Is it just and fair that the will of as many as 30 or 40 or even 49 percent of the people be ignored? Should not the majority and the minority both give a little to effect a compromise, so that the wills of all the people are represented in each decision? And, since the majority has more room to spare, should it not magnanimously give a little more than the minority?

We would answer that compromise is fine, *if* one can be effected, but that too often a compromise turns out to be a solution that really satisfies no one at all. Or very few. Also, that there inevitably come times when compromise is simply not possible: a road may fork to the east and to the west with nothing but unscalable mountain in between.

Furthermore, the Japanese preference for this form of compromise is such that it frequently results in coercion of the minority dissenters to achieve apparent unanimity, leaving the minority in an even more untenable position because they have been pressured into paying lip service to a proposed action that in their hearts they do not like.

One hot summer day in 1946, we were driving south over a

pitted dirt road in Kyushu, trying to find our way to Kumamoto. As we were leaving the town of Kurume, I stopped the jeep while one of the other two Americans with me asked a girl in kimono which road we should take. She did not know but obligingly offered to take us to her house nearby, where she promised to inquire of her father: a Japanese diplomat in enforced inactivity because of the war. He proved to be quite friendly and hospitable and suggested that we pass an hour or so of the sweltering afternoon with him drinking beer.

The thought of anything cold to drink in that heat would have easily persuaded the three of us to accept his invitation, but actually no such persuasion was necessary. One look at our eighteen-year-old girl guide had been enough to convince us that few prices would have been too high to pay for the privilege of remaining in her vicinity even a short while longer. She was exquisitely, ineffably beautiful. Her face, her skin, her eyes, and her figure combined to form a sheer, un-exampled loveliness. She was a Eurasian.

By lucky coincidence, she had two sisters, almost as pretty, so her semiretired diplomat-father did not have to wait long for an affirmative answer when he further suggested, after two rounds of beer, that we abandon our projected weekend pleasure trip to Kumamoto and pass Saturday and Sunday in his home. After accepting, we were introduced to his French wife, whom he had met and married while assigned to the Japanese Embassy in Paris.

I wish I could report that the three of us courted and married those three Eurasian girls and lived happily ever after, but the plain truth is that we never saw them again after what was a most pleasant weekend in their Kurume home. All of us kept intending to go back, but soon thereafter I was given eight weekends of O.D. duty as punishment for a fracas I was involved in with two churlish Marine M.P.'s, and as that two-month period was ending, one of my two friends was hospitalized for exposure and exhaustion after a sailboat accident. And so it went.

Anyway, I mention the Kurume weekend by way of introduction to the subject of Eurasians—surely another manifestation of the failure of democracy to measure up to its
ideals in Japan—for those three French-Japanese girls were
the first *ainoko* (Eurasians) I met in Japan and because they,
with all their beauty and charm, have always typified these
people for me.

Children of Japanese-European or Japanese-American
unions were rare in prewar Japan, especially in comparison
with the more numerous Anglo-Indians of India and the half-
Dutch Eurasians of Indonesia. Because their number was
small, they were curiosities, and it has always been difficult to
be a curiosity in Japan.

An example of the tragedy that can befall these mixed
bloods is the case of a certain young man with a Japanese
father and an English mother. Like many other Eurasians, he
was never allowed—by the community around him—to feel
that he really belonged to either of his parents' countries, but
when the war with the anti-Axis powers began to appear inevitable, he had to make a choice. At first he opted to go to
England, to live there, and, if called on, to fight in its forces;
but when his English mother changed her mind and elected
to remain at the side of her Japanese husband, she was finally
able to persuade her son to stay with them. Later, during the
war, he was drafted into the Japanese Air Force and trained
as a fighter pilot. Although his first inclination had been to
fight for a country that was now one of his enemies, he managed to stifle the memory of this preference and prepared to
do his duty by the Rising Sun flag under which he was now
serving.

The war was nearing its end by the time he completed his
flight training and was assigned to a fighter squadron based
in the home islands. His first two patrol flights were unevent-
ful, but his third sortie was against a group of attacking
American B-29's. The critical shortage of spare parts rendered
his Zero a less efficient fighter craft than it would otherwise

have been, and he was shot down in flames during his second pass at the underbelly of one of the B-29's.

Parachuting out of the Zero, the Eurasian pilot found that he was wounded in the shoulder and that his flight suit was on fire in three places. While floating earthward, he succeeded in extinguishing the flames but sustained painful burns in so doing. Off to his right, he chanced to see one of the B-29's going down in flames and two parachutes suddenly blossom near it.

The Eurasian hit the ground hard and lay there under the folds of his parachute, momentarily stunned. In a few minutes, however, he staggered to his feet and struggled out of both his parachute and his badly charred flight suit. Clad only in his underwear, he started to stumble across the fields toward a road visible in the distance, but halfway there he collapsed and fainted from loss of blood and the pain of his burns and bullet wound.

Japanese farmers found him where he lay. Seeing his somewhat foreign features, they assumed that he was one of the Americans who had jumped from the burning B-29. They beat him to death with shovels.

Estimates of the number of Eurasian (or, more accurately, Amerasian) children that Americans have fathered in Japan since the end of the war range from five thousand to fifty thousand and even higher. Pearl Buck, our most distinguished woman of letters and a compassionate human being who has devoted much of her time and money to the plight of Amerasian orphans in Asia, has written that by conservative estimates one in every ten American men stationed in the Far East since 1945 has fathered a half-caste child.

Japan has no reliable statistics on the number of *konketsuji* (literally, mixed-blood children) within her borders. These children do not become the objects of statistical interest until they enter orphan homes or entangle themselves with the police. But whether they number ten thousand or one hundred thousand, they are our responsibility. We American men who fought and worked—and loved—in Asia are the ones responsible for the presence on earth of these hapless, innocent chilren.

Not all of us, of course. But the children are there in irrefutable proof that some among us gave them life. Can we afford to shrug it off and say that it must have been the other fellow? Almost any among us, except Kipling's plaster saints, may be guilty. I may be. If you are a man and if you were there, you, too, may be. We may never know.

The undeniable physical attractiveness with which many Amerasians and Eurasians are blessed (perhaps in partial compensation for the hard lot fate has handed them) has eased their way into the movies and onto the stage. Their Oriental blood softens the sometimes harsh features inherited from the West, while our blood relieves the comparative flatness of Oriental faces. Pearl Buck has called them "a new breed of people who can be the strongest, most beautiful, and most intelligent in history. . . ." She suggests survival of the fittest as a reason for this superiority: Half of these mixed-blood children die before they reach the age of five because of the neglect and poverty in which they are raised.

Some of these Amerasians have found fame and comparative affluence in the entertainment and fashion worlds, but they are a pitifully small percentage of the total. Most of the others are poor, ill-educated, and mistreated by the society in which they must live. True or not, they are usually assumed to be the illegitimate offspring of prostitute mothers and cruel, low-class fathers, which only increases the hostility with which the surrounding society views them. They are strangers in their own world, strangers who have no home to which they can ever turn.

They do not understand why the world does not accept them. Nor do I. Not really. I am familiar enough with some of the explanations—for instance, what certain Japanese said reproachfully to Mrs. Miki Sawada when she started her home for Amerasian orphans in Japan: "Why do you bother to help them? Their fathers are the ones who dropped the atom bomb on Hiroshima, aren't they?" Although I know of this and other explanations, I am unable to comprehend such cruelty in human beings. I know that it must be there, but the concept appalls me, and I shrink from it in revulsion.

In addition to the thousands of Amerasians in Japan, there are many more elsewhere in the Far East. In Okinawa. In the Philippines. In Korea. In Thailand. And in Viet Nam, in ever-growing numbers.

More than twenty thousand live—or at least survive—in Korea, with five or six hundred more being born every year. Annie Park is one of these. When she was only six, she witnessed her Korean mother in the act of selling her body to an American soldier. Immediately, in a state of semishock, Annie ran out into the night, only to be lured into an alley and assaulted. By the time she was sixteen, Annie had become a full-time prostitute catering to American servicemen. By the age of nineteen, she had prostituted herself to thousands of Americans and had undergone six abortions. Annie Park's case is exceptional—but only because, in 1965, she wrote a book telling what had happened to her, and the book, with all its lurid details, became a best-seller. (Its title was *My Forsaken Star*.) There are only too many other Annie Parks whose stories may never be known. Do we, as a people, really care to know them, to concern ourselves with the miseries of such youngsters?

Some of the Amerasians have already reached adulthood, but many are still in their impressionable teens. It is only natural for these youngsters to tend to completely identify themselves with either their mother's or their father's country. Having no fathers and living, for example, in Japan, many would understandably like to become fully accepted Japanese, but the Japanese themselves will not allow that. In their bitter despair and frustration, some Amerasians resort to extreme courses.

In early 1967, a sixteen-year-old boy of Japanese-Negro parentage raped and strangled three young women in Japan. When caught and interrogated by the police, he would say only, "I did it because I hate my kinky hair and the color of my skin."

There are good reasons (human decency, responsibility, compassion, among others) why we should help these Amerasian children. If we do not, they may easily turn to crime—or to communism. Their tattered presence in Asia will always serve to remind the Japanese, Koreans, Vietnamese, and other Orientals that we Americans have abandoned our own offspring. While we spend billions of dollars and many long years supporting, for example, the Chinese Nationalist regime on Taiwan mainly to prove to the people of Asia that we abide by our commitments, we are destroying the impression we have been trying to create by callously ignoring the children our men have fathered and forgotten throughout the Far East. And yet we could save them by the expenditure of only a small fraction of the money we have spent on behalf of Chiang Kai-shek's government.

Until recently these Amerasians were all children, mostly tucked away out of sight in orphanages or running wild and hungry in slum districts that Americans seldom visit. But more and more, as they become men and women, they will be seen and heard. To a large extent, we still have the power, if we act now, to influence whether these "forgotten mementoes of our momentary passions" become leaders of decent society or leaders of Communist cells or leaders of criminal gangs. . . . Or simply ill-used, wretched outcasts.

14

Their Future—and Ours

In considering the future of American-Japanese relations, we would do well to regard first our views of each other in the past, both distant and recent, since these may be productive of guidelines to successful commercial, diplomatic, and cultural exchange henceforth.

Early Japanese views of American and European visitors to their shores depicted us as outsized men with long, pointed noses and much—often red—hair. They prefixed their word for hair (*ke*) to one of their words for foreigners from China (*tojin*) and named us *ketojin* or "hairy foreigners." Shortened to *keto,* this pejorative is still in common use, but no more so, perhaps, than the equally offensive "Jap" is in the United States. (It escapes me why Americans who blithely say "Jap" will not do other foreigners, including ex-enemies, the same courtesy and say "Hun" for German, "Wop" for Italian, "Spik" for Spaniard, and "Chink" for Chinese.)

Even when we weren't so hairy, the Japanese insisted on so viewing us, as in the case of contemporary Japanese drawings of Commodore Matthew Perry, who was actually clean-shaven, in which he was shown as a slanty-eyed ogre with a heavy beard and moustache. Even nowadays Westerners are sometimes described in Japanese as *komo gaijin* (literally, red-haired outsiders), although Americans with red hair are no more numerous, comparatively speaking, in Japan than in their own country. (Sometimes it seems that the Japanese see things through oddly-tinted glasses: For example, they call brown sugar *akazato,* or red sugar, and green signal lights *ao-shingo,* or blue lights.)

In the 119 years that have passed since Perry first visited Japan, our physical image has not improved greatly in Japanese eyes. While granting that we are generally larger and stronger, the Japanese have grave misgivings about some of our habits of personal cleanliness. In the words of Ichiro Kawasaki, the remarkably candid ex-diplomat who wrote *The Japanese Are Like That* and *Japan Unmasked,* "Westerners have a strong body odor that is quite nauseating." This smell, of which we are blissfully unaware, is apparently caused by our consumption of animal fats, which produce butyric acid in perspiration.

Furthermore, the Japanese regard our repeated discharge of nasal mucus into the same piece of folded cloth as unspeakably filthy. Instead, they use and then discard thin sheets of paper. Because we wear our shoes indoors, they feel that our houses are no cleaner than public streets. By using disposable chopsticks in public eating places, they believe that they lessen the hazard of the contagion that might otherwise come from poorly washed utensils. When they have a cold, they often wear gauze masks, like those used by surgeons, over their noses and mouths to protect others from their germs. If they shake hands at all, they do so only with a noticeable lack of enthusiasm, for they tend to shrink from such bodily contact.

If these are among the Japanese views of our physical characteristics, what then of our spiritual qualities? Do they think we are generous or miserly, kind or cruel, wise or foolish, forthright or devious, forgiving or vindictive? Do they genuinely like or despise us?

Obviously, the answers to such questions can be neither simple nor pat. Few Japanese wholly condemn or completely support us. Each has his own mixture of resentment and appreciation, of praise and censure, of superiority and inferiority convictions, all of which are subject to barometric changes brought on by international developments and Japanese inter-pretations of them, and to geographic considerations. (The nearer the U.S. military base, the lower the regard in which we are held.)

To examine their opinions of us, we should first consider our views of them since the two are interactive and reciprocal. As a nation, we have gone through rather distinct stages in our kaleidoscopic and often unrealistic images of the people of Japan. From the "heathen Japanee" of pre-Perry days, we progressed to the giggling, shuffling Three Little Maids from School of Gilbert and Sullivan's *Mikado* and on to the quaint, colorful, unreal, toylike Japanese of *Madama Butterfly*. Then Lafcadio Hearn gave us the Japan he saw through his uniquely tinted glasses—a charming, romantic, mystic country with a misty, other-world atmosphere. Later their immigration to our West Coast fixed in our consciousness a concept of the Japa-nese as a race of gardeners, valets, and truck farmers. When these immigrants began to compete economically and success-fully with our own natives, we started to talk in worried tones about the Yellow Peril. And all this while Western writers were turning out books whose very titles reflected our atti-tudes toward the Japanese: *Mysterious Japan, Behind the Japanese Mask, Unfathomed Japan, Behind the Smile in Real Japan, Japan's Islands of Mystery, Queer Things About Japan, Glimpses at Quaint Nippon,* and others.

Next came the *Panay* Incident ("So sorry, please") and the Rape of Nanking, when we were told about Japanese soldiers who callously bayoneted Chinese babies. Our growing suspi-cions of the Thirties turned diamond-hard on the seventh of December in 1941, and after that our mental picture of the Japanese became the caricature we saw in "Slap the Jap" and similar wartime posters: a grinning, buck-toothed, bespecta-cled, bow-legged, monkeylike dwarf from whose pores dripped cunning, treachery, cruelty, arrogance, and brutality.

When the war had ended and some of our bitterness began to diminish, still another image of the Japanese took shape.

Almost imperceptibly at first, a different kind of Japanese appeared on our mental screens. We had been surprised and pleased by the lack of resistance to our Occupation Forces. Loaded with samurai swords and bartered kimono, our men in uniform returned from Occupation duty in Japan with favorable reports: The Japanese aren't so bad after all, they said. More than a few of our veterans even reenlisted in order to go back to Japan. Others brought Japanese wives home with them. During the Korean war, great numbers of our service personnel took their Rest and Recreation leaves in Japan, which became to them a kind of earthly paradise after the hell of war in Korea. During this conflict, our offshore procurement of military supplies in Japan gave that country's industry the boost it needed to break out of the doldrums of defeat and destruction and start on its way to what became the most outstanding instance of economic recovery in modern times. Japan began exporting to the United States and Europe a river of merchandise, much of which was of surprisingly high quality: cultured pearls, cloisonné, brocade, silk, cameras, binoculars, motorcycles, transistorized radios, portable TV sets, small cars, and mammoth ships.

A Japan boom of formidable dimensions was in the making. *Hibachi, ikebana, o-shibori, kabuki, netsuke, ukiyo-e, kakemono, zen, tokonoma, fusuma, koto, shibui, haiku, maiko, sayonara, zori, shoji, happi* (coats), *sukiyaki, sashimi,* and *tempura* became familiar words to many in this country. National magazines devoted entire issues to Japan. Japanese restaurants became popular and increased significantly in number. Japanese entertainers toured the United States with financial and critical success. More and more American tourists visited Japan, as did our military men en route to and from Viet Nam and other Far East stations. Hundreds of technical assistance tie-ups and joint ventures between Japanese and American companies were formed. Ever-increasing numbers of Japanese businessmen, students, exchange professors, and tourists came to the United States. The vast majority of these were neatly dressed men and women carrying cameras and transistor radios, who were anxious to learn, eager to buy and sell, and ready to be friendly. They worked hard, behaved themselves, and left good impressions.

Unfortunately, while we were becoming fonder of (or, in some cases, less bitter toward) the Japanese, they were beginning to think less of us. From a peak of admiration and appreciation in the immediate postwar period, their opinion of us has followed an uneven road that has generally led downhill over the subsequent years. Partly the blame is ours, but part of it should also be laid at the feet of their national capacity for resentment, which is based on a suspicion of their own inferiority in certain fields.

Shortly after the close of the war in the Pacific and the landing of our Occupation Forces, the Japanese realized that, contrary to their propaganda predictions, we were not going to rape their daughters or ravish their land. They saw that we intended to leave their Imperial family and their mechanism of government essentially intact. They had been prepared for worse. When it did not come, their gratitude was heartfelt. The defeat had already caused many of them to jettison their traditional values and concepts en masse. The principles that they had been trained all their lives to respect suddenly became worthless. And into this vacuum marched the victorious Americans and their allies.

If they are nothing else, the Japanese are adaptable. Supremely adaptable. The same men and women who had planned with deadly seriousness to arm themselves with bamboo spears and charge our troops landing on their beaches now undertook, with equal dedication, to enshrine us as leaders, teachers, guardians, and elder-brother figures in the newly emptied niches of their hierarchy. Since we had won the war, it was easy for them to conclude that ours must be, in many ways, a superior culture. They genuinely admired a victor, and the fact that we fed instead of slaughtered them suggested that we were willing to enter into one of their traditional elder brother-younger brother relationships. If so, then they were more than ready to become, as a nation, our younger brothers. (The fact that, in later years, we did not always behave as they believed an elder brother should behave is a factor in the subsequent decline of our reputation in their eyes.)

If only we could have withdrawn from the game after two or three years of Occupation and let the Japanese solidify their then existing opinions of us. . . . In 1949, I was working in the GHQ Censorship Detachment in Osaka with considerable access to unguarded Japanese opinions on a wide variety of subjects, as expressed in their personal correspondence and telephone conversations, and the information that we gathered thereby generally confirmed that the Japanese sincerely admired us as a people and appreciated what we were doing for them.

To relate an instance of this admiration, I drove from Osaka to Shirahama one summer weekend to go fishing. Before leaving, I had bought a new Japanese-made fishing rod and other assorted angling equipment in a shop in Osaka. In Shirahama, I gathered this tackle late one afternoon and decided to try my luck from a small rocky peninsula jutting out into the bay. Before long a crowd of a dozen or so Japanese had collected quietly behind me to watch. These people had no possible way of knowing that I could understand what they were saying, and I am confident that they assumed that I could not. Soon they began talking among themselves about the fishing tackle I was using, and I overheard such comments as "Just look at that fine tackle!" "Anyone can tell at a glance that it was all made in America!" "Why can't we Japanese make fishing equipment like that?" "No wonder the Americans do things better than we do; they have such superior tools."

After a few distraught casts, I collected my gear, smiled weakly at the bystanders, and left. I was afraid that if I stayed any longer, one of them would get close enough to read the Japanese maker's name on my fishing rod.

Such incidents were not uncommon. To the average Japanese, we were then a mythical race of magicians who could do almost no wrong. The very height of the pedestal on which they placed us made our fall from glory all the farther—and harder.

During the Occupation we made mistakes (such as the October 10, 1945, release from prison of 276 hard-core Communist leaders) that laid the groundwork for later events and conditions that were to contribute to the tarnishing of our reputation, although they were not apparent to many at the time of commission. The years after the Occupation witnessed a series of disconnected incidents (the Girard case, the Happy Dragon incident, the Sunakawa Base extension problem, the Kujukurihama Firing Range difficulty, the Mito Bombing Range dispute, etc.) which chipped away, bit by bit, at the fund of good will that the Japanese held for us. Japan's vitriolic, nonobjective press, with its mania for opposition to the political party in power in Japan—and to the United States— frequently gave such incidents a twisted emotional interpretation that illuminated the American role most unfavorably. In this they were abetted substantially by Japan's many irresponsible intellectuals, teachers, and students. The visits of our nuclear submarines to the ports of Sasebo and Yokosuka inspired shrill and violent protests from Japan's hard core of professional anti-American agitators and gave the average Japanese, who was neither left-leaning nor anti-American, cause to wonder if our nuclear submarine visits were not perhaps a potential source of real danger to his country after all. Despite the fact that we had been responsible for the inclusion of the no-war clause in Japan's 1946 Constitution, we began to work for Japan's rearmament and participation in the free world's line of defense on the rim of Asia, which occasioned the Japanese to ask, How cynical can they be? Especially since most Japanese doubt that they would be in any active danger of a Communist takeover even if the United States withdrew its bases. (They also believe that Red China can be contained economically.)

A recent public opinion poll taken by Japan's largest news service (Kyodo) revealed the following: When asked about U.S. military bases and personnel in Japan, only 2.9 percent of those Japanese polled regarded our presence as "natural and reassuring." When asked if they thought that the United States would come to Japan's aid in case of armed foreign aggression, 51.8 percent thought that we would do so *only if* such assistance coincided with our own strategic considerations, 17.4 percent believed that we would let them down, and only 11.6 percent believed in our faithfulness without reservation.

For the United States to undertake to protect a nation in which a substantial majority of its citizens do not want our forces there, do not believe that their country is in any danger, and doubt that we would stand by our commitment to help them if they should be attacked cannot be regarded as anything less than a grievous fatuity.

Our war in Viet Nam has also raised grave doubts about our national purposes in the minds of many Japanese, even as it disturbs many Americans. For one thing, they tend to view it as a war of white men killing poorly armed Asians in their own homeland. For another, they fear that they may be drawn into this war or into other U.S. conflicts in Asia against their will because of American bases and sources of supply within their borders.

But more than any other single factor, the most contributory element in the deteriorating regard in which the Japanese hold us is simply overexposure. Given our aims and commitments, some of it has been unavoidable—but not all. Unfortunately, too often our policies and actions have been guided by a persistent, fundamental American delusion: that to know us is to love us. We tend to believe that the down-to-earth, person-to-person diplomacy of the average American G.I., tourist, and businessman is such that foreigners, upon acquaintance, cannot help being charmed; that although government-level relations may be strained, the common man in countries outside the Iron Curtain will at least appreciate and understand us if given a chance. We have an unlimited, almost childlike, faith in the efficacy of our personal good will and generosity.

But in the case of Japan—and most other Asian countries —this assumption is false. Granted, all of them do not hate Americans, but to automatically and consistently assume that any Japanese or other Oriental will like us once he gets to know our man on the streets is a folk myth that is unfounded, unilateral, and downright dangerous. To substantiate this, one has only to gauge our popularity in towns near U.S. military bases in Japan in comparison to towns without American presence. Or to note the surprisingly large number of Japanese students and teachers who become anti-American after sojourns in our country. (A related irony is that those Japanese who have studied or worked in the United States do not generally advance as quickly in their fields of endeavor in Japan as those of equivalent education who stayed at home.)

I am reminded of what a Spanish general once said when asked to explain why he was restricting the free movements of his soldiery in Mexico some years after the conquest of that country: "If our soldiers were free to move about Mexico, they would sooner convert the natives to their vices than attract them to their virtues." This has, I believe, considerable pertinence to many Americans who spend time in the Far East. Partly this can be blamed on extreme cultural differences: Our breezy, to-hell-with-tradition-and-formality approach does not sit well with most Orientals. (Consider, for instance, the incident in which a prominent captain of U.S. industry asked the Emperor of Japan to autograph a ¥10,000 bill at a palace reception, or the time when a vice-president gave voice to the Rebel Yell in the Taj Mahal.) Partly it can be blamed on language difficulties. And partly on the fact that many Americans are simply not well-behaved while abroad.

During the two years that I worked in Yokosuka, I frequently went up to Tokyo (about an hour's ride) Saturday morning and returned that evening aboard one of the late trains, which were in those days crowded with American sailors on their way back to the Yokosuka Navy Base after an evening on the town. What our sailors did to harass, insult, and torment the hapless Japanese passengers on those trains was such that I often got off in Yokohama, the midway point, in disgust and shame and took a taxi the rest of the way from there. And even among those Americans who do not carouse and fight in foreign streets and bars, there is too often an overlay of unconscious arrogance and thinly veiled condescension that the Japanese sense and resent. (That the Vice-President of the United States should publicly use an offensive expression like "fat Jap" during a political campaign in Hawaii, with its large population of Japanese extraction, is a manifestation of this arrogance.)

While quite a few of us were thus engaged in losing friends and alienating people, many Japanese commentators, reporters, writers, teachers, playwrights, moviemakers, and assorted intellectuals were having a field day working us over in print with no holds barred. Although it was largely uncoordinated, thousands of key Japanese in the communication media set out on a vengeful crusade to thoroughly discredit the United States. (Their individual reasons were many and varied, but prominent among them was the fact that the freedom to criticize had long been denied them. Once it was regained, they cast about for a likely target to test the sharpness of their knives on—and the United States happened to loom large in the field before them.) Because these scathing attacks were entirely in the vernacular, they generally escaped American attention. The number of Americans in Japan who could read the Japanese newspapers and magazines was—and remains—

pitifully small, while the English language dailies either ignored these diatribes or toned them down. And few English-speaking Japanese wanted to upset their American friends with detailed accounts of what was going on.

Plays like *The Tachikawa Base: Ten Years of Rape* clearly suggested that the average American soldier in Japan was a confirmed rape-artist. Movies like *Buta to Gunkan* (*Pigs and Battleships*) delineated our sailors as a depraved, shallow, and foolish lot. Others like *Hiroshima, Nara Base, Konketsuji* (*Half-Caste Children*), *Kichi No Kotachi* (*Military Base Children*), and *Akasen Kichi* (*Red-Line Base*) were equally vitriolic and rancorous in their condemnation of Americans. Magazines like the respected *Bungei Shunju* blamed us for a plethora of chicanery from the Japan Air Lines crash on Oshima to the Shiratori Incident in Sapporo. Other magazines, less respected but perhaps even more widely read, took us to task for anything their writers happened to be upset about that day. Many well-known Americans—particularly entertainers—were a prime target, usually shortly after they had performed in Japan.

The classic hatchet job that was done on us, however, was a series of thirty-seven newspaper articles that were later published in book form. The articles in this series indicted our military forces, banks, airlines, steamship companies, F.B.I., movie studios, oil companies, soft-drink bottlers, and international businessmen. The articles pulled no punches and spared no feelings. They named names and spelled out their accusations with the utmost clarity. Typical of their allegations were these three: 1) The F.B.I. obtains a substantial percentage of its operating funds from the international white-slave ring that it clandestinely operates, 2) Coca-Cola contains a habit-forming drug that makes the drink a valuable tool in the "arsenal of American imperialism," 3) The U.S. Embassy in Tokyo maintains a torture chamber in its basement where it deals with Japanese agents who have failed in their missions.

Condensed to two words, the message of this whole series

was "Hate Americans!" To understand its potential impact, one must bear in mind that the newspaper that printed it has a circulation of 4,000,000 in several regional editions and that the U.S. equivalent would be for *The New York Times* (850,000 circulation), *The Washington Post* (480,000), *The Chicago Daily Tribune* (805,000), *The Los Angeles Times* (950,000), and *The Wall Street Journal* (1,165,000) each to carry in thirty-seven editions, usually on the front page, a venom-dripping, savage attack on the Japanese people and their institutions that was mostly false or exaggerated. (Considering that our population is twice theirs, these circulation figures actually should be doubled to be a valid comparison.)

Even if the Japanese had been eminently fair-minded and favorably inclined toward us, such a series of mendacious articles would have doubtless done us great harm, but given their growing resentment and suspicion of the United States, the harm became incalculable.

After a massive effort of that scope, one might reasonably have expected our detractors in Japan to rest on their laurels for a while, but they did not. By no means. Encouraged by the success of this series, they girded their loins, sharpened their flensing knives, and fell to their task with renewed will.

Denunciations like these clearly did not reach entirely unreceptive ears, since the Japanese have feelings of ambivalence about Americans, anyway. Most of them admire the materialistic advantages of our culture, our technological advances, and our comparative lack of guile, but they do not admire American racial prejudices, missionary zeal to convert the world to our way of life, and unemotional, "logical" approaches to matters of mutual concern.

The March 13, 1969, issue of the *Asahi* newspaper, which I have before me, carries a most revealing article by Mr. Akiyuki Nozaka, a well-known author and commentator, and a remarkably candid and introspective man. I will not pretend that Mr. Nozaka's views are typical, for not many Japanese have analyzed and revealed their innermost selves with the stark frankness that Mr. Nozaka has. I do believe, however, that the contradictory aspect of his feelings may well be typical of most Japanese and that this very ambivalence is a key to understanding their views of us.

This is what he wrote: ". . . When I see their [the Americans'] large bodies and healthy complexions and when I hear them talking, I become uneasy and emotionally upset. They cause me to act arrogantly without good reason or they cause me to smile at them flatteringly and obsequiously. At other times, they make me want to grind their proud noses in the dirt and rough them up. If one of them should come and sit down at my table in a beer hall, I am sure that I would immediately become nervous and lose my composure. For that reason, I never wanted to go to the United States, but when I finally did go last year, I lost thirteen pounds in one week because I felt that I would lose my mind if I did not keep on drinking whiskey all the time.

"In comparison to the Americans, I am still convinced that the Japanese are an inferior race. Therefore, I become impotent when I go to bed with an American woman. Facing their men, I feel strongly that I am the underdog. I am ashamed of this, and when I come upon something at which the Japanese can beat the Americans, I grow ecstatic. . . . If a Japanese boxer wins over an American opponent, tears of happiness come to my eyes. . . .

"I sometimes wonder what I would do if we were to fight another war against the United States. If Japan were invaded and if an American soldier were to suddenly appear right in front of me, would I jump at him, using various judo tricks, even though I knew that I would be no match for him? Or would I smile slavishly and say, 'Hello,' 'Thank you,' and so forth? . . . Sometimes I fear that I might act in the latter way. Now and then I lose myself in a reverie, masochistically imagining myself being thoroughly abused by Americans. I sincerely feel that I would rather dream my life away, like a lotus-eater, than for Japan to have any more dealings with

America, even though it might mean that Japan would be relegated to the status of a primitive country. I pray that Japan will retire into a kind of hermitlike existence, because I do not want American democracy, freedom, or human rights. . . ."

While more than a few Japanese may feel the desire to return to the "hermitlike existence" Japan led before Perry's squadron forced open their long-closed doors, they have not —fortunately or otherwise—allowed this to deter them from the startling advances they have chalked up on international scoreboards since 1945, when they had been brought about as low—short of literal genocide—as it was possible for a people to fall.

The very depth and diffusion of their defeat, however, brought with it certain advantages. In numerous instances it proved more beneficial, in the long view, to rebuild where there was nothing but flat, empty ground than where part of the old foundation remained. Many steel plants, for example, were so completely destroyed that when time for reconstruction came, the factory owners were forced to install completely new equipment—at, of course, painful expense. Now these same factories can undersell American steel mills in our own market partly because their equipment is more modern than that of their U.S. competitors. The mental slate had also been largely wiped clean of the fallacious ideas that were the underlying cause of this ultimate in disasters. The Japanese were starting out again, this time from nothing. Eventually this proved to have been the best starting point.

The twenty-seven years that followed witnessed Japan's miracle of economic recovery and resurgence as a leading industrial power. She has risen to be the second-strongest non-Communist nation economically and has the highest rate of sustained economic growth on earth. She leads all countries (both Communist and non-Communist) in shipbuilding, textile exports, sewing-machine manufacture, cultured-pearl production, cement exports, transistor output, daily transactions in securities, copper consumption, and manufacture of umbrella frames, electronic microscopes, zippers, pianos, and home thermometers. Japan has this planet's largest blast furnace, trading company, air-conditioning plant, privately owned gas company, and the first electric power company to record a ten-million-kilowatt level of power generation. An Osaka manufacturer, Matsushita Electric, holds the international record for the largest number of TV sets and radios produced in one year. Nihon Rayon's plant in Uji is the largest producer of nylon, making one hundred tons a day or enough for 200,000,000 pairs of hose. With a daily output of 1,624 tons, the Tomakomai mill of Oji Paper is the world's largest paper producer.

With the most patent applications anywhere, the Japanese are shaking off the old stigma of imitation with such inventions, innovations, and technological breakthroughs as the Esaki diode, the world's first brushless motor, a wrinkle-proof fabric, the Parametronic Electronic Brain, Vinylon, and a mass-produced practicable rotary engine for automobiles, among many others. During the past several years she has begun to send her own experts and technicians abroad to teach others what she has learned—not only to underdeveloped nations but also to Europe and even the United States.

Another stigma that the Japanese have been largely successful in erasing in recent years is that of being an exporter of low-quality merchandise. To be sure, such merchandise is still being made in Japan, which is one of the most forcible reasons behind the Japanese fondness for imports. And some of it is still being exported—but less and less with each passing year.

Realizing that this was the one black mark that could hurt more than almost any other, the Japanese have used all the resources at their command to create a well-founded image of a producer of high-quality goods selling at competitive prices. To accomplish this, the Ministry of Finance extended low-interest, long-term loans to exporters, while reducing their tax bite, to enable them to improve production facilities. The

Ministry of International Trade and Industry encouraged the development of quality-control associations by industry, which double-checked the work of the quality-control inspectors in each factory. Foreign buyers, still wary of Japan's past reputation for shoddiness, employed independent inspection companies with branches in Japan to make yet another inspection of the merchandise between factory and port and insisted that such certification be shown to the bank before final payment could be made.

In addition to the new industrial facilities mentioned above, the Japanese lost no opportunity to learn more technologically from advanced countries. They bought foreign technology in massive quantities, scoured foreign publications for word of new developments and inventions, and sent teams of eager, curious engineers to thousands of foreign factories.

As profits accrued, they began to build up their own research and development departments, which were in turn responsible for more and more techniques and devices that gave Japan a competitive edge where it counted. (For instance, automobile manufacturers have developed roll-on, roll-off ships that permit cars to be loaded and unloaded four times as fast as with the usual carriers. This means a savings of about one hundred dollars for each car delivered.)

In transportation, Japan has also won significant trophies: She makes more motorcycles than any other country. She has the fastest trains—and the most punctual. Her annual total of railway passenger-miles is the highest. Electric trains on the Chuo Line out of Tokyo Station depart every two minutes, a world's record. The Ginza Station, which serves four subway lines, is the largest on earth, with twenty-eight ticket-punching or ticket-taking entrances and exits. Japan has the longest and fastest monorail. She builds half of all merchant ships launched every year. Her oceangoing tugboats are the world's most powerful, only one being needed to tow a 150,000-ton tanker from the Persian Gulf to Tokyo Bay. She has the biggest shipyard and drydock. In the Thirties she built *Yamato* and *Musashi,* which were, at 72,200 tons each, the largest battleships ever launched. Her aircraft carrier *Shinano* at 72,000 tons held history's record for size until the construction of the U.S.S. *Enterprise* (85,350 tons) in more recent years. She has built the largest tanker (372,400 d.w.t.) and is planning to build another (500,000 d.w.t.) that will dwarf the giants she has already let slip down her ways. Worthy of particular note is the fact that her records in ship construction have been achieved not by exploited labor but by automation, efficiency, and such innovations as self-propelled welders and computer-controlled cutting torches. (It takes Great Britain twice as many man-hours to construct a mammoth tanker as it takes Japan, while in the United States it costs twice as much.)

In 1939, Japan began to dig the Seikan Tunnel but was interrupted by the war and subsequent defeat. Construction has now been resumed, and, when it is completed in 1975, it will be at 13.6 miles the longest underwater tunnel, easily surpassing the present record-holder: the 4.35-mile-long tunnel under the River Severn in Great Britain. (Also under construction between Nagano and Gifu Prefectures is what will be the second-longest road tunnel.)

Earthquakes have long kept Japan out of competition in tall buildings with a government-imposed limitation of 102 feet, or about ten stories, but new steels and construction techniques have achieved a breakthrough resulting in one Tokyo building that is forty-seven stories high, with taller structures being erected or planned. The statue of the Buddha in Nara is housed in what is the world's largest wooden building, and not far from it is the oldest wooden structure: the Horyuji, a Buddhist temple built in the early eighth century. The statue of the Goddess of Kannon in Chiba is, at 170 feet, the tallest free-standing statue on our globe.

To keep these statistics in their correct perspective, we should consider the scanty endowments which the Japanese have had to use in achieving them: The defeat in 1945 deprived Japan of her largest market (China) and the sources of supply of much of her raw materials. Now she must import one-third of all the copper and aluminum her industry uses, also 20 percent of the food, 50 percent of the coking coal, two-thirds of the salt, 90 percent of the petroleum, 95 percent of the iron ore, and all of the rubber, wool, and cotton. On the average, Japan imports 40 percent of all the raw materials she consumes. Despite some large, highly efficient manufacturers, Japan is still plagued by the primitive methods of production employed in her small-scale plants: Eighty percent of the total number of her factories employ only four or five workmen, who use almost no machinery other than hand tools.

Working against such deficiencies and shortages, Japan has achieved the industrial records listed earlier as well as the world's highest rate of literacy and the highest percentage of school attendance. She has provided her people with 100 percent electrification and is second, after the United States, in the number of washing machines and TV sets in use. Japan also ranks second in the number of newspapers printed daily, although her economic newspaper circulation ranks first.

On the entertainment page of the ledger, Japan boasts the world's largest nightclub, artificial ice rink, bathhouse, brewery, bowling center (252 lanes), athletes (the sumo wrestlers), and swimming pool (the Kamogawa Outdoor Pool in Chiba, which registered an attendance of 150,000 persons on August 7, 1971). As well as the longest chorus line—and more feature films produced and novels published annually than any other country.

Her commercial fish catch is the second-largest, and as an example of her advanced methodology, Japan's scientists have conditioned young fish in fish farms along the coast to gather for feeding in response to low-frequency sound vibrations transmitted electrically underwater. Years later, after being released in open sea, these same fish will swim into nets and traps in answer to the same electric stimuli.

Among Japan's records are also some that she might prefer not to have publicized: She has the highest rate of fatal traffic accidents in the world and the largest number of both student and female suicides. Tokyo Central Station is the most crowded. (The crush aboard trains is such that false eyeballs and false teeth have been known to pop out.) The Japan Sea coast has witnessed the heaviest snowfall on record: seven feet in twenty-four hours. With 40,000 addicts, Japan is Asia's largest market for addictive drugs. (Dr. M. Kato of the Japanese National Institute of Mental Health has stated that Japan produced very large quantities of amphetamines ["speed"] during World War Two to bolster the fighting spirit of her servicemen, which led to dependency in many veterans. Also, huge stocks left over in the confusion of the war's end somehow got into civilian hands and were misused by many young people, entertainers, intellectuals, and racial minorities. The peak year of such use, however, was 1954.)

Japan may also have had the world's first hippies: Chinese records describing the Japanese in the third century after Christ report that there was among them a class of men called mourning-keepers, who did not wash, comb their hair, eat meat, or approach women. And the Emperor Meiji himself may have been the harbinger of male fashions of the future— the fearfully near future, if we consider the peacock plumage of some men's dress today. The first Westerners to have an audience with him (in 1868) described the young Emperor as wearing a white brocade coat and crimson trousers that trailed along behind him. His eyebrows had been completely shaved off, and in their place two exaggerated arcs were painted high on his forehead. His cheeks were brightly rouged. One lip was painted red, the other gold, and they opened to reveal blackened teeth.

In contrast to the generally accepted data noted above, Japan also has a few claims that may be difficult to substantiate. Being unable to refute or to verify them, I pass them along as they come to me: 1) Two American archeologists of the Smithsonian Institution believe America may have been discovered—long before Columbus or the Vikings came—by

Japanese fishermen; 2) G. S. Mitchell, an American professor teaching on the Japanese island of Shikoku, has uncovered evidence leading him to the conviction that a Japanese named Chuhachi Ninomiya flew a heavier-than-air craft twelve years before the Wright brothers did.

But entirely aside from unsubstantiated or undesirable records, Japan has enough left to convince the world that even without significant military forces, she is a power to be reckoned with.

The reasons underlying these successes also deserve mention: Prominent among them is the fact that Japan spends today less than one percent of its Gross National Product on defense, in comparison to our 8 percent. We have committed ourselves by treaty to protect Japan from attack (which most of her people do not really fear) while asking for no reciprocity from her. We have, in fact, even permitted her to dictate how we should go about providing that protection. The dilemma we face in Japan today is one entirely of our own making. We drafted her Constitution with its no-war clause, so we can hardly find fault with her for insisting that she abide by it. We signed the present Security Treaty in 1960 obviously aware of the clauses giving Japan veto power over the storage of nuclear warheads on her soil and over the direct involvement of our forces stationed there in any conflict not on Japanese soil.

Despite its later destruction, the industrial buildup of the Thirties (production increased 80 percent between 1929 and 1939) left a residue of technological knowledge and experience that proved to be of great value to Japan after 1945. Many of the same managers who had contributed their talents in the prewar decade were still on hand after 1945 to clear away the rubble and start from scratch, sustained by American blessing and aid. (But not *quite* as much aid as some would like to believe: We have given Japan no direct assistance since 1952, and for several years after that, we charged Japan for a good part of the cost of maintaining our troops there—as much as $155 million annually.) The conflict in Korea occurred at an opportune time, channeling massive procurement orders to Japanese factories and filling her entertainment districts with yen-laden allied military personnel on Rest and Recreation leaves.

Furthermore, the Japanese people are blessed with certain qualities, habits, and attitudes that must be, in any penetrating analysis, the real causes for their country's rise to prominence: Certainly their ability to sacrifice personal ambitions and desires for a given collective good is high among them. Then there is their manual dexterity. And their comparative lack of labor strife. Their amenability to leadership. The willingness of their businessmen to accept government guidance, controls, and mediation. Their racial homogeneity and their almost total lack of genuine racial disorder. (Fortunately or otherwise, the racial minorities mentioned elsewhere in this book are too downtrodden to be able to foment much dissension.) Their rate of personal savings (20 percent of disposable income), which is the highest in the world. The lifelong permanence of most employer-employee relationships. Their relatively simple and inexpensive national diet. (Japanese soldiers, for example, were able not only to subsist but also to force-march and fight on little more than tea and a few balls of rice.) Their dedicated, if often overbearing, bureaucracy. And the plain fact that more Japanese (about 50 percent) work than Americans (about 35 percent).

Other contributory factors include the world's lowest crime rate, the postwar land reform, the controlled competition of their marketplace, the low birth rate, a transportation system ideal for their topography, a stable climate (except for typhoons) that can be depended on to provide rain when the rice paddies require it, a presently undervalued currency, the ready availability of risk capital, virtually full employment, a common language, comparatively little disparity of wealth, no problems of regionalism, military forces (such as they are) that are completely under civilian control, and a minimal expenditure of social-overhead capital (meaning that big business in Japan has not yet paid its debt to society).

All these factors combine to form the basis of what economist Peter Drucker has called the "most extraordinary success story in all economic history." And despite the slowdowns and uncertainties of 1971 and 1972, it seems almost certain that Japan's economy will continue to register significant, steady advances throughout the next two decades, perhaps by 1990 achieving, according to economic forecaster Herman Kahn, a higher per-capita income than we enjoy in the United States.

It is difficult, however, to achieve such success without abrasions. With every American man, woman, and child buying in 1970 $29.50 worth of Japanese goods (in comparison, for example, with the figure of $2.50 in France), Japan sold by a margin of $2.8 billion more products to the United States than she bought—the largest trading deficit in the world's economic history. As these goods poured into the United States, dollars flooded into Japan, giving her in 1971 the second-largest (after West Germany) dollar reserves in the world and confronting Americans with the gravest economic challenge we have ever faced—to which we have reacted strongly (although somewhat belatedly). In fact, it was a similar economic threat posed by Japanese immigrants to our West Coast agricultural workers that was the beginning of our other era of trouble with Japan, thus lending particular gravity to the present situation.

As the Japanese economy continues to expand (her productive power is already twice that of all the rest of Asia combined), the low posture that has characterized her international stance throughout the postwar era will doubtless diminish, to be replaced by growing nationalism, confidence, pride, self-assertion, and—yes—hauteur as well. Many superficial changes have taken place in Japan since 1945, together with some that are deeper and more lasting; but with the notable exception of a widespread and heartfelt opposition to war, many of the social attitudes that underlay and permitted the Japanese choice of disastrous paths in the Thirties and early Forties are still rampant upon the heights, among them being arrogance and self-instilled convictions of superiority that come easily to an insular people reared to believe in the basic inequality of men.

Eighteen years ago some 20 percent of Japanese polled stated that they believed themselves superior to Westerners. Three years ago 57 percent agreed. Ten years from now that percentage will surely be a more substantial majority. Of course, it would not be in the least startling to learn that the majority of most races consider themselves better than others —with Americans more guilty than most—but the difficulty here is that when the Japanese feel that way, they tend to make such conviction manifest—although somewhat veiled under the guise of the condescending concern of the obviously superior for the patently inferior.

For it is a fundamental truth about Japan that this nation cannot long function internationally on assumptions of equal rights. Just as Japanese domestic society is a hierarchy, so the nations of the world must—in the Japanese view of things— fit themselves into upper and lower niches in a vertical ranking arrangement. The Imperial Rescript commemorating the signing of the Tripartite Treaty read in part, "The task of enabling each nation to find its proper place . . ." and this is a theme recurrent throughout Japan's modern history. Their fascination with rank in all things precludes and obviates most concepts of equality. The Japanese can accept and live with lower rankings, as they amply proved during the first fifteen or twenty years after World War Two. And they can—with equal facility—adjust to superior rankings, but it is then that they appear to many Westerners to be insufferably arrogant, although—by their own lights—they are only taking the well-earned role of a concerned elder brother or benevolent master. It is here, if anywhere, that what future difficulties foreign countries may encounter with Japan will take root and burgeon.

And as trade and tourism between the United States and Japan increase, we appear to grow perversely farther apart in spiritual regard and understanding. Our ignorance of each other's social structures and institutions leads both to embrace hopeless expectations of the other. Interpretations of mutual problems vary with the side of the Pacific you are standing on. In the matter of textiles, for instance, we are saying that textiles produced by cheap Japanese labor are forcing American textile workers out of their jobs, whereas in Japan, they are saying that Japan-made textiles account for only 2 percent of the U.S. market and that the entire tempest-in-a-teapot can be traced to a political campaign promise made by Richard Nixon to Southern textile mill operators in return for their support.

If such misunderstandings persist, the Japanese could withdraw neurotically into one of those unsettling periods of national self-reflection which have often preceded their fish-quick, yet fundamental, shifts in national policy. If this comes about, the declining years of the twentieth century could well see our fairly cordial friendship of the past quarter-century change to a mutually suspicious, coolly distant economic rivalry that would be bilaterally hurtful and disadvantageous.

It behooves us to do our part to see that this does not happen.

Index